UNION INTERNATIONALE DES SCIENCES PRÉHISTORIQUES ET PROTOHISTORIQUES
INTERNATIONAL UNION FOR PREHISTORIC AND PROTOHISTORIC SCIENCES

PROCEEDINGS OF THE XV WORLD CONGRESS (LISBON, 4-9 SEPTEMBER 2006)
ACTES DU XV CONGRÈS MONDIAL (LISBONNE, 4-9 SEPTEMBRE 2006)

Series Editor: Luiz Oosterbeek

VOL. 6

2006
lisboa
uispp
XV congresso

Session C18

Mesolithic/Neolithic Interactions in the Balkans and in the Middle Danube Basin

Edited by

Janusz Krzysztof Kozłowski
Marek Nowak

BAR International Series 1726
2007

Published in 2016 by
BAR Publishing, Oxford

BAR International Series 1726

Proceedings of the XV World Congress of the International Union for Prehistoric and Protohistoric Sciences
Actes du XV Congrès Mondial de l'Union Internationale des Sciences Préhistoriques et Protohistoriques

Outgoing President: Vítor Oliveira Jorge
Outgoing Secretary General: Jean Bourgeois
Congress Secretary General: Luiz Oosterbeek (Series Editor)
Incoming President: Pedro Ignacio Shmitz
Incoming Secretary General: Luiz Oosterbeek

Mesolithic/Neolithic Interactions in the Balkans and in the Middle Danube Basin

ISBN 978 1 4073 0168 6

Contacts: Secretary of U.I.S.P.P. – International Union for Prehistoric and Protohistoric Sciences
Instituto Politécnico de Tomar, Av. Dr. Cândido Madureira 13, 2300 TOMAR
Email: uispp@ipt.pt   www.uispp.ipt.pt

BAR Publishing is the trading name of British Archaeological Reports (Oxford) Ltd.
British Archaeological Reports was first incorporated in 1974 to publish the BAR
Series, International and British. In 1992 Hadrian Books Ltd became part of the BAR
group. This volume was originally published by Archaeopress in conjunction with
British Archaeological Reports (Oxford) Ltd / Hadrian Books Ltd, the Series principal
publisher, in 2007. This present volume is published by BAR Publishing, 2016.

Printed in England

BAR
PUBLISHING

BAR titles are available from:

BAR Publishing
122 Banbury Rd, Oxford, OX2 7BP, UK
EMAIL   info@barpublishing.com
PHONE   +44 (0)1865 310431
FAX   +44 (0)1865 316916
www.barpublishing.com

NOTE OF THE SERIES EDITOR

The present volume is part of a series of proceedings of the XV world congress of the International Union for Prehistoric and Protohistoric Sciences (UISPP / IUPPS), held in September 2006, in Lisbon.

The Union is the international organization that represents the prehistoric and protohistoric research, involving thousands of archaeologists from all over the world. It holds a major congress every five years, to present a "state of the art" in its various domains. It also includes a series of scientific commissions that pursue the Union's goals in the various specialities, in between congresses. Aiming at promoting a multidisciplinary approach to prehistory, it has several regional or thematic associations as affiliates, and on its turn it is a member of the International Council for Philosophy and Human Sciences (an organism supported by UNESCO).

Over 2500 authors have contributed to c. 1500 papers presented in 101 sessions during the XVth world Congress of UISPP, held under the organisation of the Polytechnic Institute of Tomar. 25% of these papers dealt with Palaeolithic societies, and an extra 5% were related to Human evolution and environmental adaptations. The sessions on the origins and spread of hominids, on the origins of modern humans in Europe and on the middle / upper Palaeolithic transition, attracted the largest number of contributions. The papers on Post-Palaeolithic contexts were 22% of the total, with those focusing in the early farmers and metallurgists corresponding to 12,5%. Among these, the largest session was focused on prehistoric mounds across the world. The remaining sessions crossed these chronological boundaries, and within them were most represented the regional studies (14%), the prehistoric art papers (12%) and the technological studies (mostly on lithics – 10%).

The Congress staged the participation of many other international organisations (such as IFRAO, INQUA, WAC, CAA or HERITY) stressing the value of IUPPS as the common ground representative of prehistoric and protohistoric research. It also served for a relevant renewal of the Union: the fact that more than 50% of the sessions were organised by younger scholars, and the support of 150 volunteers (with the support of the European Forum of Heritage Organisations) were in line with the renewal of the Permanent Council (40 new members) and of the Executive Committee (5 new members). Several Scientific Commissions were also established.

Finally, the Congress decided to hold its next world congress in Brazil, in 2011. It elected Pe. Ignácio Shmitz as new President, Luiz Oosterbeek as Secretary General and Rossano Lopes Bastos as Congress secretary.

L.O.

TABLE OF CONTENTS

LIST OF FIGURES

LIST OF TABLES

MESOLITHIC-NEOLITHIC INTERACTIONS IN THE BALKAN PENINSULA AND IN THE CARPATHIAN BASIN: AN INTRODUCTION

Marek NOWAK

Institute of Archaeology, Jagiellonian University, Gołębia 11, 31-007 Kraków, Poland,
mniauj@interia.pl

The linear vision of neolithization processes, assuming the relatively fast and total transformation of generalized foragers to the Neolithic stage, with a possible transitional link viz. complex hunter-gatherers, cannot be, at present, accepted. It seems that, basically in every situation – whatever the primary cause or mechanism – neolithization is associated with the coexistence of the Mesolithic/Epipalaeolithic and the Neolithic. Consequently, different kinds of contacts and interactions must have taken place between the communities assigned to these categories. We are increasingly aware that terms such as "Mesolithic" or "Neolithic" (in their classical sense) do not fully describe the real economic-cultural diversity of the early and middle Holocene populations in Europe and in the Mediterranean zone. These terms should be regarded as – so to speak – extremes, with a whole gamut of intermediate stages in between them. Clearly, the question of contacts and interactions is, in this light, further complicated.

Neolithization was, to a large extent, the effect of social contacts and interactions (with the exception of quite sporadic instances when Neolithic settlement embraced territories that had been previously uninhabited), regardless whether its genetic determinations had an auto- or an allochtonous nature. Then, it should be born in mind that the complete neolithization of a given territory could appear after a very long coexistence of the Mesolithic and the Neolithic. During that period contacts and interactions were a standard component of everyday life. Thus, their mechanisms and effects are of interest in themselves (not only from the point of view of neolithization) and essential for a complete reconstruction of the ways the communities under discussion functioned.

Certainly, such interactions took place in the key-areas for the neolithization of Europe: the Balkans and the Carpathian Basin. However, the reconstruction of cultural relations is hindered by two factors.

Firstly, the relation between the Mesolithic and the Neolithic in this zone – regardless the understanding of these terms – were, in practice, always obscured by the fundamental question of the origin of the Neolithic, considered as a "full-package" Neolithic.

Secondly, a huge problem is the surprisingly small data on the Late Mesolithic; how to interpret this fact has been for many years a subject of controversies. Adherents of allochtonous models have assumed that the modest quantity of data on the Balkan Mesolithic reflects the extreme scarcity of the network of Mesolithic settlement, caused by environmental (Perlès 2001: 25–30) or socio-economic determinants (Kertész & Sümegi 2001: 231). The supporters of the autochthonous model, on the other hand, in the polemics with their oponents, draw attention to the fact that the absence of the Mesolithic is, largely, only apparent; first of all, Mesolithic sites are "undiscoverable" because they are covered by thick middle and late Holocene layers or were inundated when the sea level rose (Bailey 2000: 32-36; Merkyte 2003: 312; Tringham 2000: 32; Zvelebil & Lillie 2000: 69). If most of the Mesolithic population of the Balkan zone had indeed concentrated in river valleys and littoral zones, then our knowledge of their relics would be minimal. Moreover, the number of archaeologists specializing in the studies of Mesolithic is small.

In the history of investigations into the origin of the Neolithic in the Balkan Paeninsula and the Carpathian Basin and, what follows, into the Mesolithic-Neolithic relations, there are two basic approaches: the allochtonous and the autochtonous.

The former approach should be defined as classical, the first model that appeared, practically, simultaneously with the identification of the oldest Neolithic in the Balkans and the Carpathian Basin. Hypotheses related to the allochtonous model link the beginnings of the European Neolithic with migrations from Anatolia and the Near East; the role of local, Mesolithic population was practically ignored (Childe 1929: 32, 34; 1947: 17, 58, 61; Clark, Pigott 1970: 282, 284–5; Milojčić 1949; Benac et al. 1979: 13–4; Garašanin 1979: 100–1, 139–41). It was, usually, assumed that those Near Eastern immigrants were equipped with a complete Neolithic package, initially, possibly, without ceramics. The Pre-ceramic Neolithic would be an argument in favour of the similarity to the Near-East – Anatolian model and the early date of Neolithic migrations to the southern regions of the Balkan Peninsula. Neolithic package persisted consistently in its original form; minor changes in settlement and economy could appear only after a considerable time when advancing migrations reached zones that were ecologically different from the southern part of the Balkans which was similar to the Near East homeland-territories. Also in recent years the allochthonous viewpoint has been expressed by various researchers (Bojadjev *et al.* 1993; Comşa 1993: 151, 167; Demoule & Perlès 1993: 364–365; Lazaro-vici 1996: 22–25; Maxim 1999; Perlès 2001: 39–45; Runnels 2003; Starnini 2001: 396; Thiessen 2000; Van Andel & Runnels 1995: 494–498).

The lack of response of the adherents of the allochthonous model to the question of the role of local hunters-gatherers in the neolithization of the Balkan zone was caused, above all, by the exceptionally limited data on the Mesolithic. For it is hard to believe that researchers should not be aware of the possibility of the contribution of local populations to the process of neolithization. This is well expressed in the memorable work by V.G. Childe "Danube in Prehistory" (4th edition), where merely two Mesolithic sites are mentioned in the context of the whole Balkan Peninsula (Childe 1929: 18–19). Nevertheless, Childe says:

> These scattered [Mesolithic – MN] families, if they took to food production when they came in contact with the neolithic peoples in the Subboreal phase, would multiply rapidly and exercise a decisive influence on the subsequent development of civilization.
>
> [Childe 1929: 20–21]

In recent years, as Mesolithic and Neolithic chipped stone inventories are increasingly better investigated, adherents of the allochthonous scenarios point to a lack of obvious similarities in the sphere of material culture between the Late Mesolithic and the First Neolithic. Chronological and ecological evidence, too, is used as an argument in favour of migrationist hypotheses. Some of the supporters of the allochthonous approach, admitting limited participation of local populations in the process of neolithization (Perlès 2003, Vencl 1986: 45), propose a concept of "limited allochtonism".

On the other hand, the arguments of supporters of autochthonous models – especially British researchers (e.g. Bailey 2000: 114–152; Whittle 1996: 43–46) and the younger generation of Balkan archaeologists (e.g. Budja 1996; 1999; 2001; Kotsakis 2001; 2003) – have been gaining in popularity in recent years. Hypotheses

of the kind accentuate decisive importance of local Mesolithic populations for the neolithization. They strongly emphasize that it was Mesolithic population that actively played a vital role in these processes; thus, the Balkan model of the First Neolithic was not a simple continuation of the Near-East – Anatolian models. Views on this issue have been presented with varying intensity. Some researchers do not admit of a possibility of even minimal south-eastern migration; in such case the role of the Near East and Anatolian farmers would have been transmission of new, Neolithic cultural attributes (Barker 1985: 71, 98; Chapman 1994; Whittle 1996: 43–4 – though the latter author accepts an alternative solution i.e. importance of small immigrant groups). However, most of the autochthonists do not altogether negate the presence of groups from Anatolia or/and Near East (Budja 1999; 2001; Kotsakis 2001; Kyparissi-Apostolika 2000; Vlachos 2003). These constructions – although this is not often clearly formulated – interpret neolithization as a process of gradually growing significance of Neolithic traits among local, Mesolithic communities. The earliest evolutional stages of the Balkan Neolithic were, supposedly, to exhibit minor significance of these attributes; in situations that do not fit this concept the tentative existence of such a formative stage is arbitrarily assumed and regarded as yet undiscovered (Kotsakis 2003: 219). On the basis of publications presenting autochthonous scenarios it is difficult to unequivocally determine when – precisely – the role of Neolithic attributes would have become dominant. There are some views that in the Balkans, except for Greece, it ensued only during the development of the Vinča cultural complex (Kaiser & Voytek 1983; Voytek & Tringham 1989).

It is my belief that in many cases migrationist and indigenist views, in their less orthodox versions, vary de facto in a minimal degree. The discrepancies rest in differently distributed emphasis in almost identical constructions. For example, assertions of D. Vlachos (2003) and C. Perlès (2003) are identical as regards the presence of an outside component i.e. these authors accept the occurrence of minor migrations from Anatolia, but endow them with different significance. D. Vlachos sees their role as marginal, whereas Perlès claims that they were a pre-requisite condition for initiating the process of neolithization.

Views that assume the co-existence of local Mesolithic populations and immigrant Neolithic groups, and treated neolithization as the outcome of complex processes of their interactions are relatively recent (Bánffy 2004; Borič 2002; Budja 1996: 70-72; Tringham 2000; Zvelebil & Lillie 2000: 68–72). These hypotheses could, in fact, be regarded as a separate, integrationist (Zvelebil 2001) group of constructions that explain the neolithization of the Balkan zone. In the light of these hypotheses the role of Neolithic attributes is to have been highly differentiated i.e. parallel to material culture diversity, also settlement and economic mosaics are to have functioned.

Data from palaeogenetic investigations, rapidly growing in the last several years, have seriously supplemented classical archaeological data (although ambiguity of many genetic data should also be stressed – e.g. Ammerman et al. 2006; Zvelebil 2001: 13-17). These data corroborate – in my opinion – the last of the aforementioned groups of explanations referring to "Balkan" transformations in the early and middle Holocene. In the light of early genetic hypotheses (Ammerman & Cavalii-Sforza 1984; Cavalli-Sforza 1996; 1997; 2003; Cavalli-Sforza et al. 1994; Cavalli-Sforza & Cavalli-Sforza 1995) the Balkan Peninsula and, basically the whole of Europe, underwent neolithization that was brought from outside by the population originating from Anatolia, who gradually spread across the entire Europe as demic diffusion. According to C. Renfrew (1987) in terms of language this population was Indoeuropean. However, the broadening of the spectrum of genetic investigations into prehistoric populations, primarily the research into mitochondrial DNA and chromosome Y, adjusted these notions considerably. This research has shown that majority of European populations have Palaeolithic genealogy (Adams & Otte 1999; Haak et al. 2005; Richards 2003a; 2003b; Sykes 2003). On the scale of the whole Europe this research suggests that the models proposed by Cavalli-Sforza and his team have to be discarded. Simultaneously, genetic data of the kind indicate the presence of a small (about 20%) component of a foreign, post-Palaeolithic population in Europe. This "younger" substratum is recorded first of all in the Balkans and, in a lesser degree, in Central Europe. Thus, the beginnings of the Neolithic in the Balkan zone could partially be related to the influx of some groups of Anatolian-Near Eastern population.

Papers in this volume accentuate, largely, the complexity and multilinear cultural evolution. Consequently, the authors represent generally integrationist group of constructions that describe the status and transformations of communities inhabiting the Balkan Peninsula and the Carpathian Basin in the seventh and sixth millennium BC.

The paper by **I. Gatsov** and **P. Nedelcheva** dealt with the chipped stone assemblages from the site of Menteşe and their significance for the beginnings of the Neolithic in the Marmara Sea basin. The authors have convincingly shown that the inventory from Menteşe is similar, in terms of techniques of blade production (among others bullet cores), morphological

parametres and – to some extent – tool structure, to a number of other inventories from this region, dated to between 6.500 and 5.500 B.C., for example: sites with ceramics such as Ilipinar (phases IX and X), Fikir tepe and Pendik. Of greatest interest, possibly, is the similarity between the Mentese inventory and aceramic inventories from the Turkish coast of the Black Sea, in the region of Bosphorous (Ağaçli group). Another interesting fact is that these inventories exhibit distinct differences in comparison with the Early Neolithic of the Thracian Plain (Karanovo I/II). Thus, if chipped lithics are taken into account, in the Marmara Sea basin at the beginning of the Neolithic a separate techno-complex appears to have formed, where – in authors view – the component of local elements belonging to the Black Sea Epipalaeolithic/Mesolithic tradition is clearly observable.

D. Mihailović devoted his paper to the Late Mesolithic of Serbia and Montenegro and sees the Late Mesolithic in this region as a strongly varied and dynamic phenomenon, evidenced pre-Neolithic migrations. The author points to the Iron Gates Mesolithic and the Dalmatian zone as regions where the continuity of cultural development was marked. In the Iron Gates this was related to dynamic economic and ideological transformations; some influences of the pre-ceramic developmental stages in the Near East are suggested. In turn, Mesolithic hunter-gatherers in the Central Balkans integrated with the Neolithic relatively quickly, and contributed vitally to its fast expansion. The author believes that traditional models explaining the genesis of the Balkan Neolithic are inadequate. Similarly to the Near-East – Anatolian zone social and ideological determinants should, too, be taken into consideration in the zone under discussion.

D. Borić in his paper puts forward a scenario of smooth and gradual Mesolithic-Neolithic transition in the Danube Gorges which he preferably describes with a term "transformation". Frontier model is inadequate to these processes since it takes the existence of two distinct cultural realities as granted. Such fundamental discrepancies basically were not representative for the area under discussion. Foregoing transformation was under way as a consequence of interactions between inhabitants of the Iron Gates ecological niche and Early Neolithic groups that appeared in the areas around ca. 6.300/6.200 BC. The period 6.200-5.900 BC was crucial for that transformation; IGM became a component of Early Neolithic exchange network in that time. Some inclusions of foreign "Neolithic" population possibly also took place. In Author's opinion, transformations recorded in settlement, economy and symbolical behaviors should not be considered as a kind of "ideological resistance". They all provided "allegiance to new social contexts". Surprisingly enough, their nature was different even within such a small microregion. For instance, postulated increase in plant (cereals?) food refers actually to two sites only (Lepenski Vir, Ajmana); other sites have not provided traces of the kind.

According to **P. Sümegi**, a mosaic-like segmentation, visible at the macro-, meso- and micro-scale was typical for the eastern part of the Carpathian Basin from as early as the Ice Age. The emergence of such mosaicity is due to *inter alia* the overlap of four major climatic zones in the region as well as the formation of neotectonic depressions. Development of present-day Tisza valley, conditioned also by the latter factor, resulted in formation of island-like, loess-covered Pleistocene surfaces. Consequently, two types of landscape emerged: 1) river valleys and basins, 2) residual surfaces. In P. Sümegi's view, "when this natural mosaic pattern is studied close up, a structure may be recognized that is comparable to a mathematical "fractal microscope" set. This type of set is characterized by repeating an identical pattern along with increasing magnification."

The sites of the Körös culture demonstrate distinct preference for loess-covered, residual surfaces within the alluvium. These "islands" limited the subsistence possibilities of early farmers since alluvial areas beyond were flooded regularly at least twice a year. Although once spring and early summer floods receded, the drying floodplain offered excellent graze, only the "islands" were habitable at the time of high waters, even for livestock. Accordingly, the author hypothesize the existence of a Central European - Balkanic Agroecological Barrier (CEB AEB) within the central parts of the Carpathian Basin, which in essence determined the possibilities of spreading of the agro-pastoral groups during the Early Neolithic. On the other hand, he also emphasizes the important role of the river valleys acting as "meeting points" and infiltration corridors for the Mesolithic and Neolithic groups in the whole process of Neolithization within the Carpathian Basin.

E. Banffy, **W. J. Eichmann** and **T. Marton** analysed the role of Mesolithic hunter-gatherer groups in the spread of agriculture in western Hungary, against the background of Europe. The authors emphasize that the categories such as the Mesolithic and the Neolithic are ambiguous, while the trajectories of neolithization processes are diverse. Consistent with this seem the authors' view that the process of formation of the LBK in Transdanubia is, essentially, the effect of the interaction between early agriculturalists (immigrant Starčevo communities from the south) and the indigenous Late Mesolithic hunter-gatherer population, in spite of the fact that the Late Mesolithic settlement

is scanty. The sparse evidence of the Late Mesolithic could be caused by natural geomorphological process as well as by the relatively short tradition of investigations into pre-Neolithic settlement. Of interest is the authors' view that the agro-pastoral economy was of minor importance economy in case of Starčevo communities around Lake Balaton due to their successful adaptation to marshland environment. In other words, the first stage of neolithization, from the Mesolithic point of view did not mean profound changes in subsistence strategies. The different, i.e. higher, topographical location of "Linear" sites suggests that the shift to predominance of domesticated food took place at the beginning of the classical phase of the LBK (*ca*. 5.300 BC).

K. Biró discussed the Early Neolithic raw material economies in the Carpathian Basin. Spatial analysis of available data indicates the presence of two, distinct provinces of raw material supply. In Transdanubia the dominant material was radiolarite, whereas in the Tisza basin obsidian and limnoquartzite. A group of sites located in between shows a greater diversity of raw materials. The author concludes that the Early Neolithic groups commanded an excellent knowledge of the best lithic raw materials available in the Carpathian Basin. Possibly, the location of its outcrops, especially of obsidian and limnoquartzites, was a factor that stimulated "northern" migration.

In their paper **J.K. Kozłowski** and **M. Nowak** claim that the First Neolithic in the Upper Tisza basin was an allochtonous phenomenon. Typological and chronological analyses of available lithic materials indicate that even among a few inventories traditionally linked with the Late Mesolithic, a large part cannot, in fact, be assigned to this period. Some similarities of material culture of the First Neolithic in this zone with the late Körös/Criş tradition suggest that the initial areas of migrations that reached the NE part of the Carpathian Basin in 5.800–5.600 BC could have been either the central Great Hungarian Plain or Transilvania. The latter possibility seems more likely. On the other hand, further evolution of the Neolithic in the second half of the sixth millennium BC, shows a number of specific features, especially in the Eastern Slovakian Lowland. Possibly, this was the effect of the geographical location itself since the Eastern Slovakian Lowland is somewhat isolated from the central and southern parts of the Carpathian Basin, while – on the other hand – is predisposed to more intensive Transcarpathian contacts, with the territories in the upper Vistula basin and the upper Dnester. Undoubtedly, in the course of such contacts, the Late Mesolithic groups of the Janisławice culture remained in the sphere of interests of AVK communities. Theoretically, a hypothesis is also possible about close coexistence of AVK population and the Late Mesolithic people in different ecological zones in the Upper Tisza basin. In time, in the effect of contacts, the Late Mesolithic groups would have been gradually incorporated into the economic, settlement and cultural systems of the AVK. However, to confirm this scenario more Late Mesolithic remains would have to be discovered.

References

ADAMS, J. & OTTE, M. (1999) Did Indo-European languages spread before farming? *Current Anthropology* 40: pp. 73-77.

AMMERMANN, A. J. & CAVALLI-SFORZA, L. L. (1984) *The Neolithic Transition and the Genetics of Populations in Europe*. Princeton: Princeton University Press.

AMMERMAN, A. J., PINHASI, R. & BÁNFFY, E. (2006) Comment on "Ancient DNA from the First European Farmers in 7.500-Year-Old Neolithic Sites". *Science* 312: pp. 1875a

BAILEY, D. W. (2000) *Balkan Prehistory. Exclusion, Incorporation and Identity*. London: Routledge.

BÁNFFY, E. (2004) *The 6th Millennium BC Boundary in Western Transdanubia and its Role in the Central European Neolithic Transition (the Szentgyörgyvölgy-Pityerdomb Settlement)*. Budapest: Archaeological Institute of the Hungarian Academy of Sciences.

BARKER, G. W. (1985) *Prehistoric Farming in Europe*. Cambridge: Cambridge University Press.

BENAC, A., GARAŠANIN, M. & SREJOVIĆ, D. (1979) Uvod. In GARAŠANIN, M. ed., *Praistorija Jugoslavenskih Zemalja II, Neolitsko Doba*. Sarajevo: Akademija Nauka i Umjetnosti Bosne i Hercegovine. pp. 11-33.

BOJADJEV, J., DIMOV, T. & TODOROVA, H. (1993) Les Balkans Orientaux. In KOZŁOWSKI, J. K., ed. *Atlas du Néolithique européen, vol. 1. L'Europe orientale*. Liège: Université de Liège. pp. 61-110 (Études et Recherches Archéologiques de l'Université de Liège; 45).

BORIĆ, D. (2002) The Lepenski Vir conundrum: reinterpretation of the Mesolithic and Neolithic sequences in the Danube Gorges. *Antiquity* 76: pp. 1026-1039.

BUDJA, M. (1996) Neolithization in the Caput Adriae region: between Herodotus and Cavalli-Sforza. *Poročilo o raziskovanju paleolitika, neolitika in eneolitika v Sloveniji* 23: pp. 61-77.

BUDJA, M. (1999) The transition to farming in Mediterranean Europe - an indigenous response. *Documenta Praehistorica* 26: pp. 119-141.

BUDJA, M. (2001) The transition to farming in Southeast Europe: perspectives from pottery. *Documenta Praehistorica* 28: pp. 27-47.

CAVALLI-SFORZA, L. L. (1996) The spread of agriculture and nomadic pastoralism. In HARRIS, D. ed. *The Origins and Spread of Agriculture and Pastoralism in Eurasia*. London: University College of London Press. pp. 51-69.

CAVALLI-SFORZA, L. L. (1997) Genetic and cultural diversity in Europe. *Journal of Anthropological Research* 53: pp. 383-404.

CAVALLI-SFORZA, L. L. (2003) Returning to the Neolithic transition in Europe. In AMMERMAN, A. J. & BIAGI, P. eds. *The Widening Harvest. The Neolithic Transition in Europe: Looking Back, Looking Forward*. Boston: Archaeological Institute of America. pp. 297-315.

CAVALLI-SFORZA, L. L. & CAVALLI-SFORZA, F. (1995) *The Great Human Diasporas. The History of Diversity and Evolution*. Addison-Wesley.

CAVALLI-SFORZA, L. L., MENOZZI, P. & PIAZZA, A. (1994) *The History and Geography of Human Genes*. Princeton: Princeton University Press.

CHAPMAN, J. (1994) The origins of farming in south east Europe. *Prehistoire Europeenne* 6: pp. 133-157.

CHILDE, V. G. (1929) *The Danube in Prehistory*. Oxford: Clarendon Press.

CHILDE, V. G. (1947) *The Dawn of European Civilization* (4th Edition). London: Kegan Paul, Trench, Trubner & Co., Ltd.

CLARK, G. & PIGGOTT, S. (1970) *Społeczeństwa prahistoryczne*. Warszawa: Państwowe Wydawnictwo Naukowe.

COMŞA, E. (1993) La Roumanie meridionale, In KOZŁOWSKI, J. K., ed. *Atlas du Néolithique européen, vol. 1. L'Europe orientale*. Liège: Université de Liège. pp. 151-187 (Études et Recherches Archéologiques de l'Université de Liège; 45).

DEMOULE, J-P. & PERLÈS, C. (1993) The Greek Neolithic: A New Rewiev. *Journal of World Prehistory* 7: pp. 355-416.

GARAŠANIN, M. (1979) Centralnobalkanska zona. In GARAŠANIN, M. ed. *Praistorija Jugoslavenskih Zemalja II, Neolitsko Doba*. Sarajevo: Akademija Nauka i Umjetnosti Bosne i Hercegovine. pp. 79-213

HAAK, W., FORSTER, P., BRAMANTI, B., MATSUMURA, S., BRANDT, G., TÄNZER, M., VILLEMS, R., RENFREW, C., GRONENBORN, D., ALT, K. W. & BURGER, J. (2005) Ancient DNA from the First European Farmers in 7.500-Year-Old Neolithic Sites. *Science* 310: pp. 1016-1018.

KAISER, T. & VOYTEK, B. (1983) Sedentism and economic change in the Balkan Neolithic. *Journal of Anthropological Archaeology* 2: pp. 323-353.

KERTÉSZ, R. & SÜMEGI, P. (2001) Theories, critiques and a model: Why did the expansion of the Körös-Starčevo culture stop in the centre of the Carpathian Basin? In KERTÈSZ, R. & MAKKAY, J., eds. *From the Mesolithic to the Neolithic. Proceedings of the International Archaeological Conference held in the Damjanich Museum of Szolnok, September 22-27, 1996.* Budapest: Archaeolingua, pp. 225-246.

KOTSAKIS, K. (2001) Mesolithic to Neolithic in Greece. Continuity, discontinuity or change of course? *Documenta Praehistorica* 28: pp. 63-73.

KOTSAKIS, K. (2003) From the Neolithic side: the Mesolithic/Neolithic interface in Greece. In GALANIDOU, N. & PERLÈS, C. eds. *The Greek Mesolithic: Problems and Perspectives*. pp. 217-222 (British School of Athens Studies; 10).

KYPARISSI-APOSTOLIKA, N. (2000) The Mesolithic/Neolithic transition in Greece as evidenced by the data at Theopetra cave in Thessaly. *Documenta Praehistorica* 27: pp. 133-140.

LAZAROVICI, G. (1996) The process of Neolithization and the development of the first Neolithic civilisation in the Balkans. In Grifoni-Cremonesi, R., Guilaine, J. & L'Helgouac'h, J. eds. *The Colloquia of the XIII International Congress of Prehistoric and Protohistoric Sciences, Forli (Italia) 8-14 September 1996.The Neolithic in the Near East and Europe.* Forli: A.B.A.C.O. pp. 21-39.

MAXIM, Z. (1999) *Neo-Eneoliticul din Transilvania. Date Arheologice şi Matematico-Statistice.* Cluj-Napoca (Bibliotheca Musei Napocensis; 19).

MERKYTE, I. (2003) The Mesolithic syndrome in Southeastern Europe. *Acta Archaeologica* 74: pp. 307-318.

MILOJČIĆ, V. (1949) *Chronologie der jüngeren Steinzeit Mittel- und Südosteuropas.* Berlin.

PERLÈS, C. (2001) *The Early Neolithic in Greece.* Cambridge: Cambridge University Press.

PERLÈS, C. (2003) An alternate (and old-fashioned) view of Neolithisation in Greece. *Documenta Praehistorica* 30: pp. 99-113.

RENFREW, C. (1987) *Archaeology and Language. The Puzzle of Indo-European Origins.* London: Jonathan Cape.

RICHARDS, M. (2003a) The Neolithic transition in Europe: archaeological models and genetic evidence. *Documenta Praehistorica* 30: pp. 159-169.

RICHARDS, M. (2003b) The Neolithic invasion of Europe. *Annual Review of Anthropology* 32: pp. 135-162.

RUNNELS, C. (2003) The origins of the Greek Neolithic: a personal view. In AMMERMAN, A. J. & BIAGI, P. eds. *The Widening Harvest: the Neolithic Transition in Europe. Looking Back, Looking Forward.* Boston: Archaeological Institute of America. pp. 121-133.

STARNINI, E. (2001) The Mesolithic/Neolithic transition in Hungary: the lithic perspective. In KERTÈSZ, R. & MAKKAY, J., eds. *From the Mesolithic to the Neolithic. Proceedings of the International Archaeological Conference held in the Damjanich Museum of Szolnok, September 22-27, 1996.* Budapest: Archaeolingua, pp. 395-404.

SYKES, B. (2003) European ancestry: the mitochondrial landscape. In AMMERMAN, A. J. & BIAGI, P. eds. *The Widening Harvest: the Neolithic Transition in Europe. Looking Back, Looking Forward.* Boston: Archaeological Institute of America. pp. 315-327.

THISSEN, L. (2000) Thessaly, Franchti and western Turkey: clues to the Neolithisation of Greece? *Documenta Praehistorica* 27: pp. 141-154.

TRINGHAM, R. (2000) Southeastern Europe in the transition to agriculture in Europe: bridge, buffer, or mosaic. In PRICE, T. D., ed. *Europe's First Farmers*: Cambridge...: Cambridge University Press, pp. 19-57

VAN ANDEL, T. H. &. RUNNELS, C. N. (1995) The earliest farmers in Europe. *Antiquity* 69: pp. 481-500.

VENCL, S. (1986) The role of hunting-gathering populations in the transition to farming: a Central-European perspective. In ZVELEBIL, M. ed. *Hunters in Transition.* Cambridge: Cambridge University Press. pp. 43-51.

VLACHOS, D. (2003) Who did it? Perspectives on the beginning of the Neolithic in Greece. *Documenta Praehistorica* 30: pp. 131-139.

VOYTEK, B. A. & TRINGHAM, R. (1989) Rethinking the Mesolithic: the case of the South-East Europe. In BONSALL, C. ed. *The Mesolithic in Europe. Papers Presented in the Third International Symposium.* Edinburgh: Edinburgh University Press. pp. 492-499.

WHITTLE, A. (1996) *Neolithic Europe. The Creation of New Worlds.* Cambridge: Cambridge University Press.

ZVELEBIL, M. (2001) The agricultural transition and the origins of Neolithic society in Europe. *Documenta Praehistorica* 28: pp. 1-26.

ZVELEBIL, M. & LILLIE, M. (2000) Transition to agriculture in eastern Europe. In PRICE, T. D., ed. *Europe's First Farmers*: Cambridge: Cambridge University Press, pp. 57-93.

THE CHIPPED STONE ASSEMBLAGES OF MENTEŞE
AND THE PROBLEM OF THE EARLIEST OCCUPATION
OF MARMARA REGION

Ivan GATSOV

New Bulgarian University, Department of Archaeology, 1618 Sofia, 21 Montevideo, Str., Bulgaria;
Archaeological Institute and Museum, 1000 Sofia, 2 Saborna Str., Bulgaria, igatsov@yahoo.com

Petranka NEDELCHEVA

New Bulgarian University, Department of Archaeology, 1618 Sofia, 21 Montevideo Str., Bulgaria,
pnedelcheva@nbu.bg

Abstract: *It could be suggested that Early Neolithic chipped stone assemblages from South Marmara region were influenced in some degree by local technological tradition, which come from the Epipalaeolithic/Mesolithic periods. Simultaneously the Early Neolithic assemblages of Menteşe, Ilipinar, Fikir tepe and Pendik disclose totally different technological features and totally different system of procurement in respect of the Early Neolithic stone assemblages in Northern Thrace. Any parallels between the Early Neolithic chipped stone assemblages connected with white painted, dark polished and painted pottery from the territory of Northern Thrace and SW Bulgaria and those from South Marmara region have been found.*
Key-words: *Epipalaeolithic, Mesolithic, Marmara Sea, Tharce, Fikir tepe Culture, Early Neolithic, Karanovo I-II*

Resumé: *Nous sugggerons dans cette communication que les assemblages du Néolithique ancien provenant de la région au sud de la Mer Marmara ont été enracinés, au moins partiellement, par la tradition technologique, dans l'Epipaléolithique/Mésolithique local.*
En même temps les assemblages du Néolithique ancien de Menteşe, Ilipinar, Fikir tepe et Pendik sont entièrement différents, du point de vue technologique et par leur système d'approvisionnement en matières premières lithiques, des assemblages de la Thrace septentrionale.
Aucune analogie entre les industries lithiques du Néolithique ancien associées à la céramique peinte en blanc et avec celle à surface lustrée et foncée n'existe pas entre le territoire de la Thrace septentrionale et le Sud-Ouest de la Bulgarie et la région au sud de la Mer Marmara.
Mots-clés: *Epipaléolithique, Mésolithique, Mer Marmara, Thrace, Fikir tepe Culture, Néolithique ancien, Karanovo I-II.*

The mound of Menteşe is located ca. 27 km south of Ilipinat settlement in the plain of Yenisehir, Northwestern Anatolia. Within the framework of Ilipinar multidisciplinary research project small excavation has been undertaken at the mound of Menteşe led by Dr. J. Roodenberg (Fig. 1.1). As a result some quantity of flint and obsidian artifacts has been obtained.

The artifacts have been separated according to the levels of occupation. The formers have been distinguished by the excavator as follow: 1- upper, 2- middle and 3 – basal one. The artifact distribution' by levels is presented bellow (Table 1.1). From the total number of 1.113 artifacts in this report only the specimens from upper, middle and basal layers are included -704 artifacts.

All artifacts have been separated by the type of raw material – flint and obsidian and related to the categories of cores, cortical specimens, crested specimens, debris, flakes, blades and retouched tools as well.

Table 1.1. Distribution of flint and obsidian artifacts

	Obsidian	**flint**	**Total**
1	29	231	260
2	47	337	384
3	19	41	60
Total	95	609	704

OBSIDIAN ARTIFACTS

Due to the fact the material come from small sounding the artifact distribution by categories doesn't show any regularity (Table 1.2). Almost half of the artefacts are presented by blades, followed by debris, while the other categories have been registered in single specimens (Fig. 1.2: 7; Fig. 1.4: 3). The number of the cores is relatively high. The above presented assemblages structures' reflected core reduction on spot - all activities connected with core preparation and exploitation were done in frame of the settlement.

Fig. 1.1. Location of the Menteşe site (1).

Table 1.2. Distribution of obsidian artifacts by levels and categories

	LEVEL			Total
	1	2	3	
Cores	2	2	1	5
cortical specimens	0	0	1	1
crested specimens	3	4	2	9
Debris	7	11	8	26
Flakes	0	3	4	7
Blades	16	25	3	44
retouched tools	1	2	0	3
Total	29	47	19	95

Cores

The obsidian cores are presented by single platform items, for blades and bladelets mainly and in final stage of exploitation. Some examples are closed to the prismatic ones. The core processing was carried out from one platform. Most of the cores present flat or semi rounded striking surface. As a rule the core length is between 5-7cm. (Fig. 1.7: 5; Fig. 1.8: 4)

Blades

The preserve parts of the blade proximal fragments and entire specimens present linear (punctiform) butts. The way of detachment is connected with punch applying and in lesser degree by soft hammer stone (Table 1.3). It is interesting the very low frequency of pressure blades and total lack of specimens with trace of hard hammer stone using.

Table 1.3. Ways of detachment and butts of obsidian blades

	flat	linear (punctiform)	unde-termined	Total
Pressure	0	3	0	3
Punch	1	12	1	14
soft hammer stone	0	8	0	8
Total	1	23	1	25

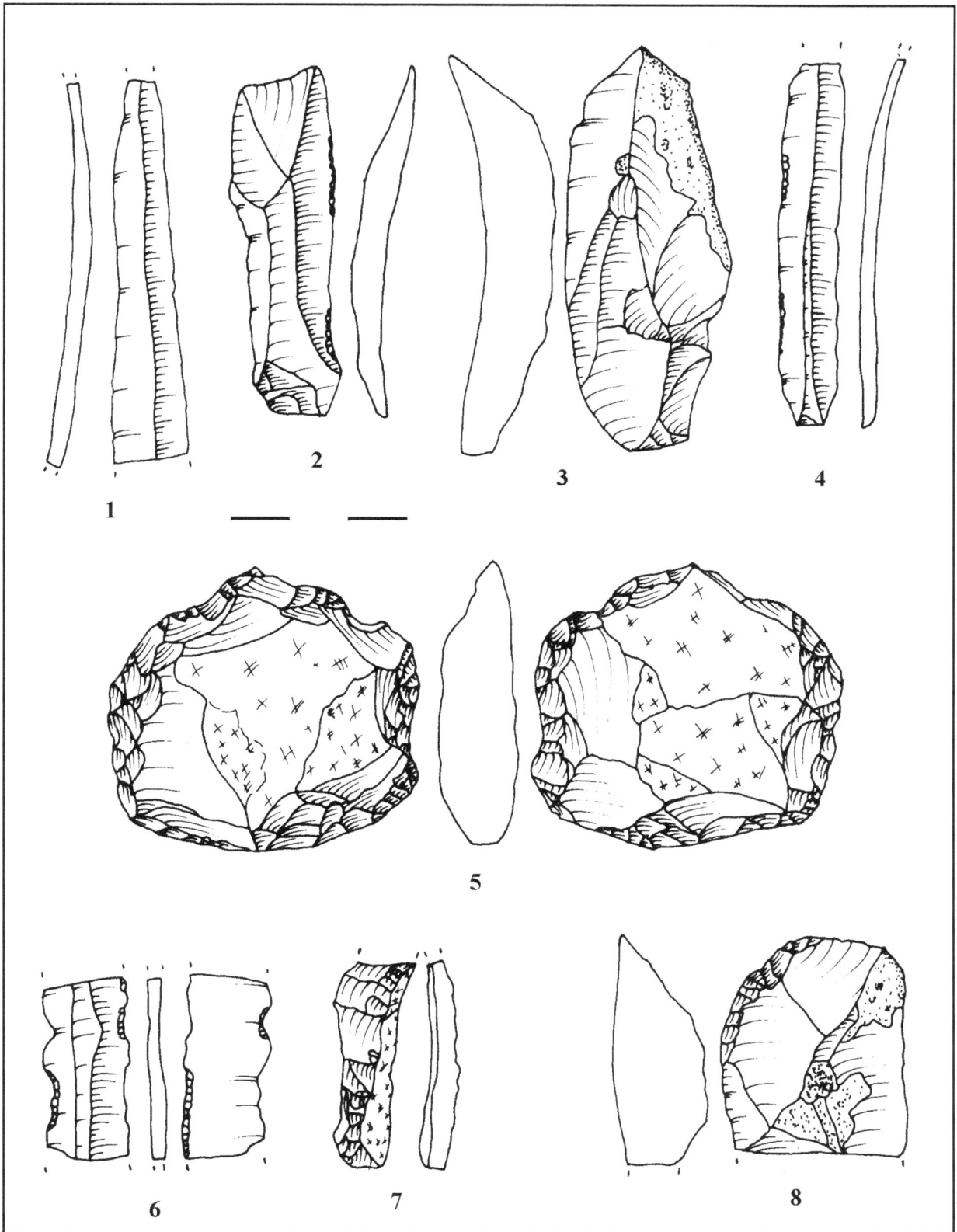

Fig. 1.2. Menteşe. Chipped disk -5; End scraper- 8; Crested specimens- 3, 7; Retouched blades-2, 4; Notched tool-6; Blade-1. (1 – 6, 8 - flint; 7 – obsidian; 4, 8 - without stratigraphy; level 1 - 5; level 2 - 1, 3, 6, 7).

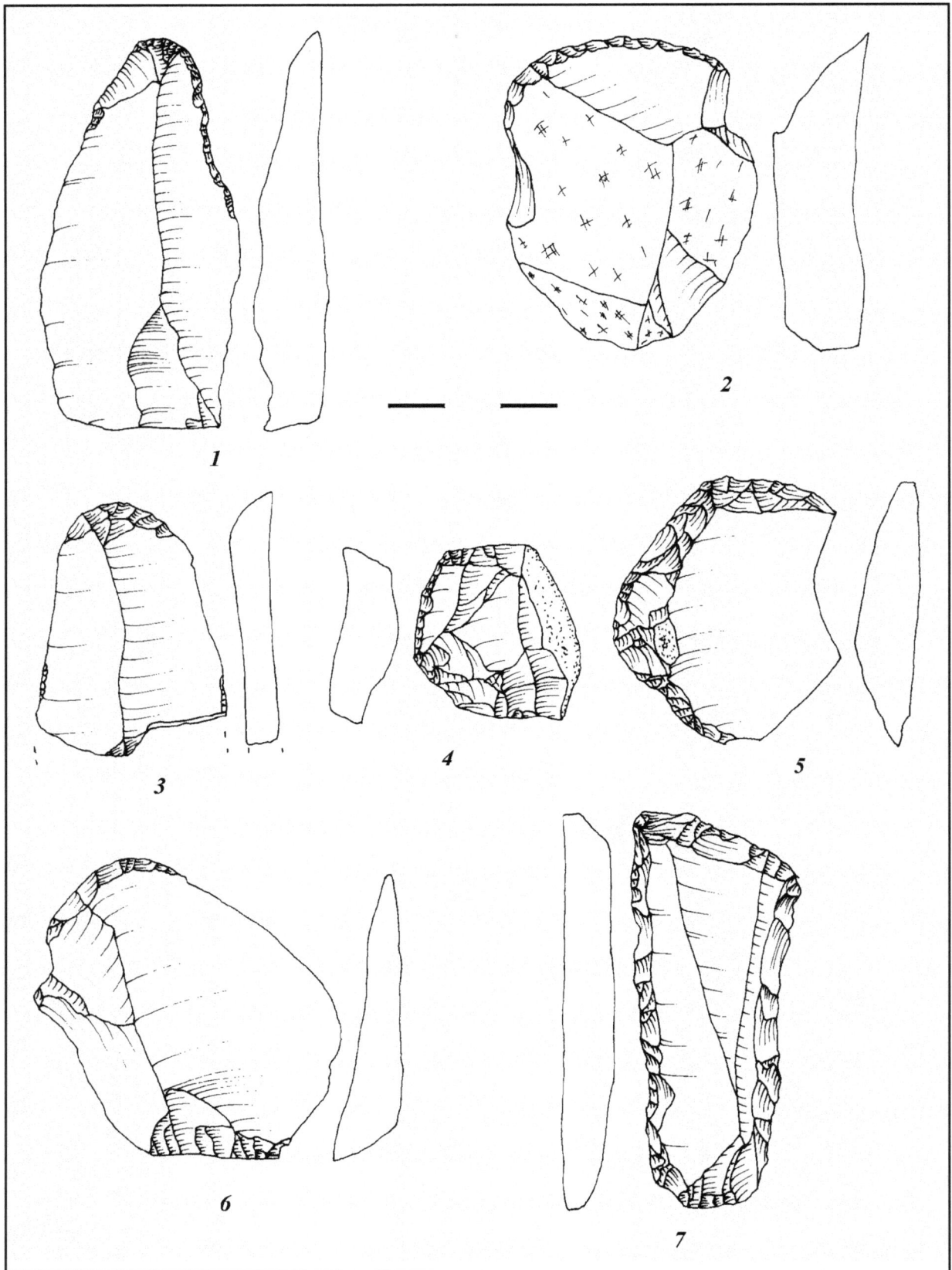

Fig. 1.3. Menteşe. End scraper-1-3; 5 -7; divers - 4. (1 - 7 flint; level 2 - 1, 3, 4, 5, 6, 7; level 3 – 2).

The estimation of mean value of width and thickness (Table 1.4) shows typical for this region obsidian blade debitage with small sizes.

Table 1.4. Metrical values of obsidian blades

	Minimum	Maximum	Mean	Std. Deviation
Width	5	15	8,07	2,223
Thickness	1	5	2,21	0,767

Obsidian blades from all assemblages under study are featured by unidirectional specimens (Table 1.6); most of them are with triangular cross section and come from advanced stage of core reduction and parallel edges (Table 1.5) (Fig. 1.5: 8, 10; Fig. 1.6: 5, 9; Fig. 1.7: 3).

Table 1.5. Relation of edges and shape of cross section of obsidian blades

	triangular	trapeze	multifaceted	Total
parallel	4	17	2	23
convergent	1	7	1	9
divergent	0	2	0	2
irregular	3	3	4	10
Total	8	29	7	44

Table 1.6. Direction of scars on obsidian blades

	Fr.	%
unidirectional	43	97,8
Double platform	1	2,2
Total	44	100,0

FLINT ARTIFACTS

The distribution of flint artifact categories' followed almost the same schema as in case of obsidian specimens (Table 1.7). The blade frequency reaches around 50% in respect of entire quantity of artifacts (Fig. 1.2: 3; Fig. 1.4: 1), come after debris and retouched tools.

Cores

The flint cores like the obsidian ones are presented by single platform items, for blades and bladelets. Some

of the specimens have cortex on one of their side, the dimensions of the analyzed specimens range between 10-5 cm, and were connected with final stage of exploitation, like the obsidian ones. (Fig. 1.7: 4; Fig. 1.8: 8)

Table 1.7. Distribution of flint specimens by levels and categories

	LEVEL			Total
	1	2	3	
Cores	3	6	1	10
cortical specimens	3	1	0	4
crested specimens	6	15	0	21
Debris	46	89	13	148
Flakes	18	35	6	59
Blades	111	137	9	257
retouched tools	44	54	12	110
Total	231	337	41	609

The mean value of blade width is higher in respect of obsidian specimens, while the value of thickness is practically the same (Table 1.8).

Table 1.8. Metrical values of flint blades

	Minimum	Maximum	Mean	Std. Deviation
Width	2	29	12,45	3,647
Thickness	2	15	3,38	1,352

Flint blades are characterized by irregular shape and trapeze and multifaceted cross section (Table 1.10). The specimens were detached by pressure, punch and soft hammer stone (Table 1.9). The frequency of blades obtaining by hard hammer stone is practically zero (Fig. 1.2: 1)

Table 1.9. Ways of detachment and butts of flint blades

	flat	linear (punctiform)	Total
pressure	4	59	63
punch	20	34	54
hard hammer stone	10	3	13
soft hammer stone	15	37	52
Total	49	133	182

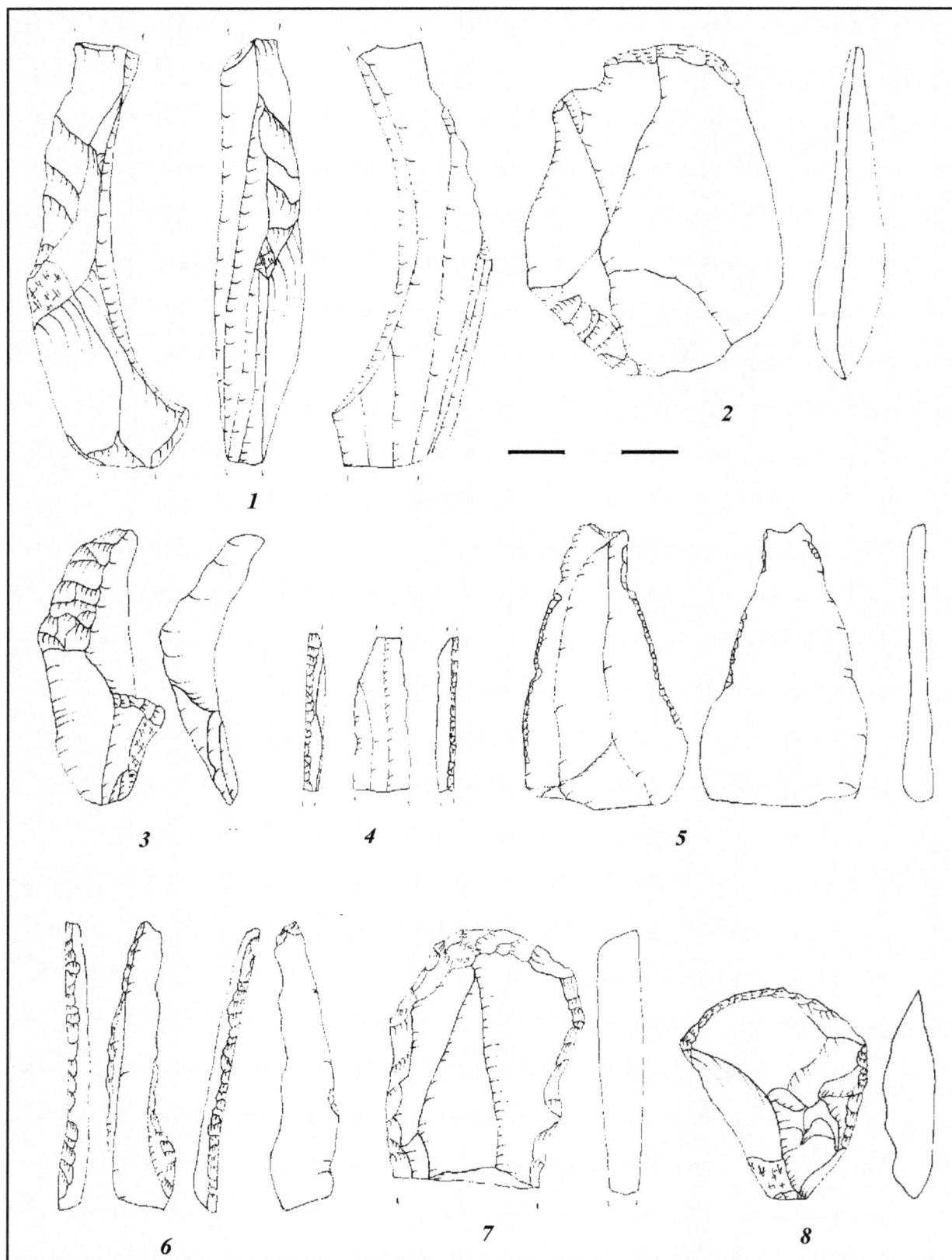

Fig. 1.4. Menteşe. Crested specimen -1, 3; End scraper on blade-7; Retouched flake-5; End –scraper on flake-2, 8; perforator on blade - 4, 6; (1, 2, 4, 5, 6, 7, 8 – flint; 3 – obsidian; level 1 –1, 6, 7; level 2 – 2, 5, 8; level 3-3, 4).

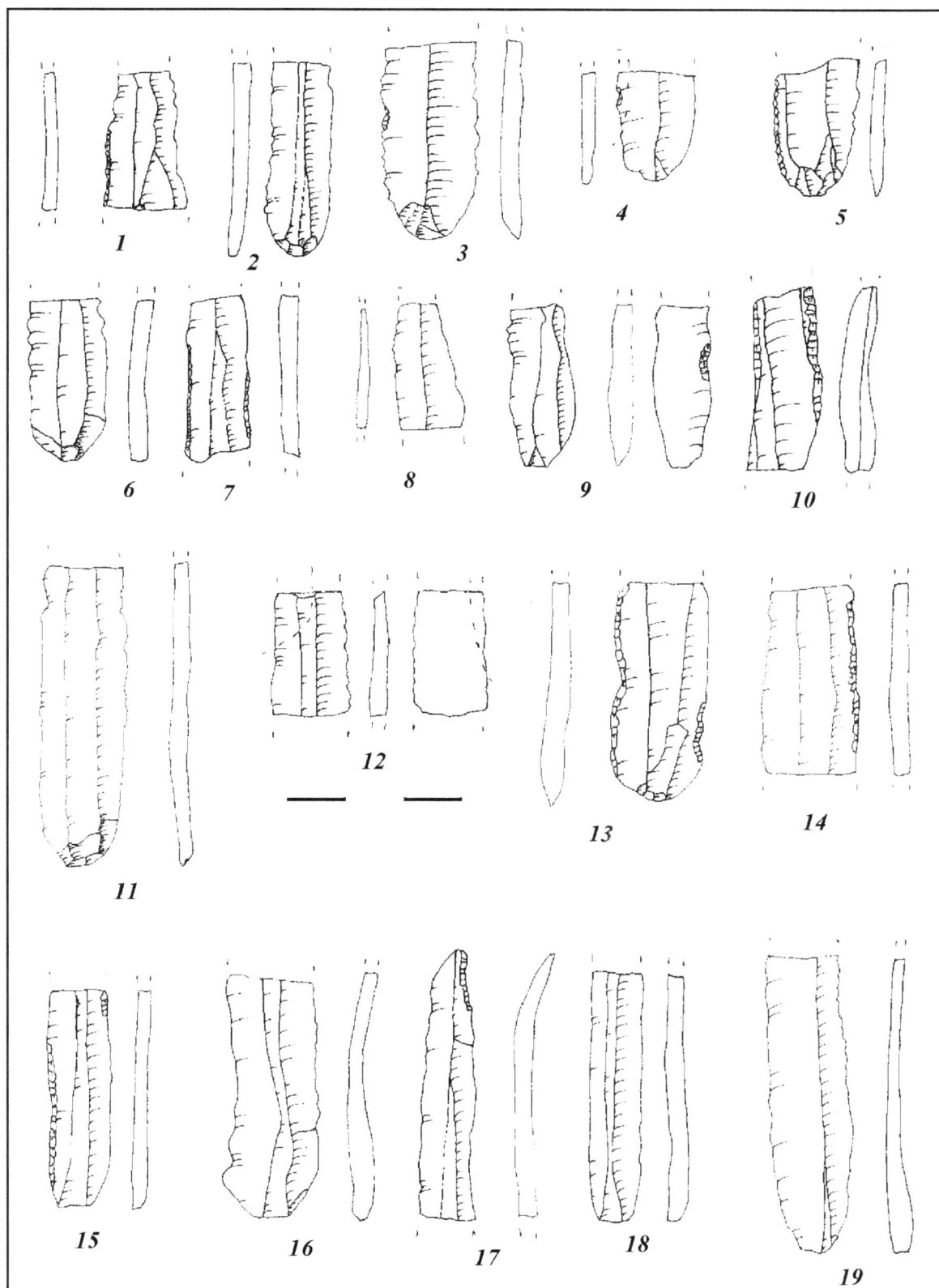

Fig. 1.5. Menteşe. Blade with denticulated retouch -1-3, 5, 6, 11-14, 16, 17, 19; Blade with micro retouch- 9, 7,15; Blade with marginal retouch-10; Blade-8, 18; Fragment of retouched tool - 4. (1 – 7, 9, 11 – 19 – flint; 8, 10 – obsidian; 16 - without stratigraphy; level 1 – 1, 2, 5, 9, 10, 12 - 15, 17, 18; level 2 – 3, 4, 6 - 8, 11, 19).

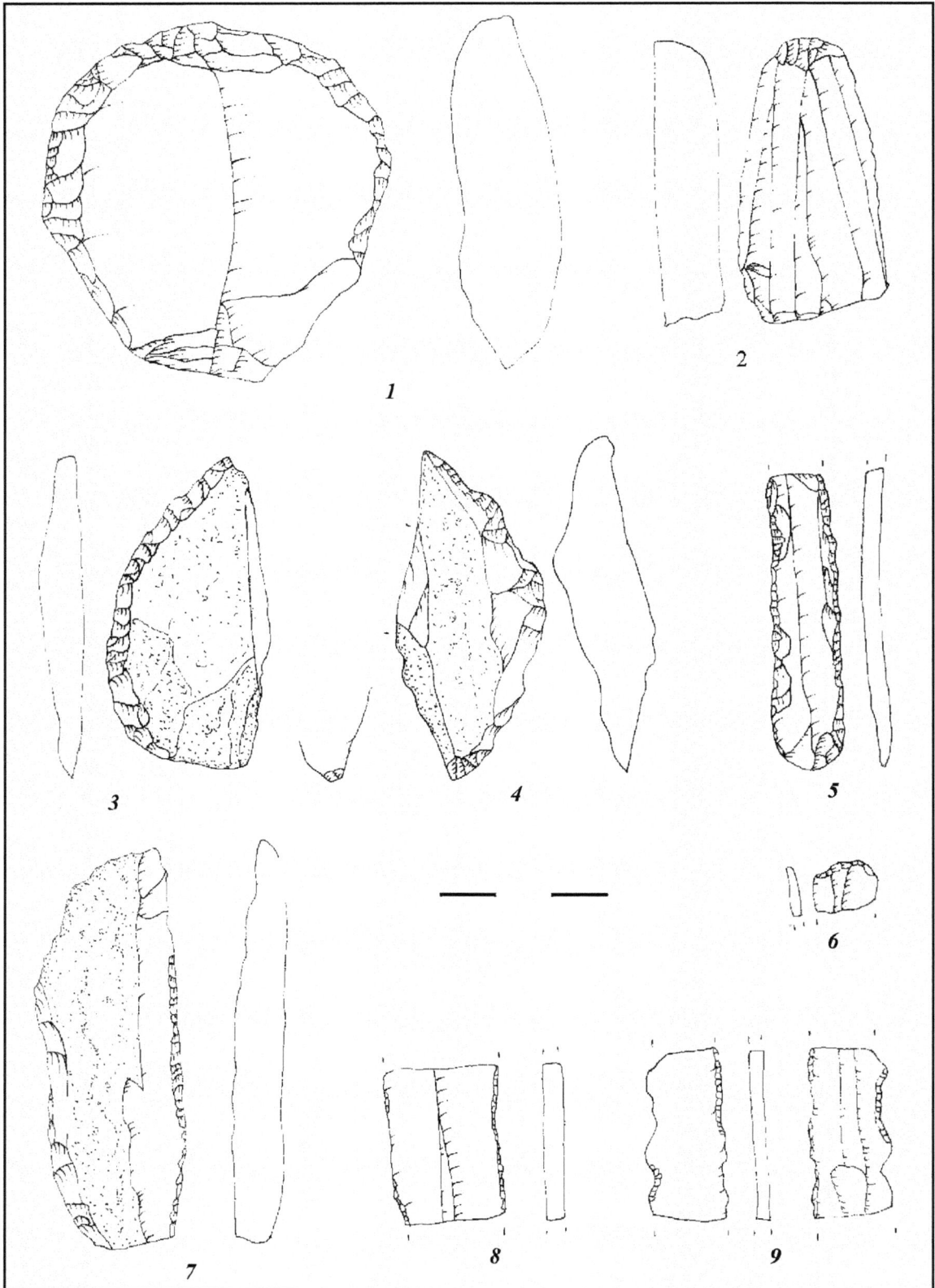

Fig. 1.6. Menteşe. End scraper on flake-1-3; Fragment of retouched tool -6; Blade with marginal retouch -7; Blade with micro retouch-8, 9; Blade with denticulated retouch - 5; Alternated perforator-4. (1 – 4, 6 – 8 - flint; 5, 9 – obsidian; 1, 5, 8 - without stratigraphy; level 1 – 4; level 2 – 2, 3, 6, 7; level 3 – 3.

Table 1.10. Relation of edges and shape of cross section of flint blades

	triangular	trapeze	multifaceted	Total
parallel	17	39	4	60
convergent	23	27	26	76
divergent	2	6	9	17
irregular	28	45	31	104
Total	70	117	70	257

The flint retouched tools (Table 1.11) are presented mostly by blade specimens, among the tools blades with denticulated retouch are prevailing, following by blades with micro and marginal retouch, perforators and drills and end-scrapers on blades. The flake tools are presented by end-scraper on flakes and retouched flakes. There were found also two chipped disks in level 1 and 2. (Fig. 1.2: 2, 4- 6, 8; Fig. 1.3: 1-7; Fig. 1.4: 2, 4-8; Fig. 1.5: 1-7, 9, 11-19; Fig. 1.6 1-4, 6-8; Fig. 1.7: 1, 2)

Table 1.11. Distribution of flint retouched tools by levels and types

	LEVEL			Total
	1	2	3	
blades with marginal retouch	1	2	0	3
fragments of retouched tool	4	3	1	8
end-scrapers on blade	1	1	0	2
end-scrapers on flake	6	11	2	19
divers	1	4	1	6
blades with micro retouch	5	6	0	11
retouched flakes	0	4	0	4
perforators and drills	2	0	2	4
blades with denticulated retouch	23	22	6	51
chipped disks	1	1	0	2
Total	44	54	12	110

The already obtained radiocarbon dates of Menteşe - defined the basal layer of this settlement as "the oldest village in Northwestern Anatolia" (Roodenberg et al. 2003, 36). Up to now the radiocarbon dates from the basal layer of Menteşe referred the beginning of the settlement in second half of VII mill. BC or just before the Ilipinar sequence – phase X.

In other words the earliest chipped stone material from Menteşe as an earliest evidence of human activities in the region under study could be considered. The fact

that the basal layer of Mentese settlement has been dated at 6.400 cal. BC supports the idea of M. Özdoğan about the possibilities in the end of VII mill BC to exist also land roads for the western expansion of Neolithic cultures.

From the other hand the main technological and typological features of Menteşe chipped stone assemblages allow to consider them as a part of the techno complex. To the former the assemblages from Ilipinar – phases X and IX, Pendik and Fikir tepe could be related as well (Fig. 1.10). The base of this suggestion is the exploitation of blade and blade single platform cores, conical, semi-conical and bullet ones for by pressure and punch techniques in the assemblages mentioned above. About the most common tool types in all assemblages it should be pointed out the occurrence of flat rounded and semi-rounded end scraper and characteristic blade perforators shaped by semi steep retouches.

Between the chipped stone assemblages of Fikir tepe, Pendik and Ilipinar-phases X and IX defined parallels in their technological and typological characteristics can be detected. In these assemblages core knapping process is based on the similar blade reduction sequences, pressure and punch or indirect percussion blade and bladeletes single platform conical cores, including bullet ones with rounded or semi rounded striking surfaces and platform situated at almost 90 degree. (Fig. 1.8: 1-3, 5-7, 9)

The typological structures of the assemblages from Pendik and Fikir tepe and Ilipinar (Fig. 1.9: 1-10) is featured by similar morphological parameters of some retouched tools such as flat circular or semi circular flat end scrapers and blade perforators with well distinguished working parts.

The opinion of M. Özdoğan support the idea of similarity between the assemblages mentioned above "...An absolute dating for the Fikir tepe culture is given by the C14 dates from Iipinar and Yarimburgaz, which yield a range c. 6.100-5.600 BC" (Özdoğan 1995).

In this connection further down some results concerning the technology of pottery are presented. The research work on the Mentese pottery allows Dr. A. van As and Dr. M.-H. Wijnen to noticed... "The pottery from Menteşe Höyük, excavated in 2000, was manufactured by a combination of modeling and coiling techniques and fired in an open fire in reducing to neutral conditions. As a result the pottery has mostly a light grey-brown tot dark grey brown colour, although clear reds occur. In the upper levels deep

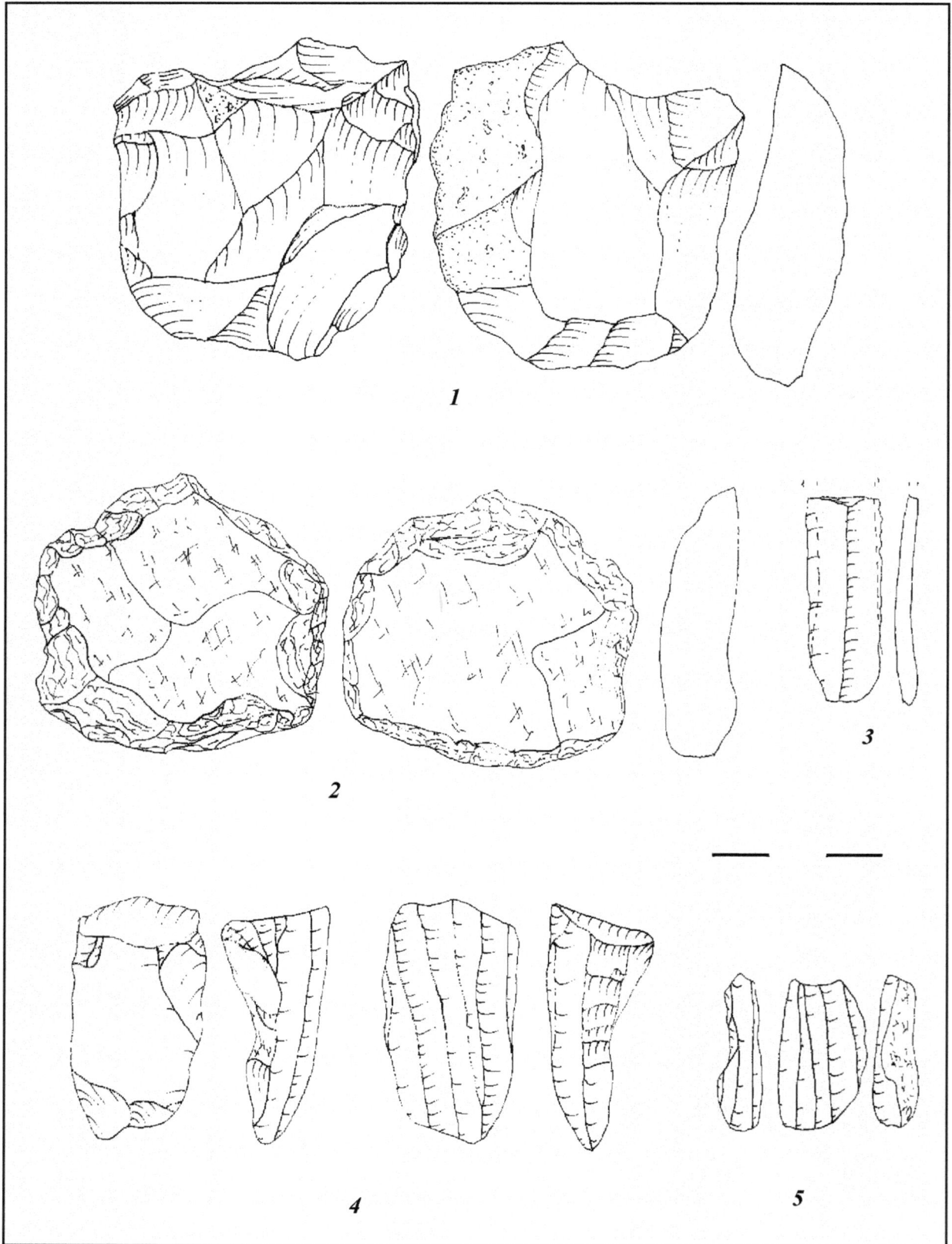

Fig. 1.7. Menteşe. Chipped disk -2; Blade with denticulated retouch-3; Core-4, 5; Various – 1
(1, 2, 4 – flint; 3, 5 – obsidian; level 1 – 5; level 2 - 1 – 4).

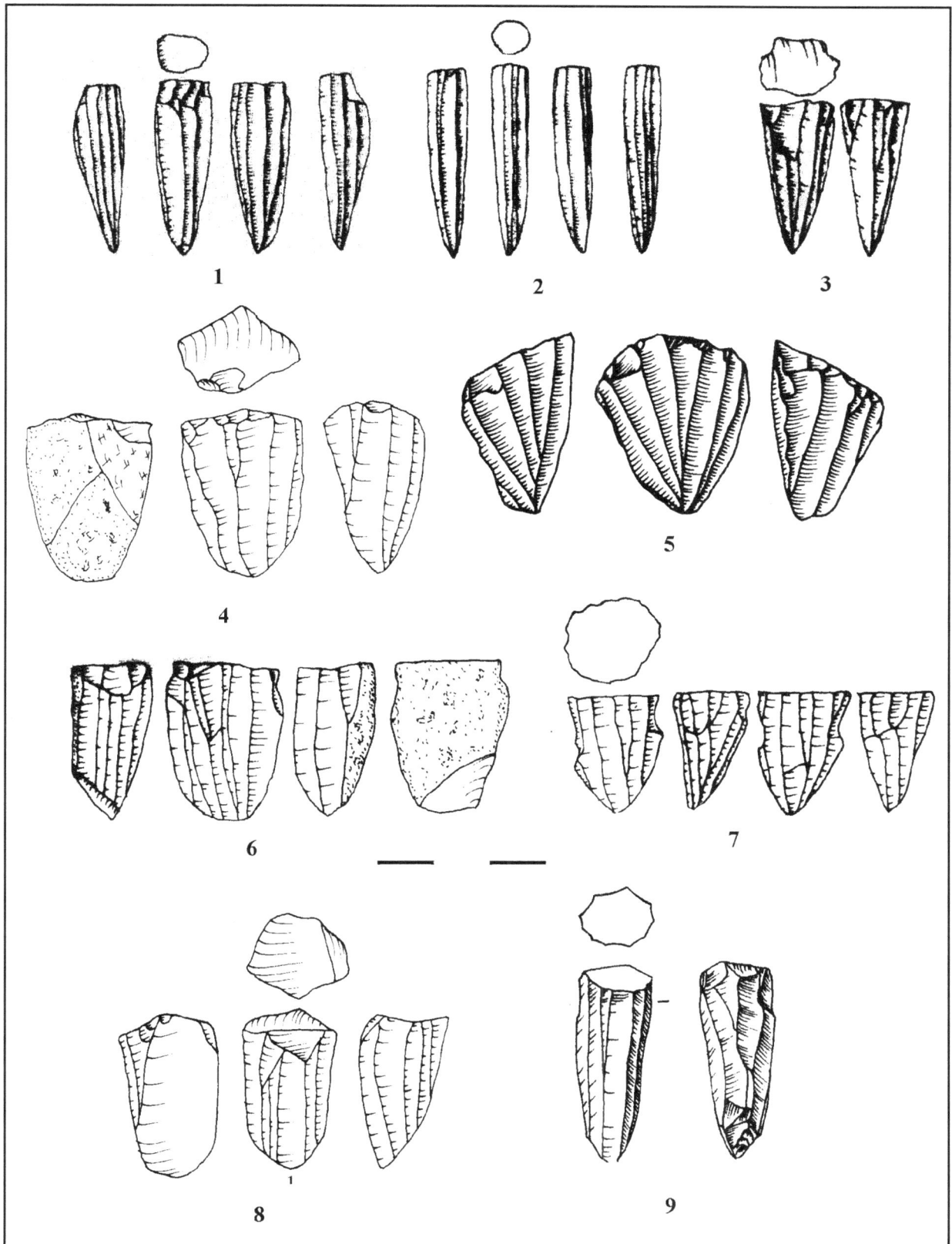

Fig. 1.8. Bullet cores. Ilipinar 1-3; Mentese 4, 8 (4- flint; 8- obsidian level 2 -4; without stratigraphy-8;)
Pendik 5; Agacli 6, 7; Fikir Tepe 9.

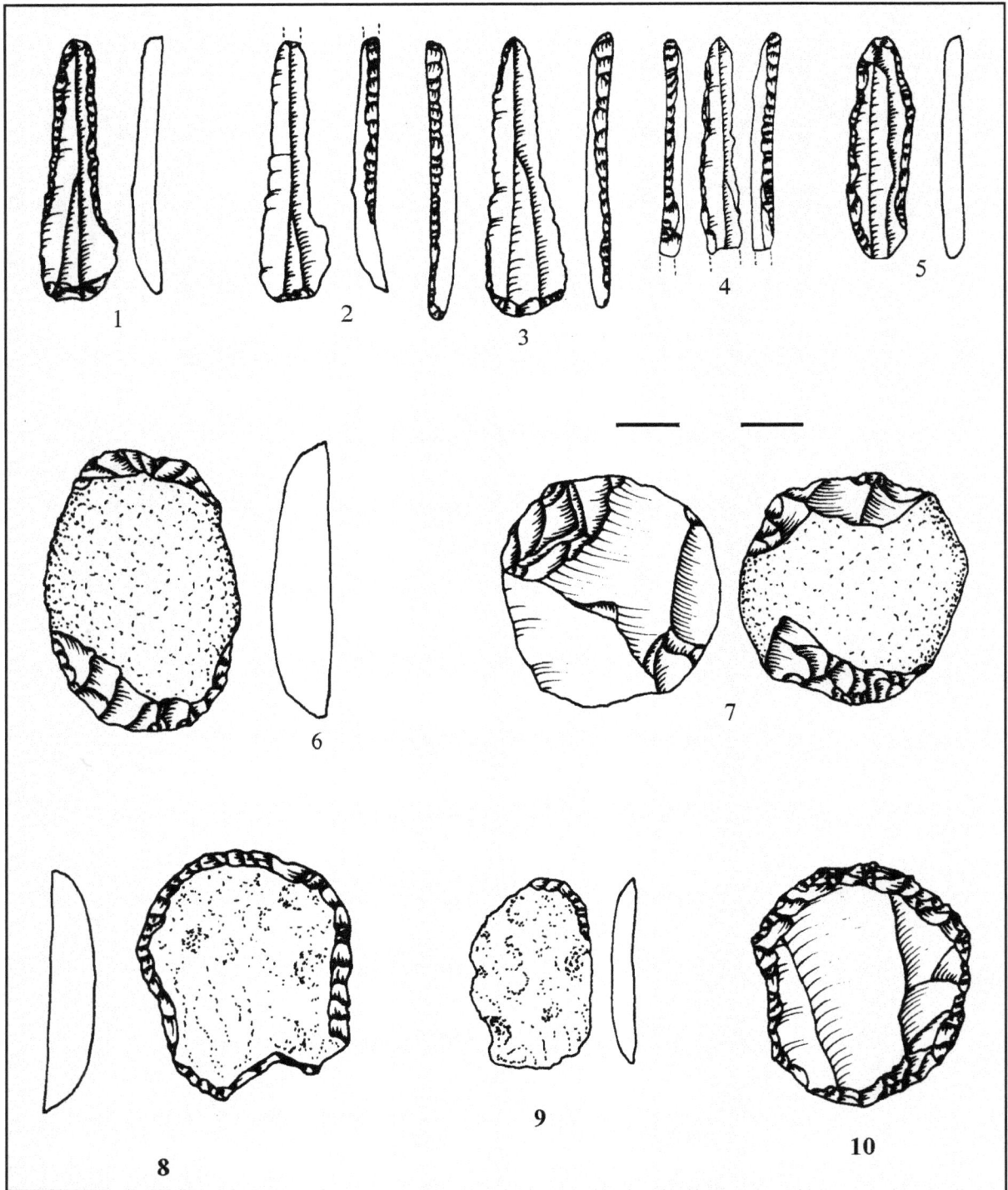

Fig. 1.9. Ilipinar. Combined tools – end – scraper + perforator 1-3;
Perforators 4, 5; end – scrapers 6, 7, 8, 9, 10.

black becomes more common. A large amount of the pottery had a high glossy burnished outer surface. In the upper levels vessels with a S-shaped profile were very common; preliminary result indicate that in the lower levels the S-shape was far less pronounced, whereas the simple plain rimmed hole mouth vessel became more common. Vessels had in general a flat base; the whole sample yielded only one ring-base.

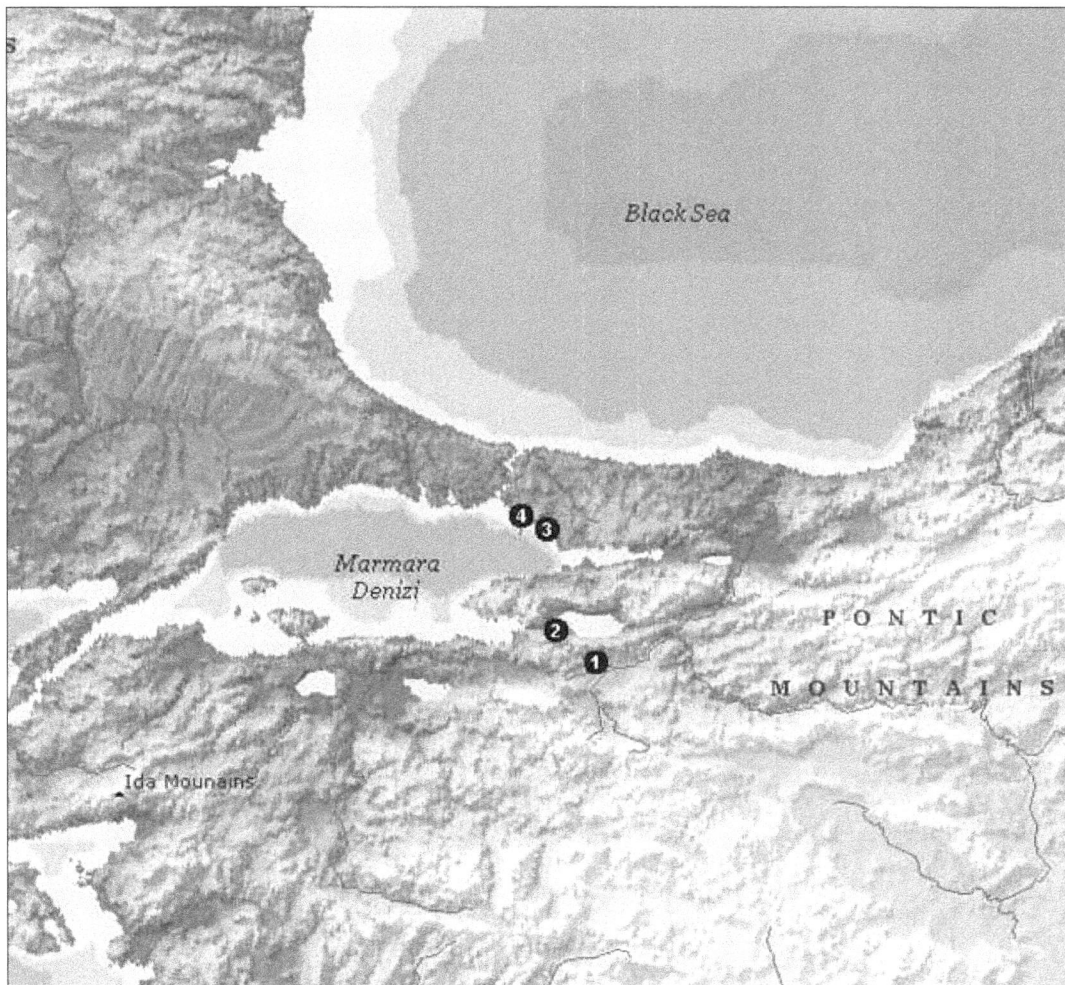

Fig. 1.10. Location of the sites: 1- Menteşe; 2- Ilipinar; 3- Pendik; 4- Fikir tepe.

Decoration is relatively sparse – maximal 2% of the total sample. It always consists of shallow incised groves arranged in simple geometric patterns. The higher levels yielded also the remains of at least two rectangular boxes on feet, decorated with incised geometric patterns. Concluding it can be said that the pottery from Menteşe fits perfectly in the Fikir tepe-sequence" (Gatsov 2006, 153-158).

The other problem occurs with the appearance and distribution of bullet cores. The former spread out from the Prut - Seret basin to the Crimean Peninsula including during the Mesolithic period. The bullet cores in the area of Turkish Black Sea shore during the Epipalaeolithic/Mesolithic transition have been registerred. As far as Turkish Black sea shore is concerned these are the assemblages from Ağaçli group. The chipped stone assemblages from this group present some links with the local Black Sea Epipalaeo-lithic/Mesolithic cultures. At the present stage it could

be considered that the inventories of Ağaçli group are connected with the local Epipalaeolithic/Mesolithic traditions which took place in the area of Black Sea shore during the time VIII/VII mill BC.

From the other hand the bullet cores could be detected also in all chipped stone assemblages from the Early Neolithic settlements during the Early Neolithic period also in the area of South and Eastern Marmara region Ilipinar, Fikir tepe, Pendik and Menteşe as well. All assemblages analyzed from the Marmara region show some similarity with Agacli group and the argument for this suggestion is the appearance of bullet cores in all of the inventories presented above.

About M. Özdoğan the chipped stone industries of Fikir tepe and Pendik "...are very significant in general terms and they appear to be a direct offspring of the Epipalaeolithic industries of the region... The amount of obsidian collected from the surface of the Pendik site is greater than the quality recovered during the Fikir tepe excavations..." (Özdoğan 1983).

As a consequence it could be suggested the Early Neolithic assemblages from South Marmara region were influenced in some degree by local technological tradition, which come from the Epipalaeolithic/Mesolithic periods.

Simultaneously the Early Neolithic assemblages of Menteşe, Ilipinar, Fikir tepe and Pendik disclose totally different technological features and totally different system of procurement in respect of the Early Neolithic stone assemblages in Northern Thrace. (Roodenberg J.J., L.C. Thissen (eds, 2001). The chipped stone assemblages from this part of Thrace – for example Karanovo I and II, Azmak Early Neolithic Layer, Cap. Dimitrievo, etc. are featured by macro blade technology and as a matter a fact flakes and flake tools are missing. Blade tools in shape of retouched blades, blade perforators, blade truncations, blade specimens with rounded end – type Karanovo I and II had been shaped by high semi steep or steep retouch.

As a rule the artifacts connected with the Early Neolithic period in South and Southwest Bulgaria had been done on a very high quality yellow flint with or without inclusions. It is very likely that the sources of this raw material lie in the region of Northern Thrace – somewhere not far a way from the settlements of Karanovo and Azmak (Gatsov I. and V. Kurchatov, 1997).

Any parallels between the Early Neolithic chipped stone assemblages connected with white painted, dark polished and painted pottery from the territory of Northern Thrace and SW Bulgaria and those from South Marmara region have been found.

References

ROODENBERG, J.; VAN AS, A.; JACOBS, L.; WIJNEN, M. H. (2003) Early settlement in the plain of Yenişehir (NW Anatolia). *Anatolica*. 29, p. 17-59.

ÖZDOĞAN, M. (1995). Neolithic in Turkey. In *Reading in Prehistory. Studies presented to Halet Cambel*. Istanbul. p. 53-55.

GATSOV, I.; KURCATOV, V. (1997) Neolithische Feursteinartefakte. In HILLER, S.; NIKOLOV, V., eds. lits. - *Karanovo, Die Ausgrabungen im Südsektor 1984-1992*. Salzburg, Band I.1, p. 213 – 227, Band I.2 Tafeln, Taf. 92-94.

ÖZDOĞAN, M. (1983) Pendik. A Neolithic site of Fikir tepe culture in the Marmara region. In BOEHMER, R. M.; HAUPTMAN, H., eds. lit. - *Beiträge zur Altertumskunde Kleinasiens. Festschrift für Kurt Bittel*. Mainz. p. 401- 411.

GATSOV, I. (2006) The state of research into the problem of Pleistocene-Holocene transition. In GATSOV, I.; SCHWARZBERG, H., eds. lit. - *Aegean-Marmara-Black Sea: Present State of the Research of the Early Neolithic*. Langenweissbach. p. 153-158.

ROODENBERG, J. J.; THISSEN, L. C. (eds.) (2001) *The Ilipinar excavations II*. Leiden: Nederlands Instituut Voor Het Nabije Oosten.

LATE MESOLITHIC OF SERBIA AND MONTENEGRO

Dušan MIHAILOVIĆ

University of Belgrade, Department of Archaeology, Čika Ljubina 18-20, 11000 Belgrade, Serbia;
dmihail@EUnet.yu

Abstract: The Late Mesolithic in the central Balkans has only been investigated in two regions: Montenegro and the Iron Gates area. In Late Mesolithic Montenegro there occurs the Castelnovian which is of local derivation and characterized by many distinctive features. It has been established that the emergence of Castelnovian tool types precedes microbladelet technology, and that Castelnovian influences spread from the coast towards the Balkan interior. Contrary to earlier suggestions, there is no reliable evidence to confirm the occurrence of pottery and domestic animal bones on the sites of this date. In the Iron Gates area the Late Mesolithic shows a continuity with the previous period and is coeval with the emergence of the Neolithic in the central Balkans. It has been suggested that Near Eastern elements may have been involved in its formation.
Key words: Western and Central Balkans, Late Mesolithic, Iron Gates Mesolithic, Early Neolithic, Near Eastern influences

Résumé: Le Mésolithique récent dans les Balkans centraux n'est étudié que dans les deux régions : celles du Monténégro et du défilé du Portes de Fer. Au Monténégro, durant le Mésolithique récent, apparaît le Castelnovien fondé sur des bases locales et caractérisé par de nombreuses spécificités. On a remarqué que l'apparition des outils de type castelnovien précède celle de la technologie d'élaboration des lamelles et que les influences castelnoviennes se propageaient pénétrant des zones côtières vers les régions intérieures des Balkans. Malgré les hypothèses précédemment annoncées, la présence de la céramique et des os des animaux domestiqués provenant de ces sites n'a pas été assurément attestée. Dans le défilé du Portes de Fer le mésolithique récent apparaît en continuation de la période précédente et il est contemporain de l'apparition du Néolithique dans les Balkans centraux. On a fait remarquer que sa formation pourrait également résulter des influences des éléments proche-orientaux.
Mots-clés: Balkans centrale et occidentale, Mésolithique récent, Mésolithique du Portes de Fer, Néolithique ancien, influences Proche-Orientaux

Late Mesolithic of the central Balkans is not a uniform cultural manifestation. The sites from this period have been discovered in two distant regions: in Montenegro and in the northeastern Serbia. The Mesolithic sites in Montenegro have been discovered half a century ago (Crvena Stijena) and from that time the Mesolithic has been confirmed in many caves and rock shelters. On the other hand, Mesolithic in Serbia is known for decades only at the sites in the Iron Gates. When we take into account that central Balkan is very insufficiently investigated and the fact that Mesolithic sites have not been encountered in the most of the neighboring countries it becomes clear why the theories about low population density of the southern Balkans in the early Holocene did occur and instantly were accepted by many authors (Perlès 2003). However, it should be bore in mind that in the past (except in Greece) there were no serious attempts to discover the Mesolithic sites in the Balkans. In this paper we shall try to consider the Mesolithic of Serbia and Montenegro within broader regional context and to point to the open questions concerning the cultural circumstances in the period immediately preceding the emergence of the Neolithic in the central Balkans.

LATE MESOLITHIC OF MONTENEGRO

The investigations so far revealed that Mesolithic in Montenegro is the frequent phenomenon and that it is easy to identify at least when caves and rock shelters are concerned. Late Mesolithic is confirmed in layer IV at Crvena Stijena, in horizons Ia and Ib at Odmut and Vruća Pećina, while at Medena Stijena was encountered the industry with trapezes in the considerably disturbed horizon IV (Basler 1975; Kozłowski *et al.* 1994; Mihailović 1996, 1998; Đuričić 1997). The coastal sites are classified as the local variant of Castelnovian while the industry from Medena Stijena has not distinctive Castelnovian characteristics and could not be attributed to any of the existing techno complexes. Judging by the available absolute dates Late Mesolithic in this area commences in the middle of the 7th millennium cal BC at the latest and continues until the end of the first quarter of the 6th millennium cal BC.

Despite the fact that Late Mesolithic of Montenegro was initially defined by the finds from Odmut (Kozłowski *et al.* 1994) it is obvious that best insight in the development of the Castelnovian in this area especially when its early phase is concerned could be reached on the basis of the material from Crvena Stijena (Mihailović 1998). In the layer IVb2 at this site are prevailing the retouched flakes, splintered pieces and denticulated and notched tools on the flakes and irregular blades. The endscrapers on the flakes and other tools, which conditionally speaking have the Romanelian character are considerably frequent while the trapezes are missing.

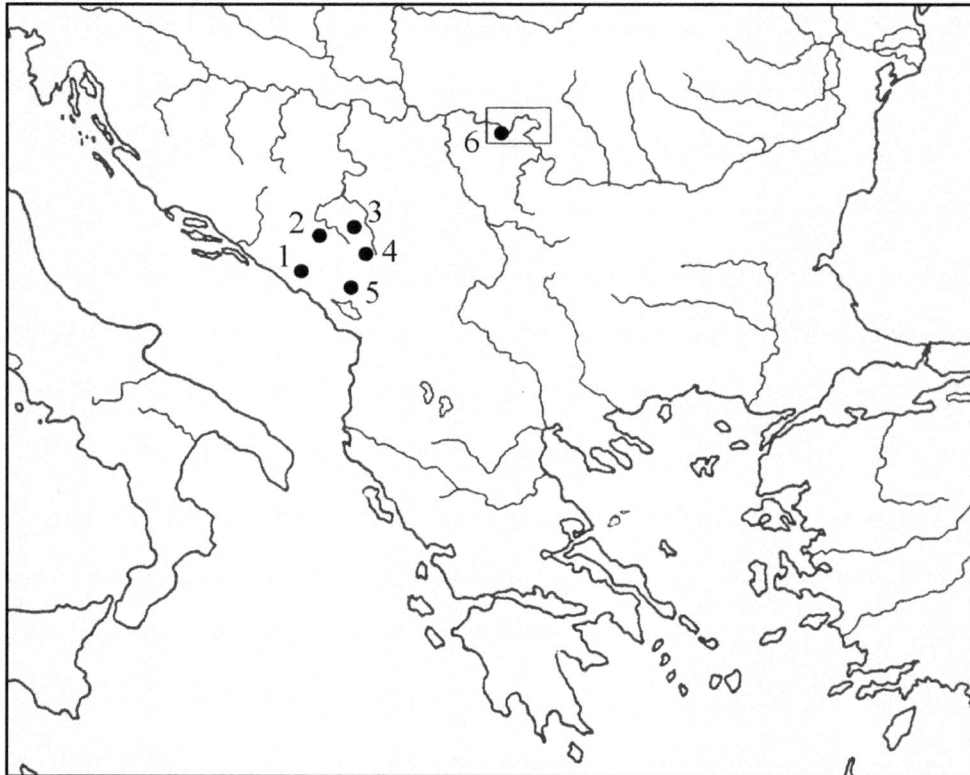

Fig. 2.1. The Mesolithic sites in the central Balkans: 1- Crvena Stijena, 2- Odmut, 3 – Medena Stijena, 4 – Trebački Krš, 5 – Vruća Pećina, 6 - Lepenski Vir and other Iron Gates sites

Great changes could be noticed in the horizon IVb1 owing to the fact that in this layer for the first time occur the specimens produced by microbladelet technology although there are still present the endscrapers and other tools on the flakes. The microbladelet technology is characterized by pressure flaking from the cores on which in the process of flaking only the platform was rejuvenated. The bladelets, which are mostly of triangular or trapezoid cross-section usually have faceted platform. They were used for production of denticulated and notched tools, tools with retouched truncation and trapezes. The microburin technique appears only in traces (only few specimens were registered). The similar situation was also encountered in the horizon IVa: the repertoire of tools on the bladelets is more restricted and there also occur slightly broader blades, which will be character-ristic of the Neolithic layer (III).

In the Mesolithic layers of Crvena Stijena, particularly in the horizon IVb1, the bone tools are rather numerous (typical are the points-projectiles with slanting base) and tools made of antler (hoes, pickaxes) and there were also found the engraved objects. Large quantity of the shells of terrestrial mollusks was collected from this horizon and many hearths were also encountered.

The situation at Odmut differs to a certain extent. The Castelnovian characteristics are less prominent. In the stone industry prevail endscrapers, retouched flakes and tools on bladelets while in the faunal remains are most frequent the remains of ibex, birds and fish. The characteristic of Odmut is the large number of flat single-filed harpoons, the harpoons with one or two barbs (over 50 specimens have been found – Srejović 1974). Similar harpoons were also found at Vruća Pećina but in the Neolithic layer (Đuričić 1997). The Mesolithic industry from this site has not been analyzed in detail but it is obvious on the basis of the published data that it is the Castelnovian industry.

And to summarize, Late Mesolithic of Montenegro originates from the Epitardigravettian basis. It includes the technologically impoverished industries from Trebački Krš and Crvena Stijena VII-V characterized by the expedient technology and with rather conspi-cuous Romanelian component (Mihailović 2001). In the beginning of the 7th millennium and perhaps even earlier the Castelnovian influences appeared first at Crvena Stijena (horizon IVb2) in such a way that changes in the repertoire preceded the introduction of the new technology. In this case it is difficult to determine whether it was a result of the cultural

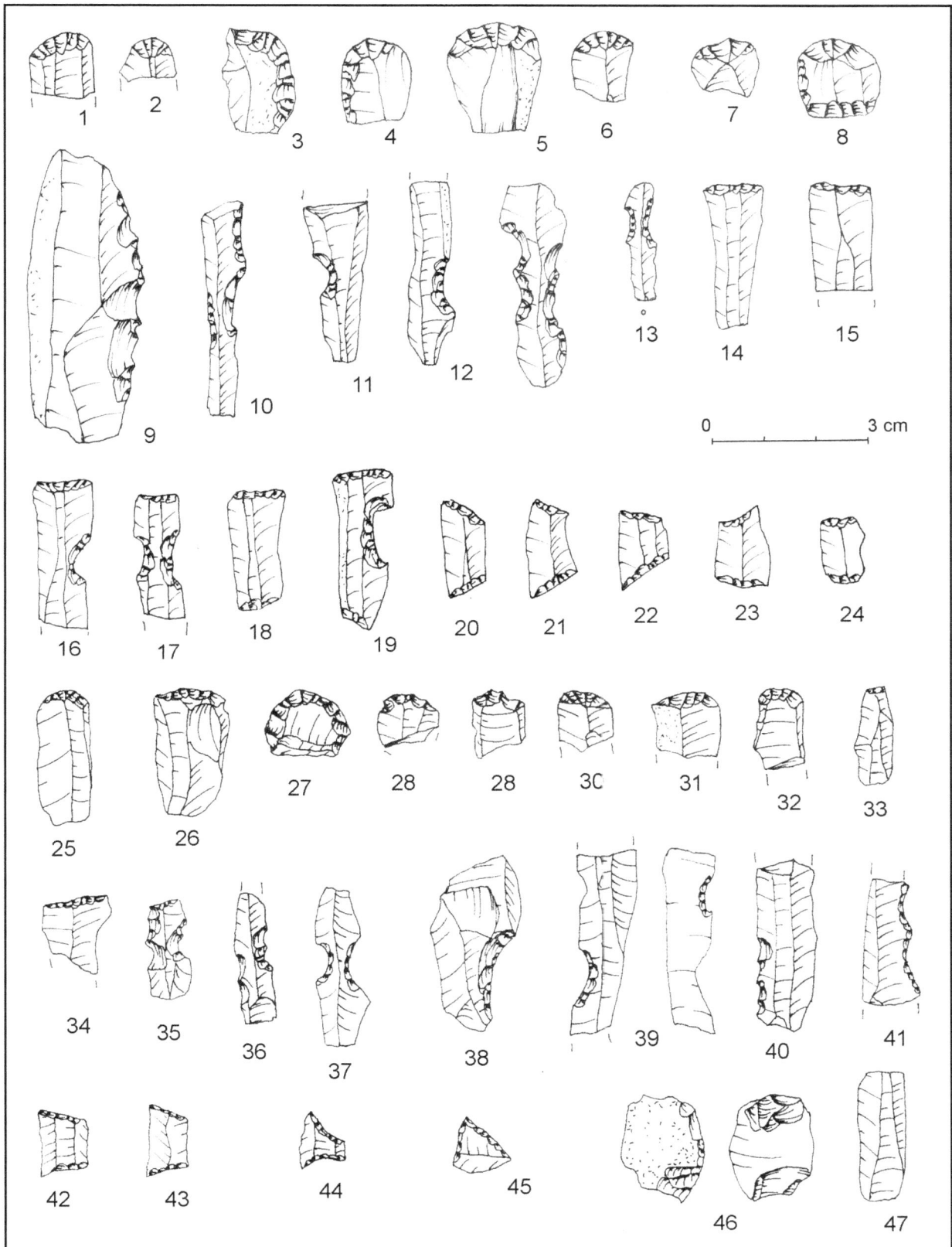

Fig. 2.2. Late Mesolithic industries from Montenegro: 1-24 - Crvena Stijena IVb1,
25-47 - Vruća Pećina (after Đuričić 1997)

influences or the need to make tools of distinct purpose (it concerns denticulated blades and blades with notches). However, it is highly probable to assume that in the later period the Castelnovian technology spread from the coast (Vrući Pećina, Crvena Stijena) to the hinterland. The Castelnovian elements are less frequent at Odmut than at Crvena Stijena and Vrući Pećina while they are completely missing at Medena Stijena. At this site the sparse trapezes and tools on the blades occur within an entirely different context. Most of the artifacts were made on flakes.

Regarding the economy the bearers of the Late Mesolithic practiced the forest fauna hunting. The hunting of birds, fishing and gathering of the mollusks (Crvena Stijena) was also registered (Basler 1975) while hunting of ibex was practiced at Odmut (Srejović 1974a) and this tradition continues also in the Neolithic (as is suggested by the finds from Spila near Perast – Marković 1985). The settlement pattern greatly resembles the one recorded in the Mesolithic of the northern Italy. There are no reliable indicators for the domesticated animals despite the fact that some time ago was published that in the layer IV were found the remains of the goat (Malez 1975). It is, however, necessary to mention that authors of the investigations at Crvena Stijena never paid serious attention to this find (Benac and Brodar 1958; Basler 1975). It is very possible that it was an intrusion from the upper layers.

LATE MESOLITHIC OF SERBIA (IRON GATES)

In contrast to the Mesolithic of Montenegro the Mesolithic of the Iron Gates was always studied as an isolated phenomenon and its chronological and cultural boundaries are more difficult to determine. There are many periodizations and different opinions concerning the definition of Epipalaeolithic, Mesolithic and Neolithic in the Iron Gates (Radovanović 1996). The main problem lies in the fact that periodization in this area could not be established only on the basis of technological and economic indicators. At many sites were discovered the remains of architecture and graves and at Lepenski Vir even the stone sculpture (Srejović 1969).

The beginning of settling in the Iron Gates region in the early Holocene dates from the middle of the 9th millennium cal BC (Radovanović 1996, Boroneanț 1999). This phase, which is usually identified as Epipalaeolithic was registered at the sites Ostrovul Banului I-II, Padina A, Terasa Veterani and probably Cuina Turcului II. Yet, it is clear that crucial changes in the material culture, economy and society of the Iron Gates communities took place already in this phase. At

that time was established the settlement pattern and way of life that is to be characteristic in the next period. The burying of the dead did appear in horizon A at Padina (Jovanović 1971, 1974, 1987; Radovanović 1996).

In the middle or advanced phase of the Iron Gates Mesolithic that spans the period from the middle of the 8th to the middle of the 6th millennium cal BC the Mesolithic culture encompassed the entire region of the Iron Gates and the sites are concentrated on the left Danube bank (Icoana, Razvrata, Scela Cladovei, Ostrovul Banului III). The cultural differentiation between the settlements in Gornja and Donja klisura are apparent and traces of projectiles in the skeletons from Vlasac and Schela Cladovei bear witness to the conflicts of the groups. From this period date the cultural horizons at Vlasac and the beginning of settling at Lepenski Vir.

The late phase of Iron Gates Mesolithic that could be called the Late Mesolithic commenced about 6.400-6.300 cal BC. It is preceded by ceasing of life at most of the settlements from the earlier phase (Lepenski Vir is an exception) (Radovanović 1996; Bonsall et al. 2002; Borić and Miracle 2004). In some settlements the Mesolithic and Neolithic elements were merging together. This phenomenon is best perceptible at Padina (Jovanović 1987; Mihailović 2004) and to a considerably smaller degree at Lepenski Vir as well (Garašanin and Radovanović 2001). Nevertheless, considering the cultural continuity and the economic basis we think that Lepenski Vir should be determined as the Mesolithic settlement.

Here a question could be asked about the factors influencing the beginning and the end of Middle and Late Mesolithic in the Iron Gates. The beginning of settling at the Danube banks should certainly be related to the increased intensity of the fishing activities. According to I. Radovanović just the fishing played the role of the resource important for the survival of the community although objectively it perhaps did not have such role. Their right to the territory the communities manifested among other things also by establishing formal burial grounds (Radovanović 1996). The beginning of the last phase also deserves our attention. For the time being it is not possible to determine whether this phase was the final result of the social and cultural integration or it occurred as a reaction to the cultural trends in the surroundings. In favor of the first assumption speaks the fact that riverside communities in the southeast Europe did not appear only in the Iron Gates but also in Moldavia (Soroki – Markevič 1974) and that it could be assumed (despite the absence of evidence) that these types of settlements were distributed throughout the wider area of the south and

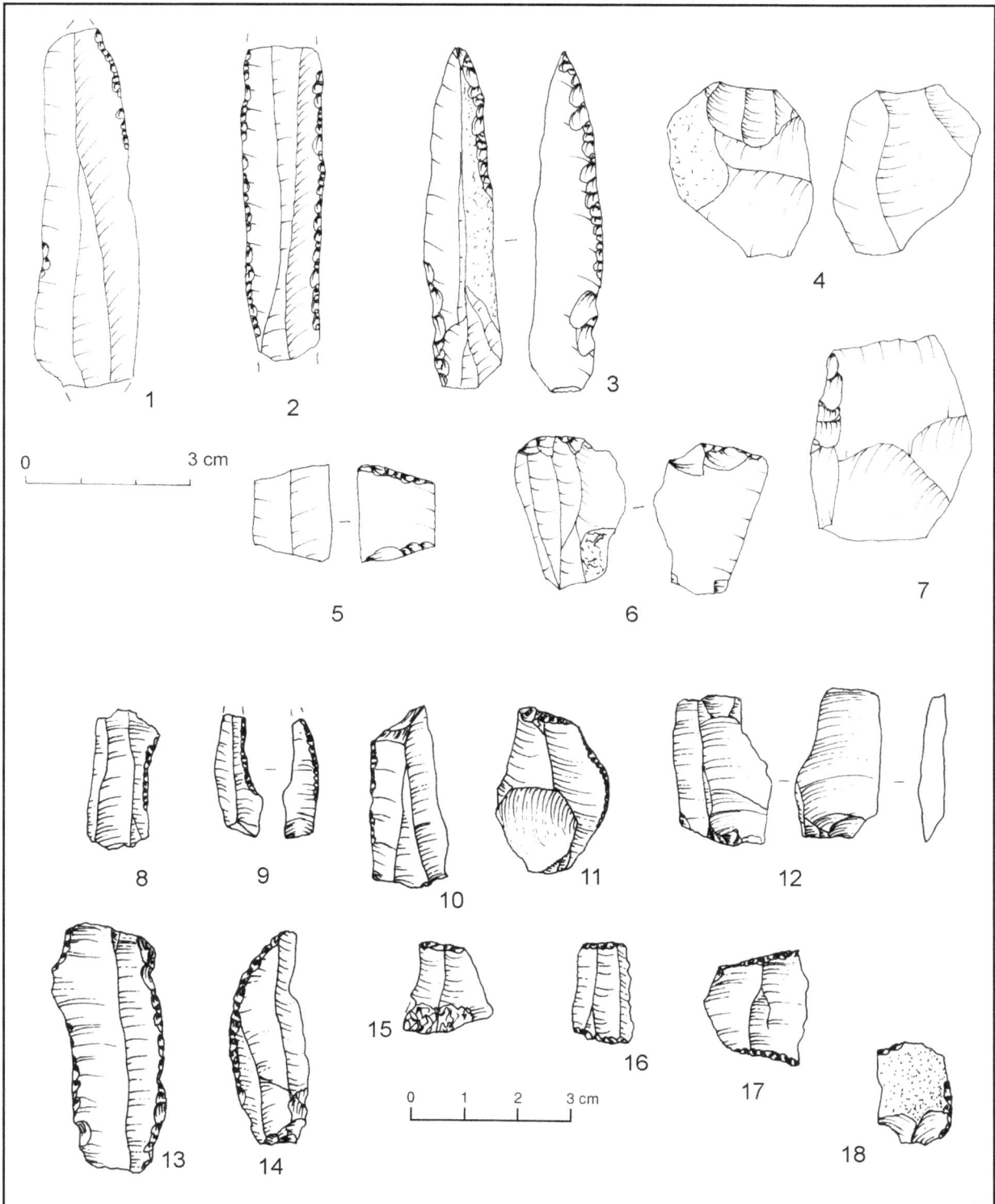

Fig. 2.3. Mesolithic-Neolithic transition in the Iron Gates: chipped stone industries from Padina B (1-7) and Lepenski Vir I (8-18) (after Kozłowski & Kozłowski 1984)

east Europe. On the other hand, it is evident that Neolithic elements at Lepenski Vir appeared simulta- neously with the occurrence of trapezoid houses and stone sculpture.

There is still another element, which could explain the distinctive character of the Iron Gates Mesolithic. It concerns the fact that great similarities between the Iron Gates Mesolithic and the Epipalaeolithic and Pre-Pottery Neolithic of the Near East had already been perceived sometime ago (Srejović 1974b; Garašanin 1997). At one time this phenomenon was explained as a result of the convergent tendencies in the cultural evolution. In the meantime the parallels multiplied and we have at our disposal also new theoretical models, which make possible different explanations.

As many authors already stated the closest analogies between the Iron Gates Mesolithic and the phenomena in the Near East could be noticed in the domain of burying the dead (Garašanin 1997). In the Iron Gates Mesolithic appears for instance burying of the sculls, which is the practice that will occur much later, i.e. at the beginning of the Neolithic in the southeastern Europe (with exception of Ukraine). Also, only in the Iron Gates Mesolithic were registered the settlements with central building and rectilinear architecture based on precise measuring of the ground plans. There is also the use of pyrotechnology (floors made of lime mortar) that had not been registered in the Mesolithic and Neolithic of the Balkans but which is typical just for the Pre-Pottery Neolithic of the Near East. Finally, it turned out that there are even analogies for the stone sculpture. Much before the occurrence of the stone sculptures in the Iron Gates Mesolithic there were settlements in southeastern Anatolia (Nevali Çori – Hauptmann 1999) with sculptures and reliefs of stone that according to the syncretism of anthropomorphic and zoomorphic motifs, technique of manufacture and even the disposition within the structures greatly resembles the sculpture of Lepenski Vir and its context.

The question of the Pre-Pottery Neolithic is not a new one and had already been raised in connection with the emergence of the pottery Neolithic in the southeastern Europe (Milojčić 1956, Tellenbach 1984). But the situation here is that in the Iron Gates Mesolithic could be observed manifestations from the early phase of the Pre-Pottery Neolithic (from the end of PPNA and early and middle phase of PPNB) which if we take into account the evidence from Vlasac also occur rather early. Therefore, the possibility could not be excluded that by the 'leapfrog' colonization (Cauvin 2000, Zvelebil 2001) part of the population from that region reached the Iron Gates area. Of course, this assertion is impossible to prove at this very moment considering the spatial and chronological distance between the Iron Gates Mesolithic and the phenomena in Anatolia and in the Near East. Yet, considering the geographical position of the Iron Gates the possibility should not be excluded that influences reached the middle Danube basin from some secondary center, perhaps on the

Black Sea coast. The connections between these areas could be observed already from the time of the Cuina Turcului-Belolesye-Shan Koba complex (Kozłowski 1989; Radovanović 1996) and the importance of the Danubian direction is suggested also by the fact that the earliest Neolithic sites in the eastern Balkans were encountered in the northern Bulgaria (Todorova and Vaisov 1993).

It is justified to assume that the Near East cultural koine at its peak did spread around much greater area. It also turned out that the bearers of the Pre-Pottery Neolithic culture after settling the distant areas were able to forsake the advanced technologies and create an authentic culture adapted to the new circumstances. The Cyprus example shows clearly that breaking with tradition happened after deteriorating of the contacts with the home region at the moment when there was no more the need for integration into larger social community and the cultural area (Simmons 1998; Cauvin 2000, Guialine et al. 2000). On the other hand, when the Iron Gates is concerned, there perhaps existed if not in the sphere of economy but in the spiritual and cultural sphere something that Srejović called the extended arch of the Fertile Crescent (Srejović 1974). Taking into consideration the geographical and cultural connections of the Balkans and the Near East we are more inclined to accept the possibility that there really existed the influences and/or contacts than to proclaim the parallels in the cultural evolution in these two areas as a coincidence or to explain them as a result of the convergent tendencies.

CONCLUDING REMARKS:
LATE MESOLITHIC AND NEOLITHIZATION
OF THE CENTRAL BALKANS

All in all, great changes took place in the end of 8th and in the first half of the 7th millennium BC in the territory inhabited by uniform Epitardigravettian technocomplex. In the Iron Gates, according to the most of the authors, commenced social integration, which would result in the emergence of the settlements with formal areas for interment while at the Adriatic coast was established Castelnovian technocomplex, which spread out towards the hinterland in the course of time. At the same time, first influences from the East reached southern Europe (Crete, Thessaly – Perlès 2001) and perhaps even the Iron Gates. At that time started cultural differentiation between the Adriatic coast and the Balkan hinterland that would increase in the ensuing period.

At the coast the continuity between the Mesolithic and Neolithic is clearly perceptible in the settlement pattern, material culture (if we leave out the occurrence of pottery) and even in the economy. It is conspicuous at the sites in Montenegro where on top of the Mesolithic horizons are encountered as a rule also the Neolithic horizons. Still, it is not clear so far how the Neolithization of this region came about. Only evident fact is that there is no chronological overlapping as the latest dates for the Mesolithic are within the range of the beginning of the 6th millennium while the Neolithic dates are couple of hundred years later (Müller 1991; Kozłowski et al. 1994).

We think that the existence of the complex hunter-gatherer communities in the central Balkans could have contributed to the rapidity of the Neolithic expansion in this region. However, it should be emphasized that there are different opinions concerning this problem. According to some authors the Neolithic could have expanded rapidly in an area scarcely populated by hunter-gatherer communities with simple social structure (Perlès 2003). On the other hand, it should be taken into account that there is a possibility that complex communities with large population and semi sedentary way of life not only had the need to accept the stable resources but also that they were able to establish more extensive social connections with the Neolithic surroundings. All this could have contributed to their early acquaintance with the Neolithic values and more rapid integration into the Neolithic society.

At this place should be underlined that new absolute dates suggest that pottery Neolithic advanced more rapidly than it was assumed in the large territory from the west Anatolia to the south Pannonia (Whittle et al. 2002; Reingruber and Thissen 2005). It is particularly conspicuous in the area from the west Anatolia to the north and east Balkans where Neolithic spread during only few hundred years (6.500-6.300 / 6.200 cal BC). Just this fact calls into question all the models based on the effects of long-lasting processes like the increase of population, quest for fertile soil and even acculturation. Thus, it is obvious that there is some concrete reason for the advance of the Neolithic and that it would be more advisable to formulate and test the hypotheses, which could explain this phenomenon than to stick to the paradigm about colonization that is sustainable only if we consider the Neolithization within far larger area and if we associate with this process also the earliest settlements of the Pre-Pottery Neolithic in Greece. When, however, these sites are concerned it is clear that it is a completely different phenomenon provoked by the different causes.

It is important to bear in mind that the Neolithic civilization of Anatolia and the Near East could not be judged only from the archaeological aspect. The civilization of the Pre-Pottery Neolithic represents the beginning of creation of the Near East cultural unity, which will be the focus of cultural events also in the ensuing millennia. Also, the Neolithization itself testifies not only about the economic but also about the complete social transformation. Therefore, we are of the opinion that it should be studied primarily as the social phenomenon.

If we accept the greater role of the Mesolithic communities in the process of Neolithization of the Balkans and it is indicated besides the archaeological also by the genetic indicators (Richards 2003) we must ask ourselves how their acculturation took place. Here could be applied to a certain extent the availability model of M. Zvelebil (Zvelebil 1986; 2001). There are indications that the Mesolithic communities in many parts of the Balkans where before the eventual appearance of the Neolithic had been exposed for a rather long period of time to the Neolithic influences (particularly in the domain of technology) but because of the absence of knowledge or the local tradition they were not ready to accept them. In the later phase, at some sites in the Iron Gates and especially at Padina in horizon B could be observed the dramatic phase of substitution when the Neolithic technology was merging with the Mesolithic architecture and economy. As in the caves of Montenegro, the isolated region of the Iron Gates made possible to comprehend the continuity of settling and to monitor the complete process in loco in contrast to many other regions where the impression of discontinuity was imposed by comparing the Mesolithic settlements in the caves and the Neolithic settlement in the open.

Something else should be also taken into consideration: if the Mesolithic communities tried at one moment to start experimenting with food production then they certainly did not do that by abandoning the traditional methods of food supplying. Within that context it is not difficult to assume the establishing of the satellite settlements, which could have at first been established in the vicinity of the Mesolithic camps and later they took over the function of the main settlements. Geographical position of the earliest Neolithic settlements in Bulgaria (on the lowest river terraces) and the fact that in the Iron Gates the Mesolithic and Neolithic sites are very close to each other indicate that this scenario is not far from the reality.

References

BASLER, Đ. (1975) Stariji litički periodu u Crvenoj stijeni. In BASLER, Đ., ed. - Crvena Stijena – zbornik radova. Nikšić: Zajednica kulturnih ustanova. p. 11-120.

BENAC, A.; BRODAR, M. (1958) Crvena Stijena - 1956. *Glasnik Zemaljskog Muzeja.* (Ser. A). N.S. 13. p. 21-65.

BONSALL, C.; MACLIN, M.; PAYTON, R.; BORONEANȚ, V. (2002) Climate, floods and river gods: environmental change and the Meso-Neolithic transition in southeast Europe. *Before Farming.* 3–4 (2), p. 1–15.

BORIĆ, D.; MIRACLE, P. (2004) Mesolithic and Neolithic (dis)continuities in the Danube gorges: new AMS dates from Padina and Hajdučka Vodenica (Serbia). *Oxford Journal of Archaeology.* 23(4). p. 341-371.

BORONEANȚ, V. (1999) The Mesolithic habitation complexes in the Balkans and Danube Basin. *Living Past.* 1. URL: http://www.cimec.ro/living-past/ mesolithic.htm

CAUVIN, J. (2000) *The Birth of the Gods and the Origins of Agriculture.* Cambridge: Cambridge University Press. p. 259.

ĐURIČIĆ, LJ. (1997) Vruća pećina – višeslojno nalaziše. *Starinar.* N.S. Knjiga XLVIII/1997. p. 195-199.

GARAŠANIN, M. (1997) Lepenski Vir posle trideset godina. In LAZIĆ, M. ed. – *Arheologija istočne Srbije.* Beograd: Centar za arheološka istraživanja. p. 11-20.

GARAŠANIN, M.; RADOVANOVIĆ, I. (2001) A pot in house 54 at Lepenski Vir I. *Antiquity.* 75. p. 118-125.

GUILAINE, J.; BRIOIS, F.; VIGNE, J-D.; CARRERE, I. (2000) Découverte d'un Néolithique préceramique ancien chypriote (fin 9e, debut 8e millénaires cal BC), apparenté au PPNB ancien/moyen du Levant nord. *Earth and Planetary Sciences.* 330. p. 75-82.

HAUPTMANN, H. (1999) The Urfa Region. In OZDOGAN, M. ed. – *Neolithic in Turkey – the cradle of civilization.* Istanbul: Arkeoloji ve Sanat Yaynlary. p. 65-86. (Ancient Anatolian Civilizations Series: 3)

JOVANOVIĆ, B. (1971) Elements of the Early Neolithic architecture in the Iron Gate Gorge and their functions. *Archaeologica Iugoslavica.* 9. p. 1–9.

JOVANOVIĆ, B. (1974) Praistorija Gornjeg Đerdapa. *Starinar.* N.S. 22. p. 1–22.

JOVANOVIĆ, B. (1987) Die architektur und Keramik der Siedlung Padina B am Eisernen Tor, Jugoslawien. *Germania.* 65(1). p. 1–16.

KOZŁOWSKI, J. K.; KOZŁOWSKI, S. K. (1984) Chipped stone industries from Lepenski Vir, Yugoslavia. *Preistoria Alpina.* 19. p. 259-293.

KOZŁOWSKI, J. K.; KOZŁOWSKI, S. K.; RADOVANOVIĆ, I. (1994) *Meso- and Neolithic Sequence from the Odmut Cave (Montenegro),* Warszawa: Wydawnictwa Uniwesytetu Warszawskiego. p. 72.

KOZŁOWSKI, S. K. (1989) A survey of Early Holocene Cultures of the Western Part of the Russian Plain. In BONSALL, C. ed. – *The Mesolithic in Europe.* Edinburgh: John Donald Publishers LTD. p. 424-441.

MALEZ, M. (1975) Kvartarna fauna Crvene stijene. In BASLER, Đ., ed. - *Crvena Stijena – zbornik radova.* Nikšić: Zajednica kulturnih ustanova. p. 147-203.

MARKEVIČ, V. I. (1974) *Bugo-dnestrovskaya kultura na teritorii Moldavii.* Kišinev.

MARKOVIĆ, Č. (1985) *Neolit Crne Gore,* Beograd: Centar za arheološka istraživanja, p. 105. (Knjiga 5).

MIKIĆ, Ž. (1988) *Antropološka struktura stanovništva Srbije.* Beograd: Filozofski fakultet. Odeljenje za etnologiju. p. 136.

MILOJČIĆ, V. (1956) Die erste präkeramische bäuerliche Siedlung der Jungsteinzeit in Europa. *Germania.* 34. p. 208.

MIHAILOVIĆ, D. (1996) Upper Palaeolithic and Mesolithic chipped stone industries from the rock-shelter of Medena Stijena. In SREJOVIĆ, D. ed. - *Prehistoric Settlements in Caves and Rock-shelters of Serbia and Montenegro - Fascicule I.* Belgrade: Centre for Archeological Research. p. 9-60. (Fascicule I; Vol. 16)

MIHAILOVIĆ, D. (1998) *Gornji paleolit i mezolit Crne Gore.* Unpublished Ph.D. dissertation. The University of Belgrade. Belgrade. p. 290.

MIHAILOVIĆ, D. (2001) Technological Decline of the Early Holocene Chipped Stone Industries in South-East Europe. In KERTESZ, R.; MAKKAY, J. eds.- *From the Mesolithic to the Neolithic, Proceedings of the International Archaeological Conference held in the Damjanich Museum of Solnok, Septemper 22-27, 1996.* Budapest: Archaeolingua. p. 339-347.

MIHAILOVIĆ, D. (2004) Chipped Stone Industry from horizons A and B at the site Padina in the Iron Gates. *The Mesolithic Landscape-Use During the Final-Palaeolithic and Mesolithic in NW-Europe: The Formation of Extensive Sites and Site-Complexes. Late Foragers and Early Farmers of the Lepenski Vir-Schela Cladovei Culture in the Iron Gates Gorges.* Acts of the XIVth UISPP Congress, University of Liège, Belgium, 2-8 September 2001 7 *Le Mésolithique.* Oxford: B. A.

R., p. 61-68. (British Archaeological Reports 1302).

MÜLLER, J. (1991) Die ostadriatische Impresso-Kultur: Zeitliche Gliederung und kulturelle Einbindung. *Germania*. Jahrgang 69. Halbband 2. p. 311-358.

PERLÈS, C. (2001) *The Early Neolithic in Greece*. Cambridge: Cambridge University Press. p. 356.

PERLÈS, C. (2003) An alternate (and old-fashioned) view of Neolithisation in Greece. *Documenta Prehistorica*. 30. p. 99-113.

RADOVANOVIĆ, I. (1996) *The Iron Gates Mesolithic*. Ann Arbor, Michigan: International Monographs in Prehistory. p. 382. (Archaeological Series 11).

REINGRUBER, A.; THISSEN, L. (2005) *CANeW 14C databases and 14C charts. Aegean Catchment* (E. Greece, S. Balkans, W. Turkey, 10.000-5.500 cal BC – June 2005). http://www.canew.org/aegeancatch-14cbox.html

RICHARDS, M. (2003) The Neolithic Invasion of Europe. *Annual Review of Anthropology*. 32. p. 135-162.

SIMMONS, A.H. (1998) Of tiny Hippos, Large Cows and Early Colonists in Cyprus. *Journal of Mediterranean Archaeology*. 11.2 (1998). p. 232-241.

SREJOVIĆ, D. (1974a) The Odmut Cave - a new facet of the Mesolithic Culture of the Balkan Peninsula. *Archaeologica Iugoslavica*. 15, p. 3-6.

SREJOVIĆ, D. (1969) *Lepenski Vir: nova praistorijska kultura u Podunavlju*. Beograd: Srpska knjizevna zadruga.

SREJOVIĆ, D. (1974b) Mezolitske osnove neolitskih kultura u juznom Podunavlju. In *Poceci ranih zemljoradnickih kultura u Vojvodini i srpskom Podunavlju*. Beograd: Srpsko arheolosko drustvo, Gradski muzej Subotica. p. 21-30. (Materijali X).

TELLENBACH, M. (1984) Materialen zum Präkeramischen Neolithikum in Süd-Ost Europa. Typologisch-stratigraphische Unterschungen zu lithischen Gerätschaften. *Germania*. 64 (1983). p. 21-138.

TODOROVA, H.; VAISOV, I. (1993) *Novokamennata epoha v Bulgarii*, Sofia: Nauka i Izkustvo. p. 288.

WHITTLE, A.; BARTOSZIEWICZ, L., BORIĆ, D., PETTIT, P.; RICHARDS, M. (2002) In the beginning: new radiocarbon dates for the Early Neolithic in northern Serbia and south-east Hungary. *Antaeus*. 25. p. 63-118.

ZVELEBIL, M. (1986) Mesolithic prelude and Neolithic revolution. In ZVELEBIL, M. ed. – *Hunters in Transition*. Cambridge: Cambridge University Press. p. 5-15.

ZVELEBIL, M. (2001) The agricultural transition and the origins of Neolithic society in Europe. *Documenta Praehistorica*. XXVIII. p. 1-26.

MESOLITHIC-NEOLITHIC INTERACTIONS
IN THE DANUBE GORGES

Dušan BORIĆ

Department of Archaeology, Downing Street, University of Cambridge, Cambridge CB2 3DZ;
db231@cam.ac.uk

Abstract: The exceptional character of Mesolithic-Neolithic sequences in the Danube Gorges has been recognized since the discovery of these sites in the 1960s. Yet only with a new research impetus in (re-)examining old collections from the sites such as Lepenski Vir, Padina and Vlasac in the 1990s did it become possible to ask a different set of questions about the way Mesolithic and Neolithic worlds interacted in the Danube Gorges. Were the inhabitants of trapezoidal buildings at Lepenski Vir using Early Neolithic pottery, and what role did the domesticates play in the subsistence of this community? Ultimately, in what way was the world of Lepenski Vir fisher-foragers changed by the arrival of the Neolithic? In order better to answer these questions archaeometric analyses have been employed on the material from the old collections. Most recently, new field research has been initiated in the hinterland areas of the Danube Gorges in order to define an assumed frontier between foragers and farmers, while a revision excavation of the site of Vlasac is underway. This paper reviews some of these new developments and discusses the nature of Mesolithic-Neolithic interactions in this region and the surrounding areas of the Balkans by reference to newly available data.
Key words: Mesolithic, Neolithic, Lepenski Vir, Vlasac, Danube Gorges

Resumé:Le caractère exceptionnel des séquences Mésolithique/Néolithique dans le Gorge du Danube a été réconnu depuis les années 60. Actuellement grâce aux nombreuses études et ré-examens du materiel de sites tels que Lepenski Vir, Padina et Vlasac il est possible de poser les nombreuses questions sur les interactions entre le monde Mésolithique et Néolithique dans le Gorge du Danube. Les habitants des maisons trapezoidales de Lepenski Vir ont ils produit la ceramique et quelle était le role des espèces domestiquées dans l'economie de subsistance de ces sociétés ? Enfin, dans quelle dégré l'arrivé du Néolithique avait changé le monde de Lepenski Vir ? Pour répondre mieux à ces questions les données archéométriques ont été utilisées, obtenues sur les matériaux des collections anciennes. Récemment des prospections nouvelles ont été entreprises dans le voisinage immédiat de Gorge du Danube afin de définir mieux la frontière supposée entre les chasseurs et les agriculteurs. Aussi une révision du site de Vlasac est en cours. Dans cette communication certains de ces résultats ont été discutés concernant la nature des interactions entre le Mésolithique et le Néolithique, non seulement dans le Gorge du Danube, mais aussi sur les territoires avoisinants des Balkans.
Mots-clés : Mésolithique, Néolithique, Lepenski Vir, Vlasac, Gorge du Danube

INTRODUCTION

There are several main models and each with numerous versions of these main models for the interpretation of the arrival of the Neolithic in Europe (which we assume to entail pottery use, domesticates and, among other things, new ways of daily conduct). While each of these models has a generalist agenda that tends to be applied to any given region, when it comes to the specifics of regional sequences each of the models inevitably becomes particularistic, demanding major adjustments of the generalist assumptions. One of the methodological and epistemological questions that arises from such a situation is whether it is possible to reconcile different scales of archaeological inquiry without compromising a fair presentation of all, frequently 'messy', sometimes loose, strands of archaeological evidence. In other words, in trying to fit some grand theory do we more often than not avoid or misrepresent evidence that does not fit? Taking into account several independent strands of evidence at several interdependent scales, I will provide an update of some aspects of scholarship about Mesolithic-Neolithic interactions in the Danube Gorges region of present-day Serbia and Romania (Fig. 3.1). For processes in this area that are conventionally termed the 'Mesolithic-Neolithic transition' I will insist on the use of the term 'transformations' (Borić 2005a), which may be a more precise characterization of the multiplicity of processes involved.

I shall first briefly point out the exceptional character of the regional sequence in the Danube Gorges and sum up the problems with the existing dataset, before presenting some recent breakthroughs in the understanding of the nature of Mesolithic-Neolithic transformations in this micro-region. This discussion will be based, firstly, on the results of some of the more recent archaeometric analyses of old archaeological collections, and, secondly, on the presentation of the most illuminating examples of my recent fieldwork in the Danube Gorges and its hinterlands with regard to the question of Mesolithic-Neolithic interactions.

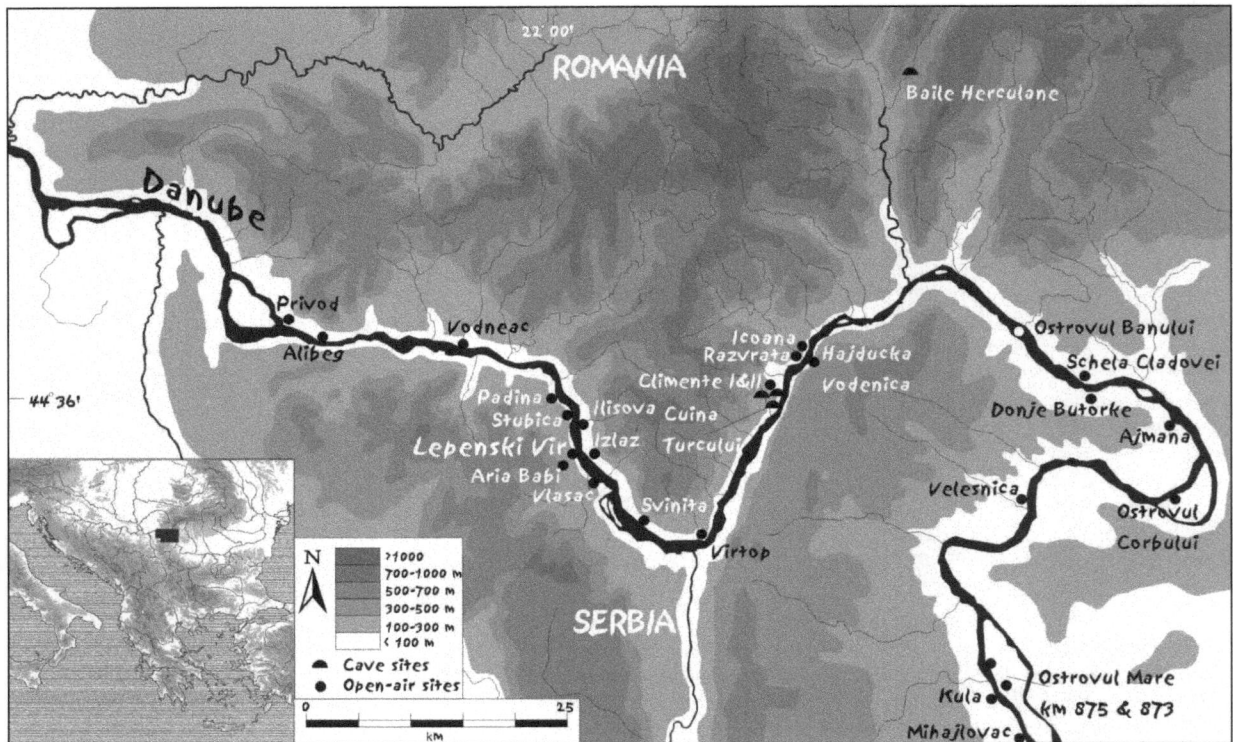

Fig. 3.1. Map of the Danube Gorges showing principal sites of Mesolithic-Neolithic date.

RESEARCH HISTORY AND BACKGROUND

The discovery of Mesolithic-Neolithic sites, including the celebrated site of Lepenski Vir, in the 1960s and 1970s brought with it previously non-existent insights into the complexity of the pre-Neolithic worlds in south-east Europe that have remained unmatched in their originality and abundance even at the present state of research. Certainly the most exciting aspect in the discovery of this phenomenon and the one directly relevant here is the fact that the richest part of the sequence in the Danube Gorges relates to the phase preceding the arrival of the first recognizably Neolithic items of material culture in this and neighbouring regions of the central Balkans. In the following I will chronologically review the developments in understanding specific aspects of the Mesolithic-Neolithic transformations in this region.

Since the discovery of the site of Lepenski Vir in 1965 with its exceptional character in architecture, burial record and symbolic expression, there remained a controversy as to the adequate dating of the most prominent phase of this site represented by trapezoidal buildings and other associated features (see Borić 1999, 2002; Garašanin & Radovanović 2001; Kozłowski & Kozłowski 2003). At first, this controversy over dating focused on the presence or absence of Early

Neolithic pottery in relation to the occupation of the trapezoidal buildings. The excavators of the neighbouring sites of Lepenski Vir (Dragoslav Srejović) and Padina (Borislav Jovanović) clashed over this question from the very beginning. At the site of Padina similar buildings were found to those of Lepenski Vir, but different from Lepenski Vir, at Padina, its excavator Jovanović (1969, 1987) reported that most, if not all, trapezoidal structures at the site had Early Neolithic pottery on their floors. Jovanović insisted that these features were to be dated to the Early Neolithic. In contrast, Srejović (1972) maintained the position that this phase represents older, Mesolithic features and regarded several instances of obvious associations of pottery on building floors of Lepenski Vir as intrusions from the upper levels (for the review of this debate see Borić 1999).

These two different empirical and stratigraphic understandings of the two sites and their respective formation processes led to different interpretations of the beginnings of the Neolithic in this region (cf. Tringham 2000). It should be noted, however, that neither of the two authors provided a developed model that would have incorporated all of the available archaeological data into a new synthesis. Srejović maintained a position favouring the idea of an autochthonous flourishing of a unique culture that might even have created a local centre of incipient domestication, and which might have contributed to the formation of the Early Neolithic of the central Balkans. Jovanović held that the greatest achievements in the Danube Gorges, including the phase with trapezoidal buildings, were influenced by the diffusion of Neolithic groups into this region and through their contact, interaction and assimilation with the Mesolithic groups that inhabited the Danube Gorges. As I will indicate later, elements of these two clashing points of view can be brought into a new synthesis.

In more recent years, the main analytical technique used for overcoming these problems was targeted radiometric dating of well-stratified materials from old excavations. The first series of radiocarbon dates on charcoal from both Lepenski Vir and Padina suggested at the time that the phase of trapezoidal buildings at both sites was relatively late and that it corresponded to the beginnings of the Early Neolithic in the southern and central Balkans (see Borić 1999). However, these new dates were met with suspicion in Srejović's camp and have frequently been ignored. In recent years, new AMS dating of the occupation of trapezoidal buildings at Lepenski Vir and Padina, confirms the validity of the first radiocarbon dates (Borić & Miracle 2004; Borić & Dimitrijević 2005, 2007; Whittle et al. 2002). Similarly, a reinterpretation of the stratigraphic relations at Lepenski Vir (Borić 1999, 2002) along with the confirmation that Early Neolithic pottery appeared during the phase characterized by trapezoidal buildings at this site (Garašanin & Radovanović 2001), puts the chronological span for the use of these structures at Padina and Lepenski Vir into the period from around 6.300 to 5.500 cal BC, possibly with two distinctive chronological phases within this period and some differences between the two sites (see below). Such dating overlaps the beginnings and the duration of the Early and Middle Neolithic in the central and north Balkans (Whittle et al. 2002; 2005). Yet there still remain two questions: (1) when exactly the pottery became available to the inhabitants of trapezoidal buildings at Lepenski Vir?; and (2) on the other hand, what prompted this particular elaboration of domestic space along with other forms of specific symbolic expression such as the proliferation of sculpted boulders and pestles? One way to solve the question of when exactly Early Neolithic pottery and other components of the 'Neolithic package' enter the Danube Gorges sites was to initiate a large-scale programme of AMS dating on the occupational residues of trapezoidal buildings at Lepenski Vir and other sites at which they have unquestionable associations with Early Neolithic pottery. In addition, dating of positively identified domesticates was the way to provide a direct date for their appearance at Lepenski Vir. While the complete results of this dating

programme are presented elsewhere (Borić & Dimitrijević 2007), it suffices to mention that it is likely that pottery became available to the inhabitants of trazpozoidal buildings from the first contact with Early Neolithic groups around 6.200 cal BC, while the introduction of domestic animals to Lepenski Vir did not take place before 5.900 cal BC. Such a partial introduction of the 'Neolithic package' to the Danube Gorges in the period between 6.300 and 5.900 cal BC bags the question about the nature of interactions between fisher-foragers and first farming groups.

Starting from the mid-1980s several authors suggested that the existing evidence from the Danube Gorges sites would best be explained by the application of the frontier model of Mesolithic-Neolithic transitions, which was growing in popularity at the time. The use of this model became particularly prominent in the course of the 1990s and suggested that there existed a long period of contacts and interactions between Mesolithic groups in the Danube Gorges and Early Neolithic groups that appear in surrounding areas of the Balkans around 6.300 cal BC (e.g. Radovanović 1996; Chapman 1993, 1994, 2000; Budja 1999; Tringham 2000; Tringham & Voytek 1989). This model accommodated the evidence of Early Neolithic pottery and some reports claiming the association of domesticates with trapezoidal buildings at these sites. Yet the details of such interactions have largely remained uncertain and problematic theoretical underpinnings persist for the application of this type of generalizing model (see Borić 2005a,b).

The frontier model differentiates foragers and farmers primarily on the mode of production and essentializes the differences between foragers and farmers in social evolutionary terms. This inherited stadial view of the past with explicit or implicit (post)colonial analogies about the processes of contact and interaction narrows one's vision with regard to the complexity that must have been involved in the transformations that took place in the central Balkans in the centuries following the arrival of the first domesticates and pottery after 6.300 cal BC. We should try to avoid falling prey to simplistic and universal descriptions of such processes of transformation. As the postcolonial culture critique suggests, 'culture contact' between different cultures can be seen as the work of 'transculturation'. Anthropologically nuanced approaches to the understanding of culture "do not see 'culture contact' as one form progressively, sometimes violently, replacing another. They focus on relational ensembles sustained through processes of cultural borrowings, appropriation, and translation–multidirectional processes (…) a 'contact zone' can never be reduced to cultural dominance or (more positively) education, acculturation, progress, etc. The concept deflects teleologies" (Clifford 2003:

34). There is a growing need to appreciate the complex workings of social processes at different scales that are frequently inadequately lumped under the proxy notions of 'culture contact' or 'acculturation' (Borić 2005a,b). In this context, one can reaffirm the point about the necessity to using our terminology more carefully in order to qualify processes we study.

In the following update of the most recent research in the Danube Gorges such a more nuanced theoretical modeling of transformations that took place in the Danube Gorges is advanced as the best way to accommodate a plethora of newly available data. I concentrate on some new AMS dates and stable isotopes as well as results of new field research.

DIETARY CHANGES AND THE MESOLITHIC-NEOLITHIC TRANSFORMATIONS: STABLE ISOTOPES

The pioneering work on stable isotopes from this region by Bonsall and his research group suggested that the diet of the inhabitants of the sites of Lepenski Vir, Vlasac and Schela Cladovei was heavily based on the consumption of fresh water fish during the Mesolithic (Bonsall et al. 1997, 2000). Such consumption of foods from an ecosystem with lower ^{14}C levels than the atmosphere obscures the age of the dated human and dog samples making them appear older due to the intake of 'old' carbon (Bonsall et al. 2000; Cook et al. 2002). Moreover, after the correction of such affected dates (cf. Cook et al. 2002; Borić & Miracle 2004) it became clear that there is a diachronic change in the intake of freshwater fish at Lepenski Vir that corresponds with the appearance of the first Early Neolithic communities across the central Balkans. Three AMS dated burials from Lepenski Vir had δ^{15}N values lighter than typical 'Mesolithic' pattern of heavy reliance on protein-rich foods. After the correction for the aquatic reservoir effect, these burials were dated in the period after 6.300 cal BC. Since the dating coincides with the start of the Neolithic in the wider region of the Balkans, Bonsall and his team connected this dietary change in the Danube Gorge's record with a take-up of newly available agricultural products that might have been coupled with a slow abandonment of fish resources among the local population.

Together with the research team led by Gisela Grupe at the Ludwig-Maximilians-University in Munich, we took on a critical re-evaluation of this data set by providing more stable isotope analyses on individuals from Lepenski Vir, Vlasac, Padina, Hajdučka Vodenica, Ajmana, Velesnica, and Kula. In addition, an enlarged sample of stable isotope measurements from the associated fauna at these sites was provided in order to reconstruct the actual foodwebs in the region (Borić et al. 2004; Grupe et al. 2003). We also examined details of particular burials and focused on the chronological patterning of faunal data. While our results are largely in agreement with the data previously presented by Bonsall's research team, we suggested that the pattern of dietary changes in the obtained stable isotope measurements cannot straightforwardly be interpreted as a reflection of the postulated shift towards abandonment of fish resources and take-up of agricultural products with the start of the Neolithic. Our research pointed out inconsistencies in the suggestion made by Bonsall and his research group that the consumption of freshwater fish was gradually and regularly decreasing over time (Borić et al. 2004: 238). More recently, Bonsall and his group similarly rejected their previous conclusions about a straightforward correlation between the lower stable isotope values and chronologically younger burials (Bonsall et al. 2004). Moreover, new AMS dates obtained on human burials from Padina, Hajdučka Vodenica and Vlasac (Price and Borić forthcoming), seem to indicate a further complication in the pattern of stable isotope data. There is a significant difference in the stable isotope patterns between Lepenski Vir and other contemporaneous sites. Dated burials from Padina, Hajdučka Vodenica and Vlasac show no dietary change in the period from around 6.300 to 5.900 cal BC, i.e. the period that saw dietary changes at the sites of Lepenski Vir and Ajmana (Fig. 3.2). Such a pattern indicates the heterogeneous nature of the process of transformation even within this micro-region. Furthermore, our re-examination of the faunal evidence from the sites of Lepenski Vir and Padina did not indicate the presence of domesticates in the period marked by the dietary change, i.e. c. 6.300-5.900 cal BC (Borić & Dimitrijević 2005), which shows that the subsistence change cannot be connected with the introduction of domestic animals as previously argued.

Thus, the apparent dietary change after 6.300 cal BC evident on several dated individuals from Lepenski Vir must have had different causes. One of the possibilities was to suggest that similar to interpretations offered in north-west Europe (e.g. Thomas 2003; see Richards and Shulting 2006), ideologically imposed taboos relating to food–'touch not the fish'–could have been responsible for such a change, as was argued previously by Radovanović (1997). However, there also might have existed other reasons for this pattern of dietary changes at this particular time. Something more complex was taking place in the centuries after 6.300 cal BC in the Danube Gorges and the neighbouring regions than a simple transition to the use of agricultural products that became available at the time. Although it may be a question of the still relatively crude chronological scale attainable when dating

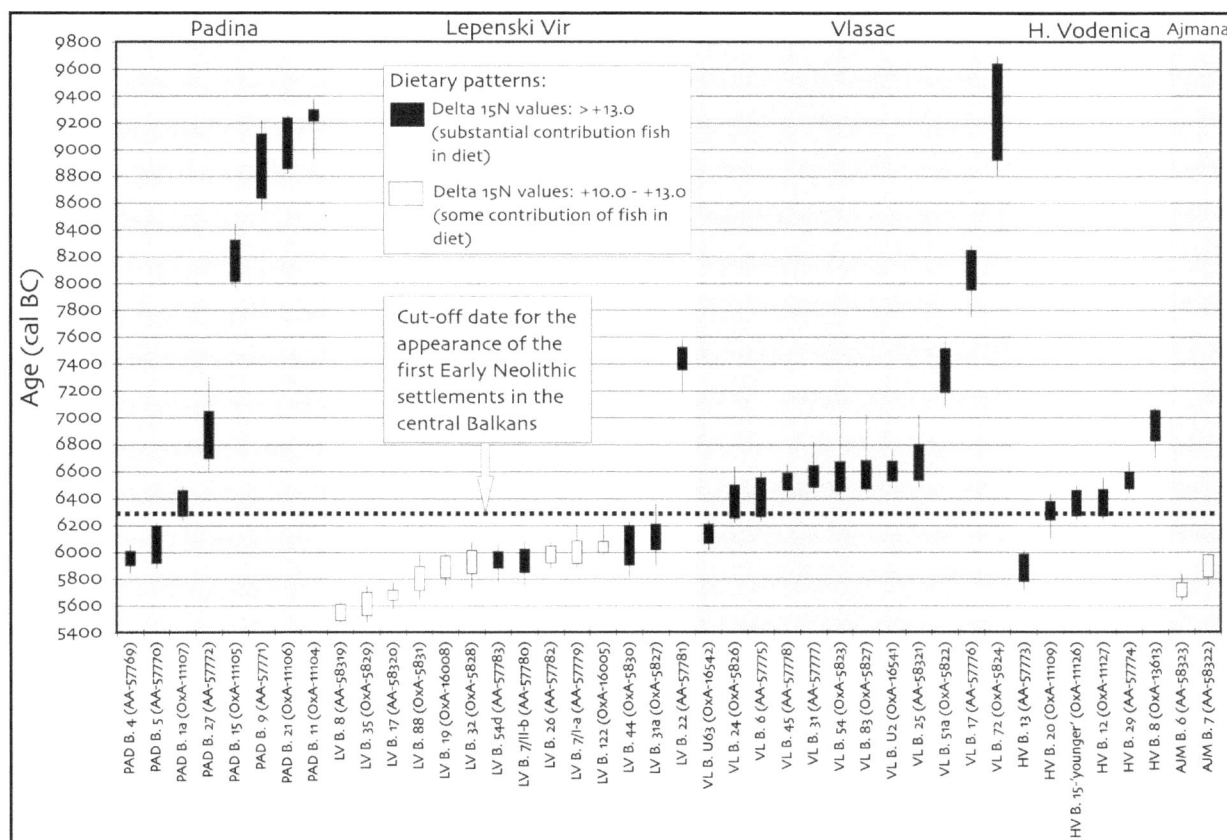

Fig. 3.2. Distribution of AMS dated burials from the Danube Gorges (Serbian side) showing diachronic changes in stable isotope patterns. Ages are corrected for those burials that have $\delta^{15}N$ values >+10‰ (affected by the aquatic reservoir effect), using Method 2 as suggested by Cook *et al.* (2002) and calibrated with OxCal v. 4.0 (Bronk Ramsey 1995, 2001). The $\delta^{15}N$ values used to estimate percentage of aquatic diet: >+13.0 ‰ = 100% reservoir correction applied (440±45 years); +10.0 – 13.0 ‰ = 50% reservoir correction applied (220±23 years). Sources for Oxford dates (OxA-): Bonsall *et al.* 1997, 2000; Cook *et al.* 2002; Borić & Miracle 2004. Four new Oxford dates (OxA-16005, -16008, -16541, -16542) were obtained as part of an AHRC/NERC funded ORADS programme: Borić & Dimitrijević 2007. New Arizona dates (AA-) were obtained as part of the strontium isotope project funded by the National Science Foundation of the USA (grant number BCS-0235465): Price & Borić forthcoming.

human burials, due to the larger standard errors of dates corrected for the aquatic reservoir effect, there might also have been important differences in the population make-up of the contemporaneous sites in the period 6.300 to 5.900 cal BC and even later. In this context, the exceptional character of Lepenski Vir, visible in various aspects of material culture (e.g. number and variety of sculpted boulders, limestone floors, etc.), is once more underlined by a likely coexistence of inhabitants with different dietary habits. New strontium data indicate an intensified mobility that probably characterizes the region on the whole in the period after 6.300 cal BC with admixtures of different groups and communities and this data set is presented in more detail elsewhere (Price and Borić forthcoming). Destabilizing our grand narratives of the

Neolithic as sedentary and Mesolithic as mobile, the current evidence from the Danube Gorges suggests that at the micro-regional level one observes a greater mobility in the Neolithic in comparison to a more regionally confined pattern of Mesolithic existence. Most recently, the pattern of interactions between the local population in the Danube Gorges and other contemporaneous communities is being addressed through new field research in the region.

NEW FIELD RESEARCH IN THE DANUBE GORGES AND ITS HINTERLANDS

New fieldwork in the Danube Gorges started in 2004 as part of a collaborative project "Prehistory of north-east Serbia" between the Department of Archaeology, University of Cambridge, England and the Department of Archaeology of the University of Belgrade, Serbia, with Dr Miloš Jevtić and the author of this text as principal investigators. A part of this wider project relating to the Stone Ages has been designed to test the notion of the Mesolithic-Neolithic frontier as a general model as well as its applicability in this regional example, by reference to known Mesolithic settlements on the Danube and largely uninvestigated hinterland areas on the Serbian side of the Danube. Previously, no systematic survey of the hinterland areas of the Danube Gorges was made after the excavation of Mesolithic-Neolithic sites belonging to the Lepenski Vir culture zone. Most of the known sites were primarily situated along a narrow strip of land along the Danube banks investigated as part of the rescue project *Đerdap I* in the 1960s and 1970s. Focusing on the hinterland areas of the previously investigated sites allows one to contextualize the existing evidence from this micro-region with other contemporaneous settlements outside the Danube Gorges in the course of the Mesolithic and Neolithic periods.

The nearest concentrations of known Early Neolithic settlements to the contemporaneous occupation of Lepenski Vir, Padina, Vlasac and other sites in the Danube Gorges, are found to the west in the Morava River valley in central Serbia (Fig. 3.3) and in Oltenia, downstream along the Danube in Romania (e.g. Cîrcea: Nica 1976). There are no positively identified Mesolithic sites in the wider region of the central Balkans. However, in the hinterlands of the Danube in Romania, the cave site of Băile Herculane (Nicolâescu-Plopsor *et al.* 1957; Dinan 1996) was inhabited during the Mesolithic period (see Fig. 3.1) and one should expect similar sites in the wider region. The closest isolated Early Neolithic settlements to the concentration of forager sites on the Danube are the sites of Kučajna (Stanojević 1988: 77-78) near the town of Bor, and Knjepište (Stanković 1986a) and Kamenički Potok (1986b), both situated near the town of Mihajlovac on the banks of the Danube downstream from the Danube Gorges (Fig. 3.3). Further investigation of these and similar sites is critical for understanding the settlement pattern during these periods and possible dynamics of an assumed frontier zone in north-east Serbia, i.e. the Danube Gorges hinterlands. The initial plan of the field project was to focus on the known and unknown caves and rockshelters of the hinterland areas of the Danube Gorges characterized by karstic features, such as the Miroč Mountain plateau (Ljubojević 2003). After the surface prospecting of speleologically known caves and test excavations in two previously unknown caves in 2004 and 2005, no Mesolithic or Early Neolithic layers were detected (Borić and Jevtić forthcoming; Kapuran *et al.* in press).

This programmatic targeting of caves and rockshelters of the region will be continued and intensified in the future, bearing in mind that several caves and rockshelters investigated on the left bank of the Danube in Romania had both Mesolithic and Early Neolithic levels. On the other hand, the best data for the Mesolithic-Early Neolithic period came through the research on newly discovered open-air sites.

Neolithic site of Aria Babi

The first positive results with regard to the investigation of forager-farmer interactions in the Danube Gorges, came with the discovery of the previously unknown Neolithic site of Aria Babi during the 2004 field survey. The site is located on the Košo Hill, above the site of Lepenski Vir, at an altitude of between 310 and 318 m asl (Fig. 3.4-3.5). The site was recognized thanks to reports from the owner of the field on which it is located. Initially, flint artifacts of yellow colour with white spots were recognized. This attractive flint also known as Balkan flint or flint from the 'pre-Balkan platform' probably originates in northern Bulgaria (e.g. Voytek 1987), and is one of the main characteristics of the Early Neolithic across the central Balkans. Surface collection on this location and subsequent excavation indicated that Starčevo type Early/Middle Neolithic pottery as well as numerous pieces of ground stone materials were spread over approximately 0.8 ha of the ploughed field. Aria Babi appears as a single occupation site with a shallow stratification of anthropogenic sediments (40-60 cm deep). Limestone bedrock is reached after 60-100 cm across the site. There were no dwelling structures discovered, which is likely due to an aggressive erosion of the upper levels of the site that might have had above-ground dwellings. There were several pits/depressions with concentrations of pottery and stone that accumulated in these depressions. A typical Early/Middle Neolithic pottery assemblage characterrizes the site (Borić & Starović forthcoming). This pottery is very similar to numerous other Early/Middle Neolithic sites in the region (e.g. Srejović 1988). There are striking similarities in shapes and decoration of pottery from Aria Babi with the recently published pottery assemblage from the 1965-1966 excavations at Lepenski Vir (Perić & Nikolić 2004). Some of the decorative motifs found at both sites are band appliqués with regular finger imprints as well as regular finger imprints on the rims of vessels. The assemblage of published pottery frag-ments from Lepenski Vir confined to the 1965-1966 field seasons largely come from deposits that could possibly be related to the period that followed the abandonment of at least some if not all trapezoidal buildings at Lepenski Vir, i.e. after 5.900 cal BC (Borić & Dimitrijević 2007).

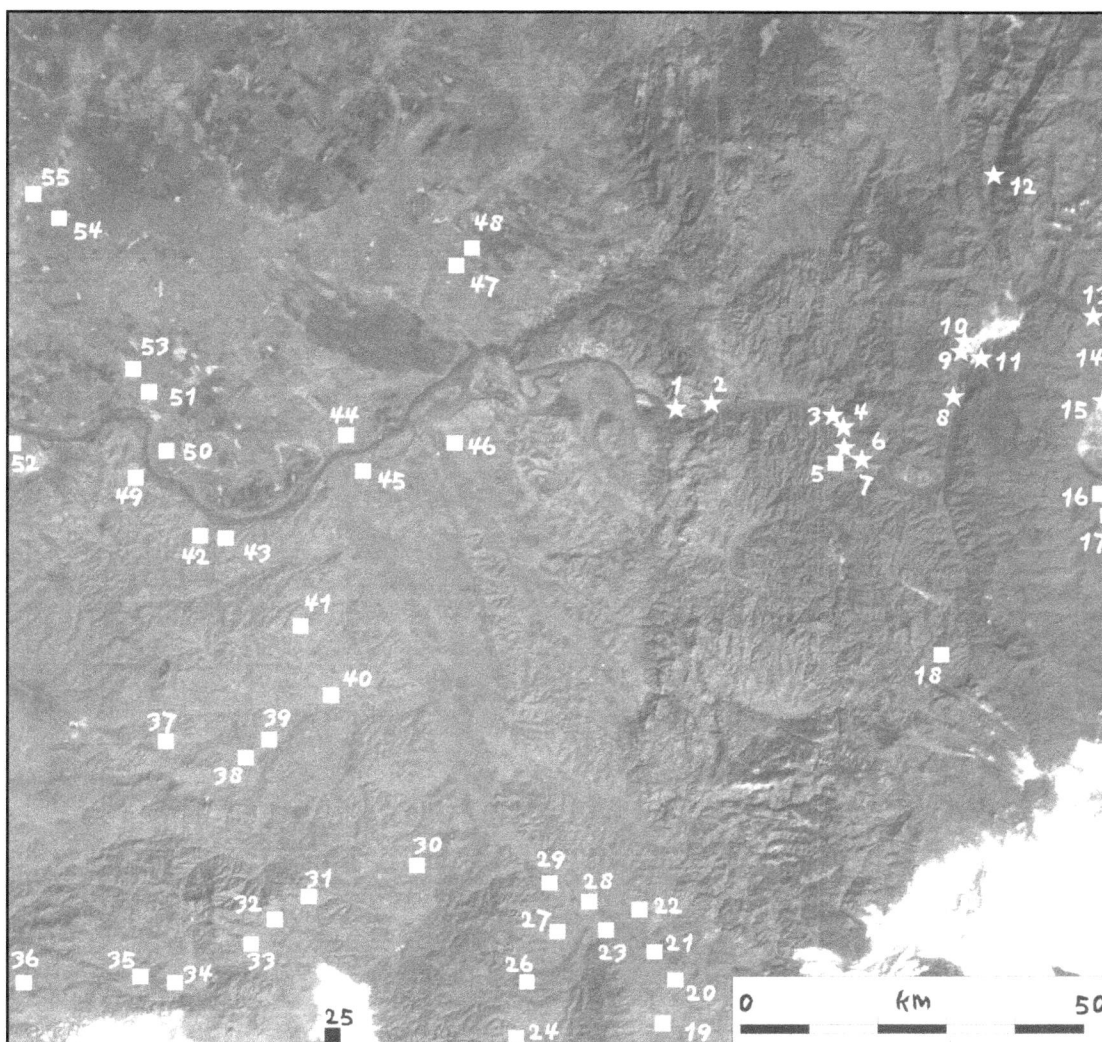

Fig. 3.3. Satellite image of north-east Serbia; sites with Mesolithic-Early Neolithic stratigraphies in the Danube Gorges shown as stars and Early Neolithic sites outside of the Danube Gorges shown as squares (site distribution supplemented after Srejović 1988: 49). 1 – Privod; 2 – Alibeg; 3 – Padina; 4 – Stubica; 5 – Aria Babi; 6 – Lepenski Vir; 7 – Vlasac; 8 – Cuina Turcului; 9 – Razvrata; 10 – Icoana; 11 – Hajdučka Vodenica; 12 – Baile Herculane; 13 – Ostrovul Banului; 14 – Schela Cladovei; 15 – Velesnica; 16 – Kamenički Potok-Mihajlovac; 17 – Knjepište-Mihajlovac; 18 – Kučajna-Bor; 19 – Slatina, Turska Česma-Drenovac; 20 – Slatina-Paraćin; 21 – Kraljevo Polje-Ivankovac; 22 – Kraljevo Polje-Ćuprija; 23 – Damjanov Kladenac-Vinorača; 24 – Tečići-Rekovac; 25 – Paljevina and Grobnice-Žune; 26 – Trnati Laz-Lukar; 27 – Bunar-Jagodina; 28 – Bukovačka Česma-Bukovče; 29 – Velika Reka-Topola; 30 – Česta-Dobrovodica; 31 – Divostin-Kragujevac; 32 – Grivac; 33 – Brdo-Kusovac; 34 – Anište-Bresnica; 35 – Ostri; 36 – Trsine-Čačak; 37 – Banja-Aranjđelovac; 38 – Kloke-Majdan; 39 – Cerovac-Zmajevac; 40 – Medvednjak-Smederevska Palanka; 41 – Staro Selo-Selevac; 42 – Dubočaj-Grocka; 43 – Rančićeva Kuća-Grocka; 44 – Manastirište-Kovin; 45 – Orašje-Dubravica; 46 – Lugovi-Drmno; 47 – Beletinci-Pavliš; 48 – At-Vršac; 49 – Belo Brdo-Vinča; 50 - Grad-Starčevo; 51 – Vatrogasni Dom-Pančevo; 52 – Ciglana-Dobanovci; 53 – Jabuka-Pančevo; 54 – Kubik-Farkaždin; 55 – Batka-Perlez.

Similarities between these two sites should not be surprising bearing in mind the proximity of the two locations. Even today, there exists a path that leads from Aria Babi to the original location of Lepenski Vir. This path also passes by Lepenski Abri, a rockshelter that is situated several meters above Lepenski Vir. Early Neolithic pottery was found at the bottom levels of this site (Jevtić 1983). Advocates of

Fig. 3.4. Position of the newly discovered Neolithic site of Aria Babi situated on the Košobrdo (Košo Hill) above the type site of Lepenski Vir.

Fig. 3.5. Archaeological excavations at the Neolithic site of Aria Babi and location of the site of Vlasac.

landscape approaches in archaeology have mentioned the importance of paths in a landscape, connecting a series of points (e.g. Tilley 1994: 30), and one could imagine that such paths are of a significant antiquity. It is likely that these three sites were contemporaneous and that people inhabiting/using each of these locations communicated with each other. Yet, what remains unclear at present is who inhabited each of these sites and at exactly what time. Due to the acidity of soil at the site of Aria Babi, no animal bones are preserved for AMS dating of these deposits. This is unfortunate since a preserved assemblage of animal bones would have been one of the most instructive indicators about the relationship between this site and those sites situated on the banks of the Danube that largely (with the exception of some pit features at Lepenski Vir, cf.

Borić & Dimitrijević 2007) lack domestic animals despite of the appearance of Early Neolithic pottery in their deposits. Information on the presence or absence of domestic taxa as well as their absolute dating would have contributed to understanding the role of Aria Babi in the settlement pattern of this region.

One could suggest two scenarios with regard to the character of this site depending on its chronological positioning. According to the first scenario, if Aria Babi is to be dated in the period from around 6.300 to 5.900 cal BC, i.e. during the phase of trapezoidal buildings at Lepenski Vir, one could suggest that the character of this site might have been strategic and that it represents a settlement of Early Neolithic farmers located in the immediate vicinity of forager sites on the Danube. The second scenario, which is at the current state of data more likely, would suggest that the likely presence of the 'full Neolithic package' at Aria Babi (but it is impossible to say whether domestic animals were present at the site although likely) may suggest that the site is contemporaneous with the phase of occupation that relates to the period after 5.900 cal BC, i.e. the period that saw a slow abandonment of at least some if not all trapezoidal buildings at Lepenski Vir. This period might have seen a significant change in the settlement pattern with the appearance of new sites, such as Aria Babi, occupying different ecological niches. However, this assumed change in the settlement pattern can only be considered a tentative scenario at present and is largely based on the lack of data for Mesolithic and 'transitional' sites in the hinterland areas that can only relate to the current state of research rather than to any 'real' pattern. Such a situation requires an intensification of survey in the hinterland areas of the Danube Gorges to locate similar sites to Aria Babi. While this kind of research in the hinterlands of the Danube Gorges remains one of the priorities in examining the assumed forager-farmer frontier in this region, the unexpected discovery of preserved levels at the site of Vlasac in the course of 2006 field season provided a completely new set of data for understanding Mesolithic-Neolithic transformations in the Danube Gorges.

Mesolithic-Neolithic site of Vlasac

The site of Vlasac is located 3 km downstream from the eponymous site of Lepenski Vir. Vlasac was partially excavated in 1970-1971 (Srejović & Letica 1978), before the location was submerged by the Danube owing to the creation of an artificial lake for a hydroelectric dam. During these two field seasons in the 1970s, almost 90 Mesolithic burials with many more individuals identified in these burials were discovered here along with the prototypes of Lepenski Vir trapezoidal buildings and rectangular stone-lined

hearths. After the first excavations, for over 35 years the Danube at this location was slowly eroding away sediments, creating a new riverbank section. During the 2005 field season in the Danube Gorges hinterlands, there were reports from local fishermen about washed out bones at this place. Checking these reports at the start of the 2006 field season, it was confirmed that certain portions of this site are still preserved and accessible for research. The possibility of excavating at this classic site of the Lepenski Vir culture bears importance on several levels. First, due to the rescue nature of the excavations in 1970-1971, contextual details are sometimes missing in the published report and excavating Vlasac in 2006 was a unique opportunity to apply rigorous excavation methodology and improve the quality of the available data. Second, the renewed excavation at Vlasac provided a possibility for reexamining formation processes at the site and its phasing as previously suggested by Srejović & Letica (1978). Finally, although the site report from the 1970-1971 excavations at Vlasac mentioned finds of Early Neolithic pottery in the upper levels of the site, such finds were never discussed in detail and no building features of Early Neolithic date were presented in the published report. Consequently, the question about the (dis)continuity between Mesolithic and Early Neolithic occupations could not be addressed. Most of the charcoal dates and in particular the more reliable AMS dates made on both human and animal bones (cf. Bonsall et al. 1997; Borić & Miracle 2004; Borić & Dimitrijević 2007; Price & Borić forthcoming) suggested that the site might have been abandoned at the end of the Late Mesolithic, i.e. around 6400 cal BC.

However, new discoveries at Vlasac strongly suggest that there was no chronological break in the occupation of this site with the appearance of Early Neolithic pottery. It seems that at least certain portions of the site were in use continuously throughout the Late Mesolithic, transformational period and into the Middle Neolithic after 5.900 cal BC. This became particularly clear on the basis of new dates for a stratigraphic sequence with a group burial excavated at Vlasac in 2006 (Borić 2006). A thin layer of vegetation humus covered an archaeologically sterile layer of eroded scree of around 60 cm in thickness. Beneath this level, the first archaeological materials were detected: an Early Neolithic level with typical Starčevo type pottery and yellow white-spotted 'Balkan' flint. This level contained the remains of a stone structure built in dry-wall technique, and a whole pot was discovered next to this construction (Fig. 3.6), suggesting an occupation level of Early Neolithic date. This stone construction was lying on top of large blocks regularly distributed close to the current section. On top of these stone

Fig. 3. 6 – Early Neolithic Starčevo pot *in situ* at the site of Vlasac excavated during the renewed work in 2006.

blocks a number of Early Neolithic pottery fragments and other materials ('Balkan' flint, animal bones, river mollusks) were found. Further excavation revealed that these large blocks of stones covered a group burial that contained seven consecutive inhumations one on top of the other. They were the remains of adults, children and neonates. No Early Neolithic pottery was found beneath the level of the stone construction put over the group burial. Stratigraphically, these two different contexts, one with pottery and one without, were clearly distinguished.

Beneath the large stone blocks that covered this burial location, there was a red deer skull with antlers and a disarticulated child's skull structurally deposited before the (ritual) 'closing' of this location. The infill of the burial consisted of dark soil from burning and decomposition of organic materials, and a large number of disarticulated human bones along with some animal bones were irregularly deposited in within it. Some of these bones were burned. Throughout the deposit of this group burial, there were a number of finds of red and white limestone beads of the kind previously only found in three burials at Lepenski Vir (Burials 54e, 87 and 46: Srejović & Babović 1983: 196-197), as well as *Spondylus* beads, also previously only found at Lepenski Vir (a necklace of *Spondylus* beads was found in Cache 1, in a Starčevo-type pot at Lepenski Vir, Srejović 1972: T. IX). These were the first indications that this feature may at least partly be contemporaneous with the phase of trapezoidal buildings at Lepenski Vir that is dated to c. 6.200 to 5.900 cal BC. Understanding what happened in the Danube Gorges during this phase is of critical importance for understanding the nature of the Mesolithic-Neolithic transformations in the region. It seems that

during this time, the indigenous population in the Danube Gorges was still characterized by inherited, typically Mesolithic cultural traits, actively interacting with Early Neolithic communities and possibly actively participating in Early Neolithic exchange networks. This suggestion has previously been advanced on the basis of some major changes characterized by (renewed?) elaboration of trapezoidal buildings, most clearly observed at Lepenski Vir and Padina. Now, it seems that other sites, such as Vlasac, can also be expected to have contemporaneous levels with evidence of new social interactions.

The ritually deposited red deer skull with antlers discovered on top of a stone plaque that covered the pelvis of the latest articulated inhumation in the group burial at Vlasac, as an act of intentional 'closing' of a feature, i.e. its abandonment, is another indication of the contemporaneous nature of deposits at Lepenski Vir and Vlasac. By directly dating this red deer skull in the range 6.006 to 5.838 cal BC at 95 per cent probability (OxA-16544) it was possible to provide a *terminus ante quem* for the group burial and *terminus post quem* for the layer with Early Neolithic pottery. This date is currently the youngest AMS date from Vlasac (see Fig. 3.2). It corresponds well with the dating of the abandonment of trapezoidal buildings at Lepenski Vir (Borić & Dimitrijević 2007), and is an independent proof for the contemporaneity of these two types of deposits at the two sites.

Due to the continuous use of this location for burial, possibly over several generations, older inhumations were disturbed significantly by the interment of new burials. These later interments also disturbed the adornment of some burials, and a number of red and white limestone beads and several *Spondylus* beads were found scattered across the upper levels of the burial tomb. However, in at least two instances it was possible to determine the precise location of these ornaments in relation to the body of the deceased. Thus, red and white limestone beads were found as a bracelet of a partly burnt child (Burial U60) that was lying facing down on the chest of a headless adult individual (Burial U63), placed parallel to the Danube with its head pointing in the downstream direction. Pierced *Cyprinidae* pharyngeal 'teeth' were found only around the neck, above both shoulders of this individual and beneath the left scapula, suggesting that these were attached to the hair or that the *Cyprinidae* 'teeth' might have been part of a headdress. The use of *Cyprinidae* 'teeth' for adornment has been well documented during the Late Mesolithic at several sites in the Danube Gorges. Next to this concentration of *Cyprinidae* 'teeth', a new item of material culture was found: a very large *Spondylus* bead, next to the neck of this individual (Fig. 3.7). This burial is dated in the

Fig. 3. 7 – *In situ Spondylus* bead found around the neck of Burial U63 in the group burial discovered at Vlasac in 2006.

range 6.232 to 6.018 cal BC at 95 per cent probability after correction for the aquatic reservoir effect (OxA-16542), which stratigraphically corresponds well with the dating of the red deer skull (OxA-16544, see above). Below Burial U63, remains of two other partly preserved articulated inhumations were found, but in these older levels of the burial tomb, no red and white limestone or *Spondylus* beads were found, suggesting a cut-off date for the changes in the adornment with the arrival of more Neolithic-like items of material culture around 6.300/6.200 cal BC. This date is in turn the date for the appearance of the first Early Neolithic communities in the central Balkans and these two phenomena can hardly be coincidental.

In sum, the group burial found during the renewed excavation work at Vlasac in 2006 seems to have been used over several generations and it chronologically overlaps the phase of trapezoidal buildings at Lepenski Vir. No pottery was found in the burial infill although this does not necessarily mean that it was not available to the community inhabiting the region at other sites from the appearance of Early Neolithic groups around 6.200 cal BC. Early Neolithic pottery and white-spotted yellow Balkan flint were found lying on top of the stone construction covering the burial tomb and their presence can at least be postulated for the period after 5.900 cal BC if not earlier. Individuals found in the burial tomb were buried according to rites character-izing the Late Mesolithic period in the Danube Gorges and their diet was characterized by a substantial intake of aquatic foods (the $\delta^{15}N$ value of dated Burial U63 with a *Spondylus* bead around the neck of the deceased is 17.0 ‰, see Fig. 3.2). Yet the appearance of new elements in the adornment, such as red and white limestone and *Spondylus* beads, seems to suggest that the people buried at this location, possibly belonging to an extended family or lineage, had become part of a new network of (Neolithic) communities inhabiting the wider region of the north-central Balkans around 6200 cal BC. The *Spondylus* network might have replaced the previous network of social interactions with distant places across the Balkans that was involved in the acquisition of another type of popular exotic marine goods during the Late Mesolithic: marine snails *Cyclope neritea* (Borić 2007b). *Cyclope neritea* ornaments were found in several Late Mesolithic burials during the previous excavations at Vlasac (Srejović & Letica 1978) as well as in one excavated burial in the course of the 2006 field season (Borić 2006). The finds of *Spondylus* and their dating in this case may suggest that here one finds the earliest examples of the *Spondylus* exchange network in Europe. As the later distribution of *Spondylus* finds, found primarily along the Danube (e.g. Willms 1985; Müller 1997), indicates, this route and a social network that seems to have been created along the Danube might have been of special importance for establishing new forms of social relatedness as well as for the diffusion of novelties since the early days of the process we call the 'Neolithization' of the Balkans.

DISCUSSION AND CONCLUSIONS

On the basis of new data coming both from the application of archaeometric analyses and new field research in the Danube Gorges, one can suggest two main stages of the transformations of fisher-foragers of the Danube and their likely incorporation into a new Neolithic social context of the central Balkans, i.e. the 'Neolithization process'. The first period can roughly be dated from around 6.300/6.200 to 5.900 cal BC. This period covers the flourishing of the site of Lepenski Vir and the appearance of one of the most recognizable features of this site: trapezoidal buildings with limestone floors and also the proliferation of sculpted boulders at this time (see Borić 2005c). Such changes seem to be related to a restructuring of the community in the Danube Gorges that might have been a reaction to expanding Neolithic social networks. Instead of seeing this change as an ideological resistance to the Neolithic world (cf. Radovanović 2006: 120), I am inclined to suggest that such changes rather might have been a way of proving allegiance to new social contexts created at the time across the Balkans (see Borić 2007, 2008). However, during this period the local Mesolithic tradition is still very strong in the whole of the Danube Gorges, and no major changes are detected in the mortuary arena. It seems that at the site of Lepenski Vir one may detect possible incomers from other regions at this time who were being buried according to the Mesolithic burial rites (Borić and Price forthcoming). It is difficult to suppose the precise identity of these incomers, and one could only speculate that these foreign individuals were of 'Neolithic' origin. At other sites that have contemporaneous deposits during this phase (Vlasac, Padina, Hajdučka Vodenica and perhaps also other sites) the way of life and subsistence practices and habits seem to be largely unaltered by the appearance of Early Neolithic communities in the surrounding regions. However, *Spondylus* beads found in the newly discovered group burial at Vlasac, dated to this phase, indicate that the local forager population across the region was aware of and in contact with a new Neolithic world. It was not an isolated population but one actively participating in changing social contexts and extended networks of exchange and acquisition of exotic items that became readily accepted. These new networks replaced similar networks that had existed for centuries across the Mesolithic Balkans. At the present state of research, the idea of a frontier between 'Mesolithic' and 'Neolithic' communities still remains elusive in this regional context. A more extensive survey for possible frontier sites in the hinterland areas of the Danube Gorges and further afield is required to test the applicability of this notion.

The second main phase of the transformation in the Danube Gorges took place after 5.900 cal BC. This second phase might have lasted until 5.500 cal BC, although the precise date for the final Neolithic abandonment of, at the time, already very old locales along the Danube is still to be determined more precisely. During this period, one could also tentatively suggest a change in the settlement pattern across the region with the appearance of new, possibly short-lived sites in new ecological niches. A candidate for such a site is the open-air site of Aria Babi on the hill above Lepenski Vir that could possibly be dated to this phase. At this time, the first domestic animals, previously absent from limestone floors of trapezoidal buildings, appear at Lepenski Vir (Borić & Dimitrijević 2007). It also seems that new waves of incomers arrived in the region and some of these were buried at Lepenski Vir. However, at this time their burial rites–crouched inhumations–are typically Neolithic. Most of the trapezoidal buildings were likely abandoned by this time. Yet in some instances there might have been an awareness and memory of the importance and previous history of this settlement site and of particular buildings. There is a difference in this respect between Lepenski Vir and Padina, since at Padina some of the trapezoidal buildings might have been occupied also after 5.900 cal BC. Although people buried at Lepenski Vir and Ajmana after 5.900 cal BC still eat fish in some quantities, their diet is less fish-dominated. A possible reliance on cereal foods could be detected for two crouched burials at Lepenski Vir, with the first appearance of caries on their teeth (Grga 1996). At the moment we are missing precise details of the character

of changes taking place during this second phase of the 'Neolithization'. For future research, it remains very important to understand what led to the final abandonment of this region by the end of the Middle Neolithic (i.e. c. 5.500 cal BC) and to its later avoidance during the Late Neolithic.

Although the precise details of the Mesolithic-Neolithic transformations in the Danube Gorges remain to be elucidated further, it is evident that processes of transformation were gradual. Despite some patterning and similarities among the sites, each site and each feature bring into sharp focus micro-historical narratives of particular social groups and individuals. This 'messiness' of converging and diverging stories is a good indication that we are on a path leading us closer to the very texture of the Mesolithic and Neolithic existence in the Danube Gorges with all of its irreducible complexity. At the moment, one could suggest a coexistence of fisher-foragers in the Danube Gorges with Early Neolithic groups in the surrounding areas for at least two to three hundred years. Contacts were made with several different 'Neolithics' that seem to have been surprisingly mobile. One could suggest a slow and phased conversion/transformation into a 'proper Neolithic' world.

Acknowledgements

I would like to thank Janusz K. Kozłowski and Marek Nowak for inviting me to participate in the UISPP session in Lisbon on September 4th, 2006 where this paper was presented. I am also grateful to the National Science Foundation of the USA (grant number BCS-0442096), British Academy (Small Grants 40967 and 42170) and the McDonald Institute for Archaeological Research for their financial support of the field project in the Danube Gorges. T. Doug Price helped a lot to start this field project and continues to provide vital support. This paper was written during my postdoctoral appointment as a Research Associate on the Leverhulme funded project "Changing Beliefs of the Human Body: Comparative Social Perspective" based at the Department of Archaeology, University of Cambridge. I would like to thank Preston Miracle and David Orton for useful comments on earlier drafts of this paper.

References

BONSALL, C.; LENNON, R.; MCSWEENEY, K.; STEWART, C; HARKNESS, D.; BORONEANȚ, V; BARTOSIEWICZ, L.; PAYTON, R.; CHAPMAN, J. (1997) – Mesolithic and early Neolithic in the Iron Gates: a palaeodietary perspective. *Journal of European Archaeology*. 5(1): p. 50-92.

BONSALL, C.; COOK, G.; LENNON, R.; HARKNESS, D.; SCOTT, M.; BARTOSIEWICZ, L.; MCSWEENEY, K. (2000) – Stable Isotopes, Radiocarbon and the Mesolithic-Neolithic Transition in the Iron Gate. *Documenta Praehistorica*. Ljubljana. 27: p. 119-132.

BONSALL, C.; COOK, G. T.; HEDGES, R. E. M.; HIGHAM, T. F. G.; PICKARD, C.; RADOVANOVIĆ, I. (2004) – Radiocarbon and stable isotope evidence of dietary changes from the Mesolithic to the Middle Ages in the Iron Gates: new results from Lepenski Vir. *Radiocarbon*. 46(1): p. 293-300.

BORIĆ, D. (1999) – Places that created time in the Danube Gorges and beyond, c. 9000-5500 Cal BC. *Documenta praehistorica*. Ljubljana. 26: p. 47-70.

BORIĆ, D. (2002) – The Lepenski Vir conundrum: reinterpretation of the Mesolithic and Neolithic sequences in the Danube Gorges. *Antiquity*. 76: p.1026-1039.

BORIĆ, D. (2005a) – Deconstructing essentialisms: unsettling frontiers of the Mesolithic-Neolithic Balkans. In BAILEY, D.; WHITTLE, A.; CUMMINGS V., eds. *(un)settling the Neolithic*. Oxford: Oxbow Books. p. 16-31.

BORIĆ, D. (2005b) – Fuzzy horizons of change: *Orientalism* and the frontier model in the Mesolithic-Neolithic transition. In MILNER, N.; WOODMAN, P. C., eds. – *Mesolithic Studies in the 21st century*. Oxford: Oxbow Books. p. 81-105.

BORIĆ, D. (2005c) – Body Metamorphosis and Animality: Volatile Bodies and Boulder Artworks from Lepenski Vir. *Cambridge Archaeological Journal*. Cambridge. 15(1): p. 35-69.

BORIĆ, D. (2006) – New discoveries at the Mesolithic-Early Neolithic site of Vlasac: Preliminary notes. *Mesolithic Miscellany*. 18(1): p. 7-14.

BORIĆ, D. (2007) – The House: Between Grand Narratives and Microhistories. In R. A. BECK, JR., ed. – *The Durable House: House Society Models in Archaeology*. Carbondale: Center for Archaeological Investigations. pp. 97-129.

BORIĆ, D. (2008) – First houses and 'houses societies' in European Prehistory. In A. JONES, ed. – *Prehistoric Europe*. Malden, MA: Blackwell Publishing.

BORIĆ, D.; MIRACLE, P. (2004) – Mesolithic and Neolithic (dis)continuities in the Danube Gorges: New AMS dates from Padina and Hajdučka Vodenica (Serbia). *Oxford Journal of Archaeology*. Oxford. 23(4): p. 341-371.

BORIĆ, D.; GRUPE, G.; PETERS, J.; MIKIĆ, Ž. (2004) – Is the Mesolithic-Neolithic subsistence dichotomy real? New stable isotope evidence from the Danube Gorges. *European Journal of Archaeology*. 7(3): p. 221-248.

BORIĆ, D.; DIMITRIJEVIĆ, V. (2005) – Continuity of foraging strategies in Mesolithic-Neolithic transformations: Dating faunal patterns at Lepenski Vir (Serbia). *Atti della Società per la preistoria e protoistoria della regione Friuli-Venezia Giulia*. Venezia. XV (2004-05): p. 33-107.

BORIĆ, D.; DIMITRIJEVIĆ, V. (2007) – When did the 'Neolithic package' reach Lepenski Vir? Radiometric and faunal evidence. *Documenta Praehistorica*. Ljubljana. XXXV. Pp. 53-72.

BORIĆ, D.; JEVTIĆ, M. (forthcoming) – Prehistory of the Danube Gorges hinterlands. *Starinar*. Beograd.

BORIĆ, D.; STAROVIĆ, A. (forthcoming) – Arheološka istraživanja lokaliteta Aria Babi u zaleđu Đerdapa. *Zbornik Narodnog muzeja*. Beograd.

BUDJA, M. (1999) – The transition to farming in Mediterranean Europe – an indigenous response. *Documenta Praehistorica*. Ljubljana. 26: p. 119-141.

BRONK RAMSEY, C. (1995) – Radiocarbon calibration and analysis of stratigraphy: the OxCal Program *Radiocarbon*. 37(2): p. 425–430.

BRONK RAMSEY, C. (2001) – Development of the radiocarbon program OxCal. *Radiocarbon*. 43. (2A): p. 355–363.

CHAPMAN, J. C. (1993) – Social Power in the Iron Gates Mesolithic. In CHAPMAN, J.; DOLUK-HANOV, P., eds. – *Cultural Transformations and Interactions in Eastern Europe*. Aldershot: Avebury. p. 71-121.

CHAPMAN, J. C. (1994) – The origins of farming in South East Europe. *Préhistoire Européenne*. 6: p. 133-156.

CHAPMAN, J. C. (2000) – *Fragmentation in Archaeology. People, places and broken objects in the prehistory of south-eastern Europe*. London & New York: Routledge.

CLIFFORD, J. (2003) – *On the Edges of Anthropology (Interviews)*. Chicago: Prickly Paradigm Press.

COOK, G.; BONSALL, C.; HEDGES, R. E. M.; MCSWEENEY, K.; BORONEANȚ, V.; BARTO-SIEWICZ, L.; PETTITT, P. B. (2002) – Problems of dating human bones from the Iron Gates. *Antiquity*. 76: p. 77-85.

DINAN, E. H. (1996) – A preliminary report on the lithic assemblages from the early Holocene level at the Iron Gates site of Băile Herculane. *Mesolithic Miscellany.* 17(2): p. 15-24.

GARAŠANIN, M.; RADOVANOVIĆ, I. (2001) – A pot in house 54 at Lepenski Vir I. *Antiquity* 75(287): p. 118-125.

GRGA, Đ. (1996) – Karijes u humanoj populaciji kulture Lepenskog Vira. *Starinar.* Beograd. XLVII: p. 177-185.

GRUPE, G.; MANHART, H.; MIKIĆ, Ž.; PETERS, J. (2003) – Vertebrate food webs and subsistence strategies of Meso- and Neolithic populations of central Europe. In GRUPE, G.; PETERS J., eds., *Documenta Archaeobiologiae 1. Yearbook of the State Collection of Anthropology and Palaeoanatomy, München, Germany.* Rahden/Westf.: Verlag M. Leidorf. p. 193-213

JEVTIĆ, M. (1983) – Lepenska potkapina, praistorijsko naselje. *Starinar.* Beograd. 33-34 (1982-1983): p. 201-207.

JOVANOVIĆ, B. (1969) – Chronological Frames of the Iron Gate Group of the Early Neolithic Period. *Archaeologica Iugoslavica.* Beograd. 10: p. 23-38.

JOVANOVIĆ, B. 1987 Die Architektur und Keramik der Siedlung Padina B am Eisernen Tor, Jugoslawien. *Germania* 65(1): p. 1-16.

LJUBOJEVIĆ, V. (2003) – Pregled speleoloških istraživanja na Miroču, Nacionalni Park Đerdap. *Zbornik 4. simpozijuma o zaštiti karsta.* Beograd. p. 109-115.

MÜLLER, J. (1997) – Neolithische und chalkolithische Spondylus-Artefakte. Anmerkungen zu Verbreitung, Tauschgebiet, und sozialer Funktion. In BECKER, C; DUNKELMANN, M. L.; METZNER-NEBELSICK, C.; PETER-RÖCHNER, H.; ROEDER, M.; TERŽAN, B., eds., - *Xrovos. Beiträge zur prähistorischen Archäeologie zwischen Nord- und Südosteuropa. Festschrift für Bernard Hänsel.* Espelkamp: Verlag Marie Leidorf Gmbh. p. 91-106.

NICA, M. (1976) – Cea Mai Veche Asezare Neolitica de la Sud de Carpati. *Studii si Cercetari de Istorie Veche si Arheologie* 27(4): 735-463.

NICOLÂESCU-PLOPSOR, C. S.; COMSA, E.; PĂUNESCU, AL. (1957) – Santierul arheologic Băile Herculane (reg. Timisoara, r. Almas). *Materiale* 3: p. 51-58.

KAPURAN, A.; JEVTIĆ, M.; BORIĆ, D. (in press) Novi nalazi keramike metalnih doba na teritoriji Đerdapa. *Glasnik srpskog arheološkog društva.*

KACZANOWSKA, M.; KOZŁOWSKI, J. K. (2003) – Origins of the Linear Pottery Complex and the Neolithic Transition in Central Europe. In AMMERMAN, A. J.; BIAGI, P., eds., – *The*

Widening Harvest. The Neolithic Transition in Europe: Looking Back, Looking Forward. Boston, Massachusetts: Archaeological Institute of America (Colloquia and Conference Papers 6). p. 227-248

PERIĆ, S.; NIKOLIĆ, D. (2004) – Stratigraphic, Cultural and Chronological Characteristics of the Pottery from Lepenski Vir – 1965 Excavations. In PERIĆ, S., ed. – *The Central Pomoravlje in Neolithisation of South-East Europe. The Neolithic in the Middle Morava Valley 1.* Belgrade: Archaeological Institute. p. 157-217

PRICE, T. D.; BORIĆ, D. (forthcoming) – Mobility in the Mesolithic-Neolithic Danube Gorges: Strontium Isotope Analyses. *Journal of Anthropological Archaeology.*

RADOVANOVIĆ, I. (1996) – *The Iron Gates Mesolithic.* Ann Arbor: International Monographs in Prehistory.

RADOVANOVIĆ, I. (1997) – The Lepenski Vir Culture: a contribution to interpretation of its ideological aspects. In *Antidoron Dragoslavo Srejović completis LXV annis ab amicis, collegis, discipulis oblatum.* Beograd: Centar za arheološka istraživanja, Filozofski fakultet, p. 85-93.

RADOVANOVIĆ, I. (2006) – Further notes on Mesolithic-Neolithic contacts in the Iron Gates Region and the Central Balkans. *Documenta Praehistorica.* Ljubljana. XXXIV: p. 111-128.

RICHARDS, M.; SHULTING, R. (2006) – Against the grain? A response to Milner *et al.* (2004). *Antiquity.* 80: p. 444-458.

SREJOVIĆ, D. (1972) – *Europe's First Monumental Sculpture: New Discoveries at Lepenski Vir.* London: Thames and Hudson.

SREJOVIĆ, D. (1988) – *Neolithic of Serbia.* Belgrade: Faculty of Philosophy, Centre for Archaeological Research.

SREJOVIĆ, D.; BABOVIĆ, LJ. (1983) – *Umetnost Lepenskog Vira.* Beograd: Jugoslavija.

SREJOVIĆ, D.; LETICA, Z. (1978) – *Vlasac. Mezolitsko naselje u Djerdapu (I arheologija).* Beograd: Srpska akademija nauka i umetnosti.

STANOJEVIĆ, Z. (1988) – Kučajna. In SREJOVIĆ, D., ed., - *Neolithic of Serbia.* Belgrade: Faculty of Philosophy, Centre for Archaeological Research. p. 77-78.

STANKOVIĆ, S. (1986a) – Knjepište – une station du grupe de Starčevo. *Đerdapske sveske.* Beograd. III: p. 447-452.

STANKOVIĆ, S. (1986b) – Embouchure du ruisseau Kamenički Potok – site du grupe Starčevo. *Đerdapske sveske.* Beograd. III: p. 467-471.

THOMAS, J. (2003) – Thoughts on the "repacked" Neolithic Revolution. *Antiquity*. 77 (295): p. 67-75.

TILLEY, C. (1994) – *A phenomenology of Landscape. Places, Paths and Monuments*. Oxford/Providence: Berg.

TRINGHAM, R. (2000) – Southeastern Europe in the transition to agriculture in Europe: bridge, buffer or mosaic. In PRICE, T. D., ed., – *Europe's first farmers*. Cambridge: Cambridge University Press. p. 19-56.

VOYTEK, B. (1987) – Analysis of lithic raw material from sites in eastern Yugoslavia. In K. T. BÍRO, ed., – *Papers for the First International Conference on Prehistoric Flint Mining and Lithic Raw Material Identification in the Carpathian Basin, Budapest-Sümeg, 1986*. Budapest. p. 287-295.

VOYTEK, B.; TRINGHAM, R. (1989) – Rethinking the Mesolithic: the Case of South-East Europe. In C. BONSALL, ed., – *The Mesolithic in Europe*. Edinburgh: John Donald Publishers Ltd. p. 492-499.

WILLMS, C. (1985) – Neolithischer *Spondylus* schmuck. Hundert Jahre Forschung. *Germania*. 65(2): p. 331-343.

WHITTLE, A.; BARTOSIEWICZ, L.; BORIĆ, D.; PETTITT, P.; RICHARDS, M. (2002) – In the beginning: new radiocarbon dates for the Early Neolithic in northern Serbia and south-east Hungary. *Antaeus*. Budapest. 25: p. 63-117.

WHITTLE, A.; BARTOSIEWICZ, L.; BORIĆ, D.; PETTITT, P.; RICHARDS, M. (2005) – New radiocarbon dates for the Early Neolithic in northern Serbia and south-east Hungary. *Antaeus*. Budapest. 28: p. 347-355.

PALAEOGEOGRAPHICAL BACKGROUND OF THE MESOLITHIC AND EARLY NEOLITHIC SETTLEMENT IN THE CARPATHIAN BASIN

Pál SÜMEGI

University of Szeged, Departament of Geology and Palaeontology, P.O.B. 658, H-6701 Szeged, Hungary,
sumegi@geo.u-szeged.hu

Abstract: Complexity or mosaicity of the climatic, faunal, floral and soil endowments developing during the Quaternary and cyclically fluctuating in space and time had a major deterministic role on the immigrating and settling human communities. Simply because it practically prevented the expansion or spreading of the gathered, hunted or even produced plants and animals giving the economic foundations of these societies to the whole of the Carpathian Basin at a given moment of time. Therefore, the immigrant groups of people from various climatic-environmental areas could occupy only certain parts of the basin at a time, which corresponded to their economic experience acquired up to that time, and which provided for their hunted, bred, foraged or cultivated animals and plants. This new geoarcheological model, conceptualized earlier, was developed for the whole of the Carpathian Basin by taking into account all the environmental and social factors, which were influencing and could have determined the spreading of the Neolithic communities bearing Balkanic-Mediterranean cultural roots and productional experiences.
Key-words: Quaternary, Holocene, environment, subsistence, Carpathian Basin, Agro-Ecological Barrier

Resumè : Le caractère complexe de la mosaique des environnements climatiques, faunistiques, pédologiques et botaniques qui ont été développé au Quaternaire et qui ont fluctué cycliquement dans le temps et dans l'éspace ont eu un role déterminant pour les migrations humaines et l'occupation du territoire. Ces conditions ont formé les obstacles dans l'extension des plantes et animaux qui ont été collecté, chassé et/ou domestiqué, formant les bases économiques des sociétés du Bassin Carpathique dans les différentes périodes (Sümegi 2003). Par conséquent les immigrants provenant des environnements et des climats différents ont pu occuper seulement certaines parties du Bassin Carpathique. C'étaient uniquement les parties qui pourrait correspondre aux conditions environnementales permettant de développer l'economie de subistance dans les zones d'origine de ces populations (Sümegi, Kertész 1998). Ce nouveau modèle geoarchéologique a été développé afin de couvrir tout le Bassin Carpathique en utilisant des facteurs aussi bien environnementaux que sociaux qui ont déterminé les conditions de l'extension des sociétés Néolithiques enracinés dans la zone Balkano-Méditerranéenne.
Mots-clés: Quaternaire, Holocène, environnement, économie de subsistence, Bassin Carpathique, frontière agro-ecologique.

According to the archaeological data one of the most important areas in the process of European Neolithization is the Carpathian-Balkanic region as it hosted the earliest representatives of the food production communities thriving out from the area of the Fertile Crescent and enabling their onward expansion to the central and western parts of the European continent. The central part of the region formed the northernmost boundary of expansion of the Anatolian – Balkan agricultural civilization, i.e. the Körös – Starčevo cultures (Kutzián 1947; Kalicz-Makkay 1977; Kalicz 1970; Kalicz et al. 1998; Bánffy 2000; 2004; Whittle 1996). North of this borderline a fundamentally different world existed with the presence of hunting-fishing-gathering Mesolithic communities (Gábori 1968; Makkay 1982). According to the archaeological and palaeoenvironmental findings available so far as a result of the mutual interaction between these two communities bearing different cultural and productionnal traditions and roots a new Neolithic culture arose termed as the Linear Pottery Complex. The western branch of this culture (known as the Linear Pottery Culture of Transdanubia) following its birth in the

Carpathian basin spread all around Europe creating a new European Neolithic culture extending from the estuary of the Rhein to the river Dnyeper and independent of any Mediterranean cultural roots and influences (Kalicz 1970; Kalicz, Makkay 1977; Kalicz et al. 1998; Bánffy 2000; 2004; Whittle 1996).

There has been an intensification of research related to the distribution of the Early Neolithic Culture and its northern boundary in the Carpathian Basin during the past few years, and numerous interpretations have been advocated explaining the possible reasons for the emergence of this borderline in the VI. millennium BC. All these processes have been univocally triggered by archeological excavations implemented at the Mesolithic sites of the Jászság (Hungary), which had been discovered by an amateur archeologist Gyula Kerékgyártó of Jászberény, under the supervision of Róbert Kertész archeologist (Kertész et al. 1994). Unfortunately, there was correct in nothing that age of the Mesolithic in the Jászság can only be determined on typological grounds (Kozlowski 2005). Therefore, the correct connections between Late Mesolithic

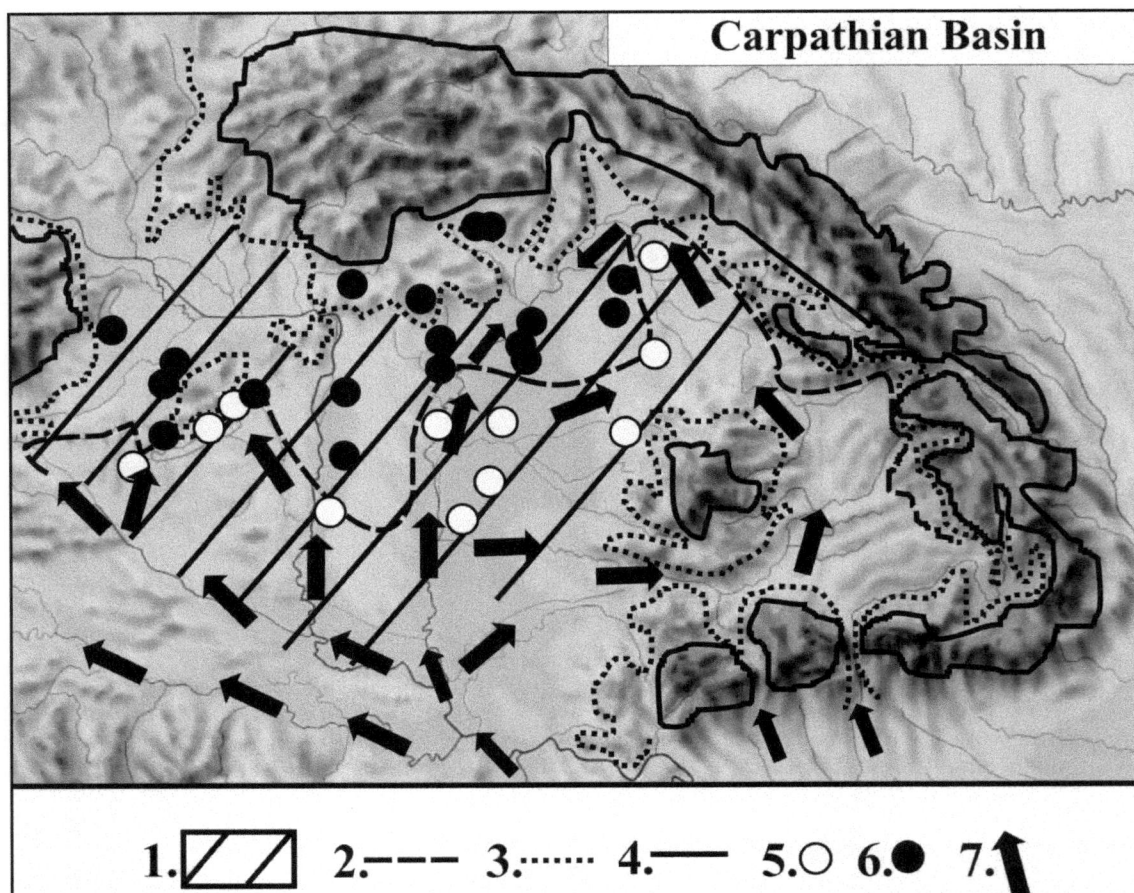

Fig. 4.1. (1. Carpathian Basin Neolithic Adaptation Zone (CABAN AZ), 2. Central European – Balkanic Agro-Ecological Barrier (CEB AEB), 3. Carpathian Piemont Agro-Ecological Barrier (CP AEB), 4. Carpathian Upland Agro-Ecological Barrier (CU AEB), 5.Catchment basin with impact of the Early Neolithic communities, 6. Catchment basin with impact of the Middle Neolithic communities, 7. Infiltration of the Early Neolithic communities)

hunters and Early Neolithic communities cannot be drawn in our days, so two highly distinct Neolithization hypotheses have been put forward for the central area of the Carpathian Basin. János Makkay (Makkay 1998) applied an approach of language history while formulating his concept of the "*Jászság boundary*", saying that it was historical-cultural factors that have finally led to the emergence of this borderline, plus the fact that the Mesolithic groups frequently encountered the Neolithic groups of the Körös culture. According to his views, the line running along the meeting points of communities bearing different technical and cultural traditions and belonging to distinct language families should mark the trajectory of this boundary. Discussing the critics of this concept is not the subject of this paper however, it must be mentioned that the emergence of a cultural interface stretching for several

hundred kilometers seems to be quite unlikely within the Carpathian Basin with data on population densities of hunting-fishing-gathering communities at hand (Deevey 1960), due to the low population numbers of the foraging Mesolithic groups inhabiting the area. The second concept of a geoarcheological model draws upon the fact that the Carpathian Basin has been characterized by a large-scale versatility during the past 10.000 years. As a result, a large-scale mosaic-like segmentation or complexity emerged, observable both at the macro-, meso- and micro-scale within the basin from as early as the Ice Age (Sümegi 1996; 2003; Sümegi, Krolopp 2002; Sümegi *et al.* 1998; 1999; Sümegi, Kertész 1998). The emergence of a macro-scale mosaicity or complexity is due to the overlap of four major climatic zones in the region (Sümegi 1995; 1996; 2000; 2003).

In addition to these three climatic zones, a sub-mediterranean influence developed in an irregular fashion from north to south. Meanwhile, continental climatic effects declined from east to west. Finally, in Transdanubia, Atlantic climatic influence may be detected, decreasing from west to east. Climatic regions may extend over thousands of square kilometers. Thanks to the cumulative interaction of these climatic zones, a mosaic-like vegetation developed in the Carpathian Basin as early as the end of the Pleistocene, and this mosaic-like complexity is observable in the composition and distribution of the modern vegetation of the basin as well (Sümegi 1996; 1999; 2000; 2003; 2004; 2005; Sümegi et al. 1998; 2002; Sümegi, Kertész 1998). The effects of the extensive overlapping climatic zones are further intensified and influenced by the regional and local morphological and hydrological conditions (Sümegi 1996; 1999; 2003; 2004; 2005). The strongest climate-modifying influences emerged within the river valleys on the one hand, as well as on the northern and southern slopes of the hills and mountains (Sümegi, Hertelendi 1998). Thus the interface of the different climatic zones does not form a clear-cut uniform boundary at the macro level, but appears as rather segmented minor puzzle pieces, restricted to adjacent smaller areas, creating a mosaic-like pattern. Furthermore, all these climatic influences followed a cyclically fluctuating trend, appearing with given frequencies throughout the course of history (Sümegi, Krolopp 2002), rendering some sort of plasticity to the boundary of the likewise periodically expanding-contracting climatic and environmental puzzle pieces (Sümegi 2003).

However, these are not homogeneous: they form local and regional mosaic patterns in accordance with geomorphologic, orographic and hydrographic features. Mosaic-like regional patterning in the Great Hungarian Plain was created by the formation of neotectonic depressions. These relatively shallow sub-basins, measuring 50-100 square kilometers each, form the deepest parts of the Great Hungarian Plain and thus defined the courses of rivers. The formation of neotectonic depressions influenced morphological and hydrogeological in at least two ways thereby influencing the quality of loose deposits on the surface of the Great Hungarian Plain and affecting pedological and vegetation conditions. On the one hand, depressions were formed with varying intensities at different times, encompassing different time intervals. Starting from the river valleys, steppe-like surfaces developed along the depressions at various altitudes above sea level.

The water tables and thus, hydrological properties of these surfaces, vary according to their respective positions. The deepest zones are river valleys and basins, usually covered by Holocene loess. These areas have the most favorable hydrological properties on the Great Hungarian Plain. This fact is of outstanding importance in an area where present-day annual precipitation varies between 500-550 mm, and reaches only 300-350 mm during the vegetation period. In fact, without its network of rivers, fed by precipitation in the Alps and the Carpathians, thus some regions of the Great Hungarian Plain would be a deforested steppe, or forest steppe under Holocene climatic conditions.

Meanwhile the asynchronous depressions of sub-basins, river valleys, shifted during the different phases of the Quaternary Period. The most significant change took place some twenty-thousand years ago, when the Tisza River, flowing in the Ér Valley, turned north and gradually formed its present day course. One of the significant consequences of the development of the present-day Tisza Valley was that earlier, loess covered Pleistocene alluvial formations became isolated as they were not affected by the lateral erosion caused by rivers. These residual surfaces formed island-like fractal structures within the basins, creating the mosaic-like local patterning of the alluvial landscape. Owing to their relatively lower lying water tables, these island-like residual surfaces are distinctly different from their more humid alluvial environment with their dry, seldom flooded, surfaces. Our data show that the development of both vegetation and soils followed this mosaic pattern characteristic of the landscape. Soils developed under the influence of water in deeper, alluvial areas while loess plateaus are covered with meadow soils. The island-like elevations within the alluvium are topped with alkali and meadow soils. The soil along their edges, however, was formed under the influence of water.

When this natural mosaic pattern is studied close up, a structure may be recognized that is comparable to a mathematical "fractal microscope" set. This type of set is characterized by repeating an identical pattern along with increasing magnification. A similar structure, the mosaic pattern, is also repeated on the Great Hungarian Plain, whether the landscape structure is studied in resolutions of several thousands of square kilometers or only a few square meters. Meanwhile, the most significant archaeological question is, whether and how these levels of mosaic patterning affected the life of Early Neolithic communities that settled in the area representing the Körös culture.

When settlement points of the Körös culture are studied more closely, an indubitable preference for loess-covered, residual islands in the alluvium may be recognized (Sümegi 2000; 2003). These areas were not flooded. That is, this one element in the mosaic pattern of the landscape had an overbearing influence on their settlement strategy. Thus, in a fundamentally dry environment, they could occupy areas in the proximity of live waters, without the settlements being threatened by regular flooding. On the basis of palaeoclimatic reconstructions it seems evident that at the end of the 7th and the beginning of the 6th millennium BC a distinct warm period followed in the Carpathian Basin as well. This must have been best characterized by an increase in the solar constant. When zones in which the solar constant evidently increased (i. e. submediterranean climatic influence expanded) are compared with the geographical distribution of Early Neolithic communities, a close spatial correlation is obtained. It shows that communities that imported domestic plants and animals (whose original gene centers had been in the Near East), could best exploit submediterranean zones in river valleys of key significance from the viewpoint of early settlement. Meanwhile island-like surfaces in the alluvium also limited the subsistence possibilities of early food producers. Beyond these features that were islands both in a morphological and ecological sense, land surfaces were covered by gallery forests, flooded regularly at least twice a year. That is, the new settlers could predictably reckon only with the island-like elevations as scenes of subsistence. Although once spring and early summer floods receded, the drying floodplain offered excellent graze, only the islands were habitable at the time of high waters, even for livestock.

The mosaic-like segmentation reached such a large-degree, that the actual borderzone or interface zone of the individual climatic and environmental units is practically resolved (Sümegi 1996; 1999; 2000; 2003; 2004; 2005). This complexity or mosaicity of the climatic, faunal, floral and soil endowments developping during the Quaternary and cyclically fluctuating in space and time had a major deterministic role on the immigrating and settling human communities. Simply because it practically prevented the expansion or spreading of the gathered, hunted or even produced plants and animals giving the economic foundations of these societies to the whole of the Carpathian Basin at a given moment of time (Sümegi 2003). Therefore, the immigrant groups of people from various climatic-environmental areas could occupy only certain parts of the basin at a time. Those parts, which corresponded to their economic experience acquired up to that time, and which provided for their hunted, bred, foraged or cultivated animals and plants (Sümegi, Kertész 1998). This new geoarcheological model, conceptualized earlier, was developed for the whole of the Carpathian Basin by taking into account all the environmental and social factors, which were influencing and could have determined the spreading of the Neolithic communities bearing Balkanic-Mediterranean cultural roots and productional experiences (Sümegi, Kertész 1998; Sümegi 2000; 2003; 2004). Based on the model, the author hypothesized the emergence of a Central European - Balkanic Agroecological Barrier (CEB AEB) within the central parts of the Carpathian Basin, which in essence determined the possibilities of spreading of the productive societies within the whole basin during the Early Neolithic (Sümegi, Kertész 1998). The ecological needs of the cultivated plants and the farmed animals of the Körös-Starcevo culture, as the earliest group engaged in agricultural production, the preservation of a dual subsistence made up of productive and improductive phases, the emergence of a sedentary lifestyle, as well as the level of technical development and productional experiences gave the basis of this new agroecological model (Sümegi, Kertész 1998). This resulted from the mosaic-like subdivision of the physical space. Since the mosaic pattern was manifested at several levels, an agroecological border zone developed at the time of the Early Neolithic. On the other hand they have also emphasized the important role of the river valleys acting as rendezvous points and infiltration zones for the Mesolithic and Neolithic groups in the whole process of Neolithization within the Carpathian Basin.

References

BÁNFFY, E. (2000) The Late Starčevo and the Earliest Linear Pottery Groups in Western Transdanubia. *Documenta Praehistorica*. 27, p. 173–185.

BÁNFFY, E. (2004) The 6th Millennium BC boundary in Western Transdanubia and its role in the Central European transition (The Szentgyörgyvölgy-Pityerdomb settlement). Budapest: Archaeological Institute of the Hungarian Academy of Sciences. (Varia Archeologica Hungarica; 15).

DEEVEY, E. S. (1960) The human population. *Scientific American*. 203, p. 194-204.

GÁBORI, M. 1968. Mesolithischer Zeltgrundriss in Sződliget. *Acta Archeologica Hungarica*. 20, p. 33-36.

KALICZ, N. (1970) *Clay gods*. Budapest: Hereditas Kiadó.

KALICZ, N.; MAKKAY, J. (1977) *Die Linienbandkeramik in der Grossen Ungarischen Tiefebene*. Budapest: Akadémiai Kiadó. (Studia Archeologica; 7).

KALICZ, N.; M. VIRÁGH, ZS.; T. BÍRÓ, K. (1998) The northern periphery of the Early Neolithic Starčevo Culture in south-western Hungary: a case study an excavation at Lake Balaton. *Documenta Praehistorica*. 25, p. 151–181.

KERTÉSZ, R.; SÜMEGI, P.; KOZÁK, M.; BRAUN, M.; FÉLEGYHÁZI, E.; HERTELENDI, E. (1994)

Archeological and Paleoecological Study of an Early Holocene Settlement in the Jászság Area (Jászberény I). *Acta Geographica Debrecina.* 32, p. 5-49.

KOZŁOWSKI, J. K. (2005) Remarks on the Mesolithic in the Northern part of the Carpathian Basin. In GÁL, E.; JUHÁSZ, I.; SÜMEGI, P. eds. lits. - *Environmental Archaeology in North-Eastern Hungary.* Budapest: Archaeological Institute of the Hungarian Academy of Sciences, p. 175-186. (Varia Archaeologica Hungarica; 19).

KUTZIÁN, I. (1947) *The Körös Culture.* Dissertationes Pannonicae, series II, No. 23.

MAKKAY, J. (1982) *New results of the Neolithic researches in Hungary.* Budapest: Akadémiai Press.

MAKKAY, J. (1996) Theories About the Origin, the Distribution and the End of the Körös Culture. In TÁLAS, L., ed. lits. - *At the Fringe of Three Worlds.* Szolnok: Damjanich Museum, p. 35-49.

SÜMEGI, P. (1996) *Comparative palaeoecological and stratigraphic values of the NE Hungarian loess region.* CSc (PhD) dissertation, p.120. Debrecen.

SÜMEGI, P. (1999) Reconstruction of flora, soil and landscape evolution, and human impact on the Bereg Plain from late-glacial up to the present, based on palaeoecological analysis. In HAMAR, J.; SÁRKÁNY-KISS, A., eds. lits. - *The Upper Tisa Valley.* Szeged: Tiscia Monograph Series, p. 173-204.

SÜMEGI, P. (2000) An environmental archaeological analysis of "Bihar-area". In SELMECZI, L., ed. lits. - *Neolithic of "Bihar-area".* Debrecen: Déri Múzeum, p. 7-18.

SÜMEGI, P. (2003) Early Neolithic man and riparian environment in the Carpathian Basin. In JEREM, E.; RACZKY, P., eds. lits. - *Morgenrot der Kulturen: Frühe Etappen der Menschheitsgeschichte in Mittel- und Südosteuropa. Festschroft für Nándor Kalicz zum 75. Geburtstag.* Budapest: Archaeolingua Press, p. 53-60.

SÜMEGI, P. (2004) The results of paleoenvironmental reconstruction and comparative geoarcheological analysis for the examined area. pp. 301-348. In SÜMEGI, P.; GULYÁS, S., eds. lits. - *The geohistory of Bátorliget Marshland.* Budapest: Archaeolingua Press, p. 301-348.

SÜMEGI, P. (2005). *Loess and Upper Paleolithic environment in Hungary.* Nagykovácsi: Aurea Kiadó.

SÜMEGI, P.; HERTELENDI, E. (1998). Reconstruction of microenvironmental changes in Kopasz Hill loess area at Tokaj (Hungary) between 15.000-70.000 BP years. *Radiocarbon.* 40, p. 855-863.

SÜMEGI, P.; HERTELENDI, E.; MAGYARI, E.; MOLNÁR, M. (1998) Evolution of the environment in the Carpathian Basin during the last 30.000 BP years and its effects on the ancient habits of the different cultures. In KÖLTŐ, L.; BARTOSIEWICZ, L., eds. lits. - *Archeometrical Research in Hungary, II.* Budapest, p. 183-197.

SÜMEGI, P.; KERTÉSZ, R. (1998) Palaeogeographic characteristic of the Carpathian Basin – an ecological trap durnig the Early Neolithic? *Jászkunság.* 44, p. 144-157.

SÜMEGI, P.; KROLOPP, E. (2002). Quartermalacological analyses for modeling of the Upper Weichselian palaeoenvironmental changes in the Carpathian Basin. *Quaternary International.* 91, p. 53-63.

WHITTLE, A. 1996. *Europe in the Neolithic.* Cambridge: Cambridge University Press.

MESOLITHIC FORAGERS AND THE SPREAD OF AGRICULTURE IN WESTERN HUNGARY

Eszter BÁNFFY

Archaeological Institute of the Hungarian Academy of Sciences, úri u. 49, 1014 Budapest, Hangary, banffy@archeo.mta.hu

William J. EICHMANN

University of Wisconsin – Madison, wjeichmann@wisc.edu

Tibor MARTON

Archaeological Institute of the Hungarian Academy of Sciences, úri u. 49, 1014 Budapest, Hangary, marton@archeo.mta.hu

Abstract: This paper examines the role of Mesolithic hunter-gatherers in the spread of agriculture in the Transdanubian region of Hungary and Europe in general. The following themes are highlighted: 1) earlier research and current status of Mesolithic studies in Hungary, with an emphasis on Transdanubia; 2) the background to the origins and spread of Early Neolithic societies; 3) possible directions for future studies on Mesolithic hunter-gatherers in Hungary; 4) preliminary results of the research on the Hungarian Mesolithic by the authors. The Mesolithic contribution to the neolithisation of the Carpathian Basin has been underrepresented for a variety of reasons and the lack of research. This situation can best be remedied by the re-examination of poorly investigated, possible Mesolithic sites in conjunction with prospection for new sites.
Key words: Mesolithic, neolithisation, Starčevo culture, Early LBK, Transdanubia (Western Hungary)

Resumé: Dans cette communication le rôle des chasseurs cueilleurs mésoiithiques dans l'extension de l'agriculture en Transdanubie a été examiné. Les auteurs se sont concentrés sur les sujets suivants : 1) l'état actuel des études sur le Mésolithique en Hongrie, en particulier en Transdanubie, 2) les bases et l'origine de l'extension des communeautés du Néolithique ancien, 3) directions possibles des études futures sur les chasseurs-cueilleurs mésolithiques en Hongrie, 4) résultats préliminaires des recherches sur le Mésolithique hongrois entreprises par les auteurs. La contribution du Mésolithique à la Néolithisation du Bassin Carpathique a été sous-estimée pour les nombreuses raisons y compris l'absence des recherches. Cette situation pourrait être changée par le ré-examen des sites peu fouillés et par les nouvelles prospections.
Mots-clés : Mésolithique, Néolithisation, Starčevo, phase ancienne de LBK, Transdanubie (Hongrie occidentale)

The earliest evidence for food-production in south-eastern Europe dates to the late 7th millennium cal BC and from the mid-6th millennium cal BC in north-central Europe. The spread of agriculture to continental Europe can be divided into two phases, both of which have traditionally been identified by the first appearance of pottery associated with an economy based on domesticated plants and animals.

In the first phase, a farming economy associated with the Starčevo culture expanded northward from Greece across the central Balkans, appearing in south-western Hungary around 5.600 cal BC (Bánffy, 2004, p. 308; Whittle *et al.*, 2002, p. 93). In the second phase of agricultural expansion, the Linearbandkeramik (LBK) spread rapidly (< 200 years) from western Hungary into central Europe, from the River Rhine in the west to the Ukraine in the east (Bogucki, 2000; Gronenborn, 1998, p. 193; Stäuble, 1995, p. 233). The north-western distribution of Starčevo sites and the south-eastern distribution of LBK sites overlap in Transdanubia in western Hungary, and thus the process of neolithisation in this region has a bearing on both the emergence and subsequent expansion of LBK.

This expansion brought with it the novel reorganisation of Early Neolithic society in the Balkans (Whittle, 1996, p. 150). Prehistorians working in Germany, Austria and the Czech Republic have demonstrated that there were direct links between Neolithic and Mesolithic cultures, and they have also found evidence for contact during both periods with western Hungary (Gronenborn, 1994, p. 138, 144; Mateiciucová, 2002, p. 176). Based on analogies from adjacent regions, it has been hypothesised that the first agriculturalists in Hungary interacted with a local Mesolithic population (Bánffy, 2000, p. 174; T. Biró, 2002, p. 129; Kalicz, 1990, p. 26).

Another major issue regarding the transition to agriculture concerns the terminology used to describe the modes of this transition and how this transition can be conceptualised. The term "Mesolithic" refers to the last hunter-gatherers, who subsisted on wild plants and animals. The beginning of the Mesolithic is associated with the onset of the Early Holocene climate around 10.000 BC (Kozłowski and Kozłowski, 1979, p. 60) and its end is generally linked to the appearance of the first food-producing, Neolithic societies. It is important to note that the beginning of the Mesolithic is linked to a global climatic event, while its end is defined in relation to an economic transition or shift within human society. The Neolithic, as most commonly used in south-eastern and central Europe, assumes a close association between the earliest domesticates and the earliest pottery.

Migration and adaptation are the two extremes on a wide scale of mechanisms (Zvelebil, 2000, p. 57–58). Disregarding now the uncertainties in defining and distinguishing between hunter-gatherers and farmers during the transitional phases, we may certainly say that agriculture spread through a variety of mechanisms, under different circumstances and for a variety of reasons in differing periods and areas (Smith, 2001). The evidence for discontinuity between pre-agricultural and agricultural societies would imply colonisation, while continuity would suggest adoption and adaptation. At the most basic level, the acceptance or rejection of either hypothesis calls for gathering the appropriate archaeological evidence from pre-agricultural and agricultural periods.

Research over the past fifty years has produced multiple lines of evidence indicating that the spread of agriculture in Europe was an extremely heterogeneous process, melting indigenous hunter-gatherers with immigrant populations (Gronenborn, 2003, p. 86). These studies have focused on the archaeological evidence from pre-agricultural and agricultural periods, such as lithic technology (Gronenborn, 1997; Taute, 1973–74) and lithic raw material supply networks (Mateiciucová, 2003). The possible role of indigenous hunter-gatherers in the spread of farming economies has not been explored in large portions of Europe and consequently, the testing of various hypothesised processes is simply not possible (Whittle, 1996, p. 10). The archaeological record for Early Neolithic settlement in Transdanubia is limited to a handful of well-investigated sites, while evidence for Mesolithic occupation remains minimal to non-existent. Therefore, the task of assessing ideological, social and economic continuity between the two periods remains purely speculative. The evidence provided by the genetics of modern European populations (Richards, 2003, p. 164) and palaeobotany (Schweitzer, 2001; Sümegi, 2004) suggests that Mesolithic hunter-gatherers were present and partook in the neolithisation of the Carpathian Basin and central Europe. However, the lack or at the best minimal direct archaeological evidence for Mesolithic hunter-gatherers has often limited discussion from moving beyond hypothetical statements (Chapman, 1985, p. 504).

Most of the Transdanubian sites, which have been assigned to the Mesolithic, have been dated on the strength of the typological traits of the lithics found there. The debitage in the lithic assemblages from these sites was omitted from the analysis of the finds, and this makes a comparison of the sites rather difficult. Another problem is that the archaeological and geological context has rarely been reported in sufficient detail. A wide range of social and economic factors undoubtedly influenced Mesolithic settlement patterns, but in the lack of detailed information on the context and content of the so-called Mesolithic sites, it is difficult to differentiate between the various sites.

Mesolithic research in the first half of 20th century was to a large extent determined by the use of French lithic typologies to identify Mesolithic materials. In Hungary, the identification of so-called "Tardenoisien" types in lithic assemblages was a hallmark of this research period. The known assemblages were surface collections, most often from sand dunes, and they were assigned to the Mesolithic on purely typological grounds, according to a framework in which Mesolithic/Tardenoisien was synonymous with "microlithic" (Gallus, 1942, p. 22; Hillebrand, 1925, p. 82; Hillebrand, 1937, p. 25). Even though many advances were made between 1950 and 1989, there was no overall research strategy for studying the Mesolithic. Another problem bedevilling research during this period and in the early 1980s, was the concept of the "Coarse Mesolithic" (Grobgerätiges Mesolithikum: Vértes, 1965, p. 216–221) and the so-called "Eger Culture" (T. Dobosi, 1975, p. 68–69). Following initial criticism (Kozłowski, 1973, p. 326), this concept was finally discarded in the late 1980s and the lithic artefacts were re-assigned to the Middle Palaeolithic (Ringer, 1983, p. 147; Simán, 1979, p. 87; Simán, 1995, p. 43). Sződliget–Vác (Gábori, 1956; Gábori, 1968) and Szekszárd–Palánk (Vértes, 1962) were the only sites excavated during this period, both of which are probably Mesolithic.

The general lack of Mesolithic finds gave led to the hypothesis that hunter-gatherers followed the large steppean animal herds and migrated northward (Simán, 1990, p. 19), and that the central regions of the Carpathian Basin remained largely depopulated until the Neolithic (Gábori, 1981, p. 106; Szathmáry, 1988).

In the late 1980s and 1990s, Róbert Kertész began a systematic survey in the Jászság region lying on the northern fringes of the Great Hungarian Plain, mainly along the Tarna and Zagyva rivers (Kertész, 1991). In the course of this survey, several sites yielding characteristic Mesolithic geometric microliths were identified along the Early Holocene (Boreal) abandoned channels and oxbows of these two rivers (Kertész, 1996, 13). Four sites were excavated: Jászberény I (Kertész, 1991, p. 29; Kertész, 1996, p. 19), Jászberény II (Kertész,

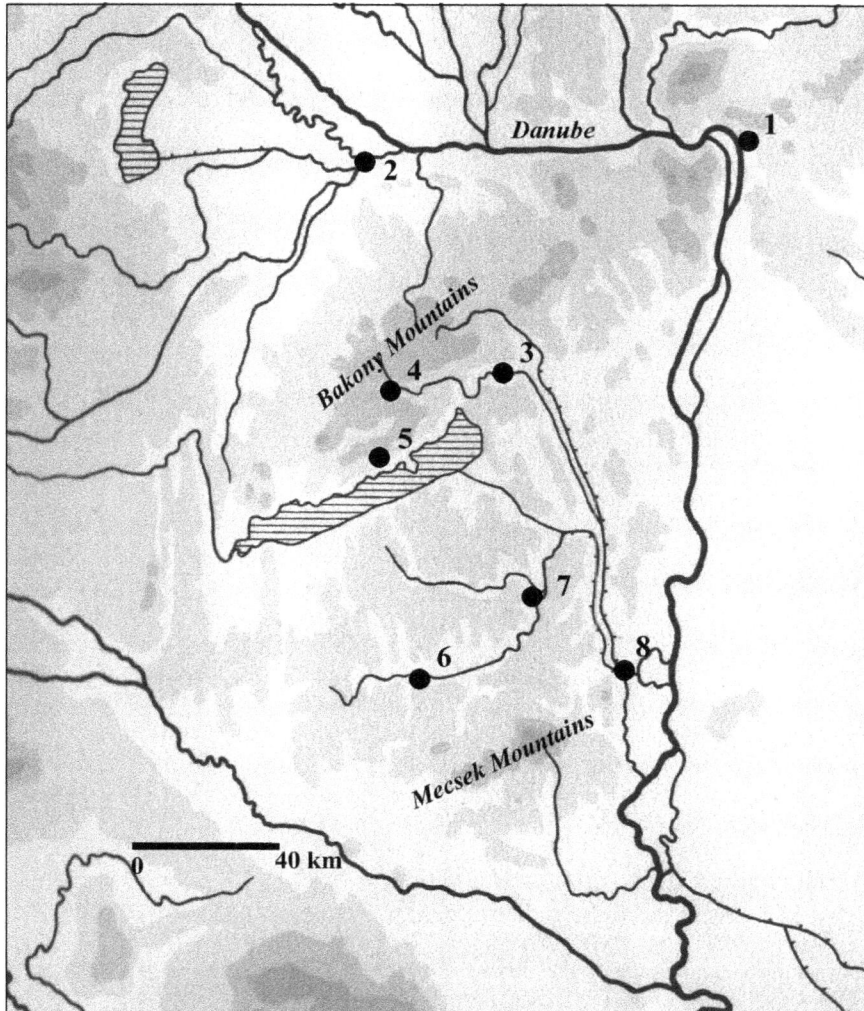

Fig. 5.1. Map of the investigated sites (1. Sződliget–Vác; 2. Győr environs;
3. Sárrét area (Nádasdladány, Csór); 4. Szentgál; 5. Vázsony Basin (Mencshely);
6. Kaposhomok; 7. Regöly; 8. Szekszárd–Palánk)

1993, p. 84), Jászberény IV (Kertész, 1996a), and Jásztelek I (Kertész, 1994; Kertész, 1996, p. 19). The lithics collected on the surface at Jászberény II and IV, and the find assemblages from the excavations at Jásztelek I and Jászberény I enabled the division of the Jászság Mesolithic into two phases based on stratigraphic observations made during the excavations: a) an Early Mesolithic, Boreal, Jászberény I phase, represented by Layers C and B2 of the Jászberény I site, the material from Layer B and Feature 1 of the Jásztelek 1 site, and b) a Late Mesolithic, Early Atlantic, Jásztelek I phase represented by surface finds from the Jásztelek site (Kertész, 1996, p. 24; Kertész, 2002, p. 289).

Over the past few years, the present authors have systematically re-examined the sites, which were previously claimed to be Mesolithic, but have only been investigated marginally (Eichmann, 2004; Eichmann et al. in press) and have conducted surveys aimed at locating potential sites (Fig. 5.1).

This paper focuses on the Mesolithic record from Hungary and, more specifically, on the quantity and quality of the evidence from western Hungary. Several interrelated factors have a bearing on this question:

– high-mobility Holocene foragers produced ephemeral sites, which leave few traces in the archaeological record;

– Mesolithic sites have been eroded, buried, or become submerged owing to rising water levels (e.g. Lake Balaton), or negatively impacted by other geological or anthropogenic processes;

– previous survey work was not sensitive enough to detect Mesolithic sites and the period has simply been insufficiently researched.

It seems likely that each of the above factors played a role in the lack of Mesolithic sites; however, if insufficient research is the prime reason for this deficiency, the contribution of forager behaviour and geological processes can hardly be studied and evaluated.

Western Hungary is one of the important nodes in the transition to the Neolithic because it witnessed the emergence of the Central European LBK from the Balkanic Early Neolithic (Starčevo culture). In the case of Transdanubia, this probably meant some forms of interaction between early agriculturalists and the indigenous Late Mesolithic hunter-gatherer population.

Until the early 1990s, the evidence for Mesolithic hunter-gatherers in Hungary was limited to poorly investigated surface collections with minimal information regarding the context from which the finds had originated (Kertész, 1991, p. 29). In numerous cases, museum collections, such as the one in Győr (Gallus, 1942, p. 22), cannot be associated with specific locations and contexts. Two probable Mesolithic harpoons recovered as stray finds during peat cutting from the Sárrét in Transdanubia (Makkay, 1970, p. 14; Marosi, 1936) have recently been dated to the Holocene based on geological stratigraphy (Sümegi, 2003, p. 379); in the future, these should be subjected to direct radiocarbon dating. In other cases, such as Mencshely in the Vázsony Basin, subsequent investigations have revealed that the sites can probably be assigned to the Neolithic (T. Biró, 1992, p. 55; Kozłowski, 2005, p. 179).

The two locations investigated at Sződliget–Vác (Gábori, 1956; Gábori, 1968) south of the Danube Bend are probably part of a single larger site. The site, which has in fact been regarded as two separate sites, is located on the left bank of the Danube just below the Danube Bend. Miklós Gábori excavated two locations, separated by 200–300 m, but the spatial and chronological relation between the two investigated areas remains uncertain. The 1955 excavation focused on an area lying on a former terrace, 100 m from the current Danube (Gábori, 1956, p. 177). Gábori reported that the excavations uncovered concentrations of gravels cracked as a result of thermal alterations, undoubtedly representing hearths, but he provided no maps or photographs of these features. The author published illustrations of some of the lithic material recovered: end scrapers, backed blades and segments, but no mention is made of their raw material. Gábori considered the 1955 Sződliget–Vác site to be assignable to the Late Epigravettian or Early Mesolithic

(Gábori, 1956, p. 181). It is important to note that the typological attributes of the artefacts recovered from the 1955 excavation does not afford a chronological assignment more specific than Late Pleistocene or Early Holocene.

The 1967 excavation at Sződliget–Vác was conducted roughly 200–300 m from the 1955 excavation. The artefacts were recovered from the humus and the underlying layer that had formed on the surface of the sand dune. Gábori interpreted the artefacts as deriving from primary, undisturbed geological context. A small, 2.4 m by 2.2 m large rectangular stone packed structure lined with flat stones associated with two external hearths was also exposed (Gábori, 1968, Taf. 1–2). The lithic assemblage was never published in detail; Gábori merely noted that it was very similar to the items recovered from the 1955 Sződliget–Vác excavations and the excavations at Szekszárd–Palánk (Gábori, 1968, p. 36).

The complete lack of maps or other detailed documenttation from the 1967 excavation limits broader conclusions, and were it not for the better documented 1955 excavations, it would not be possible to include the 1967 material in this category. Based on perceived typological similarities with the Szekszárd–Palánk site, the Sződliget–Vác sites were subsequently assigned to the Late Pleistocene (Gábori, 1968, p. 35). This chronological association is untenable after the re-examination of the unpublished 1968 Sződliget–Vác lithic collection by the authors, which contains geometric microliths (trapezes), which are typologically specific to the Late Mesolithic (Kozłowski and Kozłowski 1979, p. 68; Kozłowski, 2005, p. 180).

Prospection surveys for Mesolithic sites in the Middle Kapos Valley began in the fall of 2003. The results of the survey in the Middle Kapos region led to the discovery of several potential Mesolithic sites defined by lithic scatters without Neolithic or Copper Age ceramics, located along abandoned meanders of the River Kapos.

The Kaposhomok site, one of the earlier known sites in south-western Hungary also lies along the River Kapos (Pusztai, 1957, p. 97). The documentation of the find context of the lithic assemblage is rather unreliable, and its attribution to the Mesolithic is based on the typologically convincing Mesolithic artefacts: trapezes, steeply retouched points and triangles (Marton, 2003, p. 42).

Although the site is now generally accepted as a legitimate Mesolithic site in Transdanubia (Kozłowski and Kozłowski, 1983, p. 43; Kozłowski, 2001, p. 265; Kozłowski, 2005, p.176), many questions remain regarding the context of the finds (Marton, 2003, p. 42). According to the maps in Rezső Pusztai's article, the Kaposhomok assemblage originates from two sites (Pusztai, 1957, Fig. 1). We had some difficulties in locating the site. On Pusztai's map, the eastern site was marked on a large sand dune by an abandoned meander of the River Kapos. After consulting with Mr. Antal Trombitás, who had collected the finds published by Pusztai, it became clear that the Kaposhomok artefacts came from the eastern site (the pottery fragments were found at another location).[1]

The lithic finds from another investigated site near Regöly (Regöly 2) had been collected by a private collector, who kindly offered his entire collection of lithic material from this site (over 1200 implements) for further study.[2] The site yielded numerous lithic artefacts alongside a handful of pottery sherds (the latter could be clearly assigned to the Roman Age). The lithic assemblage is currently being analysed; the preliminary observations on the collection are as follows:

– A significant ratio of radiolarites from the Bakony Mountains (e.g. Szentgál) and Mecsek Mountains (T. Biró and Pálosi, 1986, p. 425), as well as two pieces of obsidian from the north-easterly regions of the Carpathian Basin. Radiolarite nodules with cortex suggest that the material was recovered from river gravels.

– Large number of cores, flakes, "thumbnail" scrapers, borers (Fig. 5.2. 15–16), and microblades, many of which were either informally retouched or damaged during usage. Regular blades may have been produced using either indirect percussion or pressure flaking. Sickle gloss was macroscopically observed on a few artefacts.

– Geometric microliths: trapezes (Fig. 5.2. 1–5), several backed blades (Fig. 5.2. 8–11), with abrupt dorsal and ventral retouch, of the type not reported from any Neolithic or Copper Age assemblage in western Hungary, but present in Mesolithic assemblages from adjacent regions.

– The faunal material in the surface collection included bones and some teeth of large carnivores.

– Ground stone and hammerstones, as well as flat, rounded, oval stones resembling the pieces known from Mesolithic sites throughout Europe (often with fossil inclusions). One had a small, partially drilled hole on one side.

– A single fossil dentalium shell, which may have functioned as a bead or an ornament.

The overall nature of the assemblage is one, which with a few exceptions corresponds nicely to what a Transdanubian Mesolithic assemblage would probably look like. The presence of sickle gloss on some artefacts is often the reason for assigning an assemblage to the Neolithic or later periods; however, this approach overlooks the fact that reeds and other grasses can also produce sickle gloss. The almost complete lack of pottery and the dominance of lithics strongly suggest that the site was probably occupied by non-pottery using groups.

Following this preliminary work, the intensive survey at the Regöly 2 site was begun in early April, 2004, motivated by our initial assessment of the assemblage and in order to compare a systematic surface collection with the unprofessional, non-systematic collection (Eichmann et al. in press). We were able to identify concentrations of lithics over the site and it appeared that the presence of pottery from later stone tool using cultures was minimal to non-existent.

The site was sampled by surface collection at 1 m intervals. All artefacts and ecofacts were flagged and plotted by piece in 5 m by 5 m collection units. Altogether, 130 chipped stone, ground stone, bone, and pottery pieces were recovered. We were able to identify two lithic concentrations on the surface of the site on either side of an abandoned meander of the River Koppány. The lithics included backed pieces, scrapers, blades, and other items comparable to pieces in the private collection; the assemblage also compared well with our typological concept of a Mesolithic assemblage. A few pottery sherds from later periods (Roman Age) were also recovered. The samples included an abundance of animal bones, some semi-mineralized. The relation between the bone finds, the pottery, and the lithics remains uncertain.

A small-scale test excavation was conducted during Autumn, 2004, in order to identify possible intact culture layers under the ploughzone and, also, to determine the nature of these cultural layers, if present. The three 2 m by 1 m large excavation units along a north-south transect were opened on the basis of the surface distribution of artefacts as recorded during the intensive site survey. Roughly 50 artefacts and ecofacts were recovered from both Level A (the disturbed ploughzone) and the underlying Level B. A thermally altered scalene triangle (Fig. 5.2. 6) was recovered from Level B in one unit. The poorly preserved lower metatarsal and phalanges of a large bovid (?) lying in anatomical order were also recovered from one of the units in close association with the scalene triangle.

---

[1] We would here like to thank Mr. Antal Trombitás, who collected the finds, for generously sharing with us his knowledge on the findspot of the original collection and for allowing us to study additional finds from the original collection.

[2] We are greatly indebted to Mr. Viktor Cziráky, who collected the finds, for the information he gave on the findspot and for his unfailing support during our fieldwork.

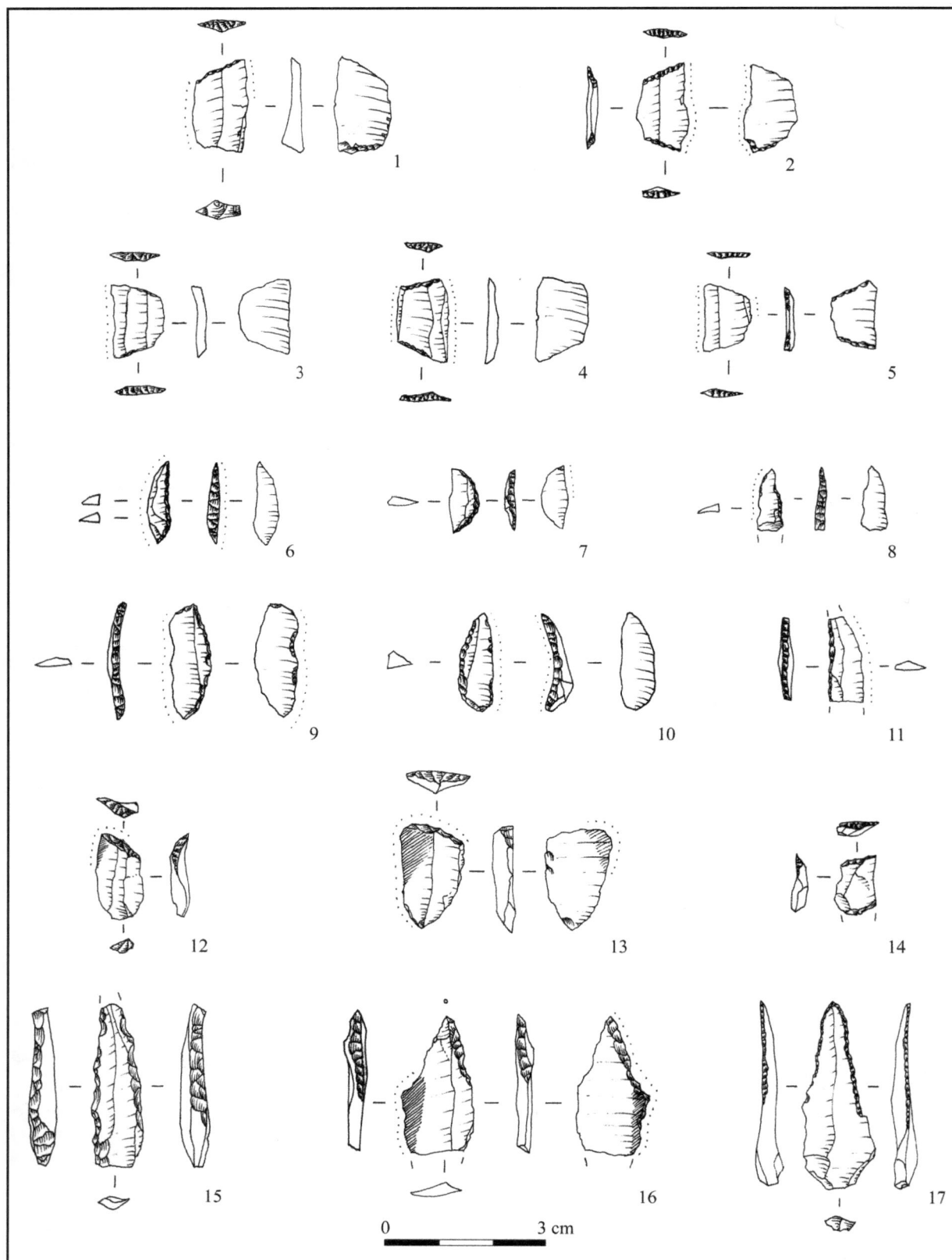

Fig. 5.2. Chipped stone artefacts from the Regöly 2 site (1–5. trapezes; 6. triangle; 7. segment; 8–11. backed blades; 12–14. truncated blades; 15–16. borers; 17. retouched blade)

In sum, the following can be said about the site:

- The scalene triangle is specific to the Mesolithic, being absent from later lithic assemblages.

- The fact that the scalene triangle had a patinated surface, reflecting thermal alteration, and was found in association with tiny pieces of charcoal suggests that the two are probably associated.

- Charcoal samples were collected, which may be used for AMS radiocarbon dating of the site.

- The recovery of faunal material in anatomical order from Horizon Level B suggests that the Regöly 2 site has intact deposits under the ploughzone, which may provide important new information on subsistence patterns and spatial behaviour at the site.

Understanding the manner in which Mesolithic foragers in western Hungary behaved during the Holocene is crucial to understanding the reaction to the Pleistocene/Holocene environmental changes and, later, the spread of agriculture in Europe. Our main goal is to provide new evidence bearing on the long-term evolutionary trajectory of Mesolithic societies. A better knowledge of the underlying general patterns of Mesolithic behaviour will greatly contribute to conceptualising the broad spectrum of interactions prior to the spread of agriculture. It is our hope that this research project will enrich the perception of this important prehistoric period among both prehistorians and the general public.

Research over the past fifty years has enriched our knowledge concerning the routes and the rate of the spread of food-producing economies, and has highlighted new regions as important nodes in this process. One of these is Transdanubia in western Hungary, the region of the Carpathian Basin west of the River Danube. In southern Transdanubia, the distribution of sites occupied by the Balkanic Early Neolithic Starčevo culture overlaps with the distribution of those of the earliest LBK, the first Neolithic culture found widely throughout central Europe north of the Alps (Bánffy, 2004; Gronenborn, 2003).

The findings of three research projects in western Transdanubia suggest that this area, including the Balaton region, were part of a frontier zone in the mid-6th millennium BC, and the setting of a long interaction between indigenous hunter-gatherer groups and immigrant Starčevo communities from the south.

It seems likely that the area south of Lake Balaton was part of this cultural interaction. After drawing together the scattered pieces of evidence (Sági and Törőcsik, 1989; Sági and Törőcsik, 1991; Eöry et al. 1991; Bánffy, 2004), it became clear that the Starčevo occu-

pation was quite dense, especially in the Kapos Valley. The recent identification of sites in areas, which in the Neolithic were covered by marshland and on islets in the former marshland along Lake Balaton indicate that these farmers of southern origin were capable of adapting to strikingly different environments. The settlements at Vörs–Máriaasszonysziget (Kalicz et al., 1998; Kalicz et al., 2002) and Tihany–Apáti (Regenye in press) reflect this different type of adaptation.

The surprising variety, but low number of cereal grains would suggest that the extent of cultivation in western Transdanubia and the Balaton region did not exceed that of horticulture (Berzsényi and Dálnoki, 2006) – the range of plants cultivated and tended in the open areas between the houses and in the narrow zone along the shore was simply broadened with the species adopted from the Starčevo communities together with the art of cultivation.

Both pre-Neolithic and Starčevo contacts had an impact on formative LBK pottery in Transdanubia. Major differences can be noted between the pottery assemblages from the late Starčevo settlements in the Balaton region and those from more southerly sites (Bánffy, 2001). This difference, reflected in the finds from Szentgyörgyvölgy–Pityerdomb and a number of other settlements, can most likely be attributed to the cultural impact of the indigenous hunter-gatherer groups.

This long-lasting process of gradual change would imply that the so-called "Neolithic revolution" i.e. the profound changes in subsistence strategies, did not occur during the initial phases of the western Transdanubian Neolithic, but one phase later. This assumption is confirmed by the observation that the shift to food-production did take place, although not in the earliest period, but at the beginning of the classical LBK phase, at the beginning of the 53rd century cal BC. The location of the sites indicates that they no longer lay directly by the lakeshore, but slightly higher, on terraces and hills overlooking rivers and lakes, and that fertile loessy areas, river and stream valleys and their lower terraces were chosen for settlement. This would suggest that in Transdanubia the major change in lifeways and subsistence patterns occurred not at the beginning of the Neolithic, as earlier believed, but some three or four generations later.

References

BÁNFFY, E. (2000) – The Late Starčevo and the Earliest Linear Pottery groups in Western Transdanubia. *Documenta Praehistorica*. Ljubljana. 27, p. 173–185.

BÁNFFY, E. (2001) – Neue Funde der Starčevo-Kultur in Südtransdanubien. In DRAŞOVEAN, F. eds. *Festschrift für Gheorghe Lazarovici.* Timişoara: Editura Mirton. p. 41-58. (Bibliotheca Historica et Archaeologica Banatica XXX.)

BÁNFFY, E. (2004) – *The 6th Millenium BC Boundary in Western Transdanubia and its Role in the Central European Neolithic Transition.* Budapest: Archaeological Institute of the Hungarian Academy of Sciences. 451 p. (Varia Archaeologica Hungarica; 15)

BERZSÉNYI, B.; DÁLNOKI, O. (2006) – Plant cultivation and crop processing in the formative LBK settlement of Szentgyörgyvölgy–Pityerdomb in Transdanubia (6th Millennium BC). *Antaeus.* Budapest. 28, p. 261-270.

BIRÓ, K T. (1992) – Mencshely–Murvagödrök kőanyaga (Steinartefakte aus neue Grabungen von Mencshely). *Tapolcai Városi Múzeum Közleményei.* Tapolca. 2, p. 51–72.

BIRÓ, K T. (2002) – Advances in the Study of Early Neolithic Lithic Materials in Hungary. *Antaeus.* Budapest. 25, p. 119–168.

BIRÓ, K T.; PÁLOSI, M. (1986) – A pattintott kőeszközök nyersanyagának forrásai Magyarországon (Sources of lithic raw materials for chipped stone artefacts in Hungary). *A Magyar Állami Földtani Intézet Jelentése 1983.* Budapest. p. 407–435.

BOGUCKI, P. (2000) – How Agriculture Came to North-central Europe. In PRICE, D. eds. *Europe's First Farmers.* Cambridge: Cambridge University Press. p. 197–218.

CHAPMAN, J. C. (1985) – Demographic Trends in Neothermal South-East Europe. In BONSALL, C. eds. *The Mesolithic in Europe.* Edinburgh: John Donald Publishers. p. 500–515.

DOBOSI, V. (1975) – Magyarország ős- és középső kőkori lelőhely katasztere. (Register of Palaeolithic and Mesolithic Sites in Hungary) *Archeológiai Értesítő.* Budapest. 102, p. 64–76.

EICHMANN W. J. (2004) – Mesolithic Hunter – Gatherers in the Carpathian Basin and the Spread of Agriculture in Europe. In HUSZÁR, I. eds. *Fulbright Student Conference Papers.* Budapest: Hungarian – American Commission for Educational Exchange. p. 161–202.

EICHMANN, W. J.; KERTÉSZ, R.; MARTON, T. (in press) – The Mesolithic in the LBK (Linienbandkeramik) Heartland of Western Hungary. In GRONENBORN, D. eds. Römisch-germanisches Zentralmuseum Mainz Tagungen, Band 2. Mainz.

EÖRY, B.; SÁGI, K.; TÖRŐCSIK, Z. (1991) – A Dunántúli Vonaldíszes Kerámia "Tapolcai csoportjának" legújabb lelőhelyei a Balaton környékéről (New sites of the "Tapolca group" of the Transdanubian Linear Pottery ware culture around the Balaton). *A Tapocai Városi Múzeum Közleményei.* Tapolca. 2, p. 7-30.

GÁBORI, M. (1956) – Mezolitikus leletek Sződligetről. (Mesolithische Funde von Sződliget) *Archeológiai Értesítő.* Budapest. 83, p. 177–182.

GÁBORI, M. (1968) – Mesolithische Zeltgrundriss in Sződliget. *Acta Archaeologica Academiae Scientiarum Hungaricae.* Budapest. 20, p. 33–36.

GÁBORI, M. (1981) – Az ősember korának kutatása Magyarországon (1969–1980). *MTA II. Osztályának Közleményei.* Budapest. 30/1. p. 91–109.

GALLUS, S. (1942) – Győr története a Kőkortól a Bronzkorig. In: GALLUS S.; MITHAY, S. eds. *Győr története a Vaskorszakig.* Győr: Győr szab. kir. város közönsége. p. 14–31.

GRONENBORN, D. (1994) – Überlegungen zur Ausbreitung der bäuerlichen Wirtschaft in Mitteleuropa – Versuch einer kulturhistorischen Interpretation ältestbandkeramischer Silexinventare. *Prähistorische Zeitschrift.* Berlin. 69 (2) p. 135–151.

GRONENBORN, D. (1997) – *Silexartefakte der ältestbandkeramischen Kultur.* Bonn: Dr. Rudolf Habelt GMBH. 243 p. (Universitätsforschungen zur prähistorischen Archäologie 37.)

GRONENBORN, D. (1998) – Ältestbandkeramische Kultur, La Hoguette, Limburg, and... What else? – Contemplating the Mesolithic – Neolithic transition in southern Central Europe. *Documenta Praehistorica.* Ljubljana. 25, p. 189–202.

GRONENBORN, D. (2003) – Migration, Acculturation and Cultural Change in Western Temperate Eurasia, 6.500–5.000 cal. BC. *Documenta Praehistorica.* Ljubljana. 30, p. 79–91.

HILLEBRAND, J. (1925) – Ungarländische Funde aus dem Mesolithikum. *Wiener Prähistorische Zeitschrift.* Wien. 12, p. 81–83.

HILLEBRAND, J. (1937) – Der Stand der Erforschung der älteren Steinzeit in Ungarn. *Bericht der Römisch-Germanishes Kommission.* Berlin. 24–25, p. 16–26.

KALICZ, N. (1990) – *Frühneolithische Siedlungsfunde aus Südwestungarn.* Budapest: Magyar Nemzeti Múzeum. 164 p. (Inventaria Praehistorica Hungariae; 4.)

KALICZ, N.; M.VIRÁG, Zs.; T.BIRÓ, K. (1998) – The northern periphery of the early neolithic Starčevo culture in south-western Hungary: a case study of an excavation at Lake Balaton. *Documenta Praehistorica*. Ljubljana. 25, p. 151-187.

KALICZ, N.; T.BIRÓ, K.; M.VIRÁG, Zs. (2002) – Vörs, Máriaasszony-sziget. In: Z. Bencze *et al.* (eds): *Régészeti kutatások Magyarországon 1999 (Archaeological investigations in Hungary 1999)*. Budapest, p. 15-26.

KERTÉSZ, R. (1991) – Preliminary Report on the Research of Early Holocene Period in the NW Part of Great Hungarian Plain. *Folia Historico-Naturalia Museum Matraensis*. Gyöngyös. 16, p. 29–44.

KERTÉSZ, R. (1993) – Data to the Mesolithic of the Great Hungarian Plain. *Tisicum*. Szolnok. 8, p. 81–104.

KERTÉSZ, R. (1994) – Late Mesolithic Chipped Stone Industry from the Site Jásztelek I (Hungary). In LŐRINCZY, G. eds. *A kőkortól a középkorig. (Von der Steinzeit bis zum Mittelalter)*. Szeged: Móra Ferenc Múzeum. p. 23–44.

KERTÉSZ, R. (1996) – The Mesolithic in the Great Hungarian Plain: A Survey of the Evidence. In TÁLAS, L. eds. *At the Fringes of Three Worlds: Hunter-Gatherers and Farmers in the Middle Tisza Valley*. Szolnok: Damjanich Múzeum. p. 5–34.

KERTÉSZ, R. (1996a) – A New Site of the Northern Hungarian Plain Mesolithic Industry in the Jászság Area (Jászberény 4). *Tisicum*. Szolnok. 9, p. 27–44.

KERTÉSZ, R. (2002) – Mesolithic Hunter-Gatherers in the Northwestern Part of the Great Hungarian Plain. *Praehistoria*. Miskolc. 3, p. 281–304.

KOZŁOWSKI, J. K. (1973) – The Problem of the So-Called Danubian Mesolithic. In KOZŁOWSKI, S. K. eds. *The Mesolithic in Europe*. Warsaw: Warsaw University Press. p. 315–330.

KOZŁOWSKI, J. K. (2005) – Remarks on the Mesolithic in the Northern part of the Carpathian Basin. In GÁL, E.; JUHÁSZ, I.; SÜMEGI, P. eds. *Environmental Archaeology in North-Eastern Hungary*. Budapest: Archaeological Institute of the Hungarian Academy of Sciences. p. 175–186. (Varia Archaeologica Hungarica; 19.)

KOZŁOWSKI, S. K. (2001) – Eco-Cultural/Stylistic Zonation of the Mesolithic/Epipaleolithic in Central Europe. In KERTÉSZ, R.; MAKKAY, J. eds. *From the Mesolithic to the Neolithic: Proceedings of the International Archaeological Conference held in the Damjanich Museum, Szolnok, September 22–27, 1996*. Budapest: Archeolingua. p. 261–282.

KOZŁOWSKI, J. K.; KOZŁOWSKI, S. K. (1979) – *Upper Palaeolithic and Mesolithic in Europe: Taxonomy and Palaeohistory*. Wrocław – Warsaw – Kraków – Gdańsk: Polska Akademia Nauk. 179 p. (Prace Komisji Archeologicnej; 18.)

KOZŁOWSKI, J. K.; KOZŁOWSKI, S. K. (1983) – Le Mésolithique à l'est Alpes. Preistoria Alpina. Trento. 19, p. 37–56.

MAKKAY, J. (1970) – A Kőkor és Rézkor Fejér megyében. In FITZ, J. eds. *Fejér megye története 1. Fejér megye története az őskortól a honfoglalásig*. Székesfehérvár: a Fejér Megyei Tanács, a Fejér Megyei Múzeumok igazgatósága és a Fejér Megyei Történelmi Társulat Keletdunántúli Csoportja. 52 p.

MAROSI, A. (1936) – A Székesfehérvári Múzeum őskori csontszigonya. *Archeológiai Értesítő*. Budapest. 54, p. 83–85.

MARTON, T. (2003) – Mezolitikum a Dél-Dunántúlon – a somogyi leletek újraértékelése. (Das Mesolithikum im südlichen Transdanubien – die Neubewertung der Funde aus dem Komitat Somogy) *Móra Ferenc Múzeum Évkönyve – Studia Archaeologica*. Szeged. 9, p. 39–48.

MATEICIUCOVÁ, I. (2002) – Silexartefakte der ältesten und älteren LBK aus Brunn am Gebirge, Niederösterreich (Vorbericht). *Antaeus*. Budapest. 25, p. 169–187.

MATEICIUCOVÁ, I. (2003) – Mesolithische Traditionen und der Ursprung der Linearbandkeramik. *Archäologische Informationen*. Tübingen. 26/2, p. 299–320.

PUSZTAI, R. (1957) – Mezolitikus leletek Somogyból. (Mesolithiche Funde im Komitat Somogy). *Janus Pannonius Múzeum Évkönyve*. Pécs. 1957, p. 96–105.

REGENYE, J. in press – A Starčevo-kultúra települése a Tihanyi-félszigeten (Settlement of the Starčevo culture in the Tihany peninsula). *Ősrégészeti Levelek – Prehistoric Newsletter*. Budapest. in press.

RICHARDS, M. (2003) – The Neolithic Transition in Europe: Archaeological Models and Genetical Evidence. *Documenta Praehistorica*. Ljubljana. 15, p. 159–167.

RINGER, Á. (1983) – *Bábonyien, eine mittelpaläolithische Blattwerkzeugindustrie in Nordost-Ungarn*. Budapest: Editio Instituti Archaeologici Universitatis de Rolando Eötvös nominatae. 206 p. (Dissertationes Archaeologicae Ser. II.; No. 11.)

SÁGI, K.; TÖRŐCSIK, Z. (1989) – A Dunántúli Vonaldíszes Kerámia "Tapolcai csoportja" (The "Tapolca group" of the Transdanubian Linear Pottery culture). *A Tapolcai Városi Múzeum Közleményei*. Tapolca. 1, p. 29-72.

SÁGI, K.; TÖRŐCSIK, Z. (1991) – *A Dunántúli Vonaldíszes kerámia kultúrája "Tapolcai csoport-jának" Balaton környéki lelőhelyei. Fundorte der* zur Kultur der Transdanubischen Linienband-keramik gehörenden "Tapolca-Gruppe" in der Balatongegend. Tapolca: Tapolcai Városi Múzeum. (Bibliotheca Musei Tapolcensis; 1.)

SCHWEIZER, A. (2001) – Archäopalynologische Untersuchungen zur Neolithisierung der nördlichen Wetterau/Hessen. Berlin – Stuttgart: J. Cramer. 158 p. (Dissertationes Botanicae 350.)

SIMÁN, K. (1979) – Kovabánya az Avason (Silex-grube am Avasberg). Herman Ottó Múzeum Évkönyve. Miskolc. 17–18, p. 87–102.

SIMÁN, K. (1990) – Population Fluctuations in the Carpathian Basin from 50 to 15 Thousand Years B.P. Acta Archaeologica Academiae Scientiarum Hungaricae. Budapest. 42, p. 13–19.

SIMÁN, K. (1995) – The Korlát–Ravaszlyuktető workshop site in North-Eastern Hungary (H4). Archaeologia Polona. Warszawa. 33, 41–58.

SMITH, B. D. (2001) – Low-Level Food Production. Journal of Archaeological Research. Springer. 9 (1), p. 1–43.

STÄUBLE, H. (1995) – Radiocarbon Date of the Earliest Neolithic in Central Europe. Radiocarbon. Tucson. 37 (2), p. 227–237.

SÜMEGI, P. (2003) – New Chronological and Mala-cological Data from the Quaternary of the Sárrét Area, Transdanubia, Hungary. Acta Geologica Hungarica. Budapest. 46 / 4, p. 371–390.

SÜMEGI, P. (2004) – Preneolitizáció – Egy Kárpát-medencei késő mezolitikum során bekövetkezett életmódbeli változás környezettörténeti rekonstruk-ciója. (Pre-Neolithization – the Environmental Historical Reconstruction of a Change in Lifestyle Occuring during the Late Mesolithicum in the Carpathian Basin) NAGY, E. Gy.; DANI, J.; HAJDÚ, Zs. eds. MΩMOS – Őskoros kutatók II. összejövetelének konferenciakötete. Debrecen:. 2000 november 6–8. Debrecen: Hajdú-Bihar Megyei Múzeumok Igazgatósága. p. 21–32.

SZATHMÁRY, L. (1988) – The Boreal (Mesolithic) Peopling in the Carpathian Basin: The Role of the Peripheries. Folia Historico-Naturalia Museum Matraensis. Gyöngyös. 13, p. 47–60.

TAUTE, W. (1973-74) – Neolithische Mikrolithen und andere neolithische Silexartefakte aus Süddeutch-land und Österreich. Archäologische Informatio-nen. Tübingen. 2/3, p. 71–124.

VÉRTES, L. (1962) – Ausgrabungen in Szekszárd Palánk und die archäologischen Funde. Swiatowit. Warszawa. 24, p. 159–202.

VÉRTES, L. (1965) – Az őskőkor és az átmeneti kőkor emlékei Magyarországon. Budapest: Akadémiai Kiadó. 385 p. (A magyar régészet kézikönyve I.)

WHITTLE, A. (1996) Europe in the Neolithic – The Creation of New Worlds. Cambridge: Cambridge University Press. (Cambridge World Archaeology). 443 p.

WHITTLE, A.; BARTOSIEWITZ, L.; BORIĆ, D.; PETTIT, P.; RICHARDS, M. (2002) – In the Beginning: New Radiocarbon Dates for the Early Neolithic in Northern Serbia and South-east Hungary. Antaeus. Budapest. 25, p. 63–118.

ZVELEBIL, M. (2000) – The Social Context of Agricultural Transition in Europe. In RENFREW, C.; BOYLE, K. eds. Archaeogenetics: DNA and the Population Prehistory of Europe. Cambridge: McDonald Institute for Archaeological Research. p. 57–79.

EARLY NEOLITHIC RAW MATERIAL ECONOMIES
IN THE CARPATHIAN BASIN

Katalin T. BIRÓ

Hungarian National Museum, tbk@ace.hu

Abstract: In the study of the Mesolithic/Neolithic transition, lithic evidence is one of the key elements for the study of continuity, discontinuity between chronologically subsequent periods of cultures using stone tools at a given area. This paper is summarising data on the Neolithic side of the time span, presenting evidences for raw material economy from Hungary, based mainly on lithic assemblages from recent excavation of the Early Neolithic / Early Middle Neolithic period. Current data suggest a sharp division between radiolarite-based assemblages in Transdanubia and obsidian-limnic quartzite based lithic industries to the East of the Danube. Centrally located sites tend to have more 'cosmopolitan' type of resources.
Keywords: Hungary, Neolithic, raw material, procurement

Resumé: Dans les recherches sur la transition Mésolithique/Néolithique les études sur le matériel lithique sont d'une importance essentielle, surtout dans l'établissement des continuités ou des discontinuités entre les périodes ou cultures. Dans cette communication les données concernant l'économie des matières premières dans le Néolithique ont été rassemblées, sur la base des sites du Néolithique ancien/début du Néolithique moyen, récemment fouillés. La structure des assemblages lithiques montre une nette différence entre la Transdanubie où les radiolarites sont dominant et la zone à l'est de Danube dominée par les obsidiennes et les quartzites limniques. Les sites entre les deux zones montrent une structure plus hétérogène des matières premières.
Mots-clés : Hongrie, néolithique, matièrre première, approvisionnement

INTRODUCTION

Lithic studies of the 'pottery periods' have received considerably less attention than desirable over long time in Hungarian research history (Patay 1976). This tendency, fortunately, seems to be over if not reversed. Intensification of raw material characterisation studies contributed to the possibilities of interpretation. Systematic studies were stimulated by Polish initiatives in the study of Early and Early/Middle Neolithic (Bácskay-Simán 1987, Biró 1987), followed by the study of Late Neolithic (Biró 1998), the Copper Age (Csongrádi 1993) and the Bronze Age, respectively (Biró 2000, Horváth 2005).

The possibility offered by large-scale excavations connected to major construction works also contributed to the accumulation of large amounts of well-dated lithic evidence. Most of the material are under current investigations and will be hopefully published in the near future.

THE CONCEPT OF EARLY NEOLITHIC

The territory of Hungary is allegedly one of the secondary centres of Neolithisation in Europe (Kalicz 1990, 1995, Bánffy 2004). During the VIth Millennium, the first bearers of Neolithic way of life appeared at the southern parts of the country. The "Neolithic package" involved a productive way of life, introduction of new species of domestic animals and plants, the knowledge and use of pottery and permanent constructions for dwelling. There is relatively little novelty in the stone industry, compared to the dramatical changes of subsistence: mainly the intensive use of polished stone implements and the appearance of harvesting tools, documented by sickle gloss blades. Contemporary to the earliest Neolithic cultures in the south, groups of local population used to live in the Northern part of the country; partly documented by sites (Jászság group, Kertész 2003), partly hypothesed on the basis of sporadic finds with no stratigraphical context (Bánffy 2004). The physical spread of the Early Neolithic population seems to stop along the line of Lake Balaton and the Tisza and its tributaries, creating a step-like barrier between stages of cultural development (Sümegi–Kertész 2001). Contemporary to the latest phase of the Early Neolithic cultures of intensive southern contacts (probably, also origins), the Starčevo-Körös-Çris complex, the Northern parts of Hungary started to develop their own, indigenous Neolithic culture together with ever growing parts of Central Europe, known as the Linearband Pottery culture which is assigned in Hungary, consequently, to Middle Neolithic, but in most parts of Europe, Early Neolithic, being, as it is, the first Neolithic culture on the territory.

Without being inclined to discuss, even more, to interfere, regional chronological systems, I am convinced that the 'Early Neolithic' lithic assemblages should really include the first known instances of productive economies at a given territory, independent

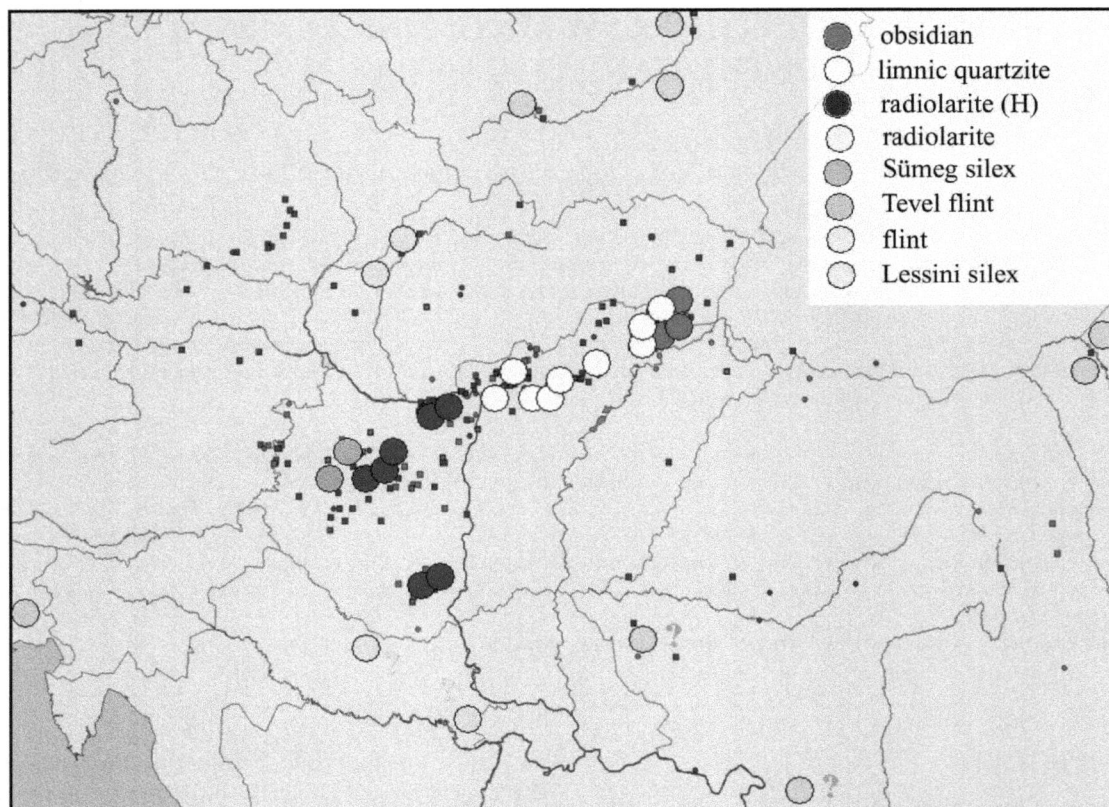

Fig. 6.1. Raw material stock for Neolithic chipped stone artefacts in Hungary.

of steps in chronological classification. Also, even with the spectacular accumulation of evidence of the past few decades, the density of sources of information is none too high and if we want to see any pattern in the data at all, we cannot disregard the early layers of lithic evidence from the LBC period. The sites discussed here therefore include, as a matter of fact, Körös and Starčevo sites together with the early (and partly, contemporary!) sites of old LBC.

THE LITHIC RAW MATERIAL STOCK

Raw materials used by the Neolithic population in Hungary based upon local raw materials within the Carpathian Basin mainly. The regional variety of rocks used by prehistoric people is fairly well known, due to systematical collecting activity and archaeometrical investigation of the prehistoric raw material stock. In this work, we can base on the comparative collection of the Hungarian National Museum, one of the first of its kind (Biró–Dobosi 1991, Biró et al. 2000, www.ace.hu/litot). The special, even eponym feature of Neolithic cultures is the large scale appearance of polished stone tools: recent interdisciplinary efforts in this field resulted in the accumulation of information in

this respect, due to the IGCP-442 project (Hovorka 2000, Biró–Szakmány 2000, www.ace.hu/igcp442). Household lithic utensils (grinders, polishers etc.) are also a developing field of interest (Szakmány-Nagy 2005, Péterdi et al. in press), and were investigated in the framework of a project partly supported by Hungarian National Science Foundation Grant and EU Culture 2000 (Biró et al. 2001, www.ace.hu/atlas).

Most of the petroarchaeological classification work is still based on macroscopic study of the lithic assemblages but we make a constant effort to support sourcing data by more objective, scientific means of analysis like petrographical thin section studies (Oravecz–Józsa 2005) or geochemical analysis of both archaeological and comparable geological material (Schléder–Biró 1999, Szakmány–Kasztovszky 2001).

The chipped stone raw material stock comprised basically similar elements like those reported for the Palaeolithic period (UISPP C-16, Biró et al. in press). The bulk supply is realised from radiolarites of the Transdanubian Mid-Mountain range and various volcanic, limnic and hydrothermal postvolcanic rock of the North Hungarian Range including obsidian (Fig. 6.1.). There are, however, some important changes. Szeletian

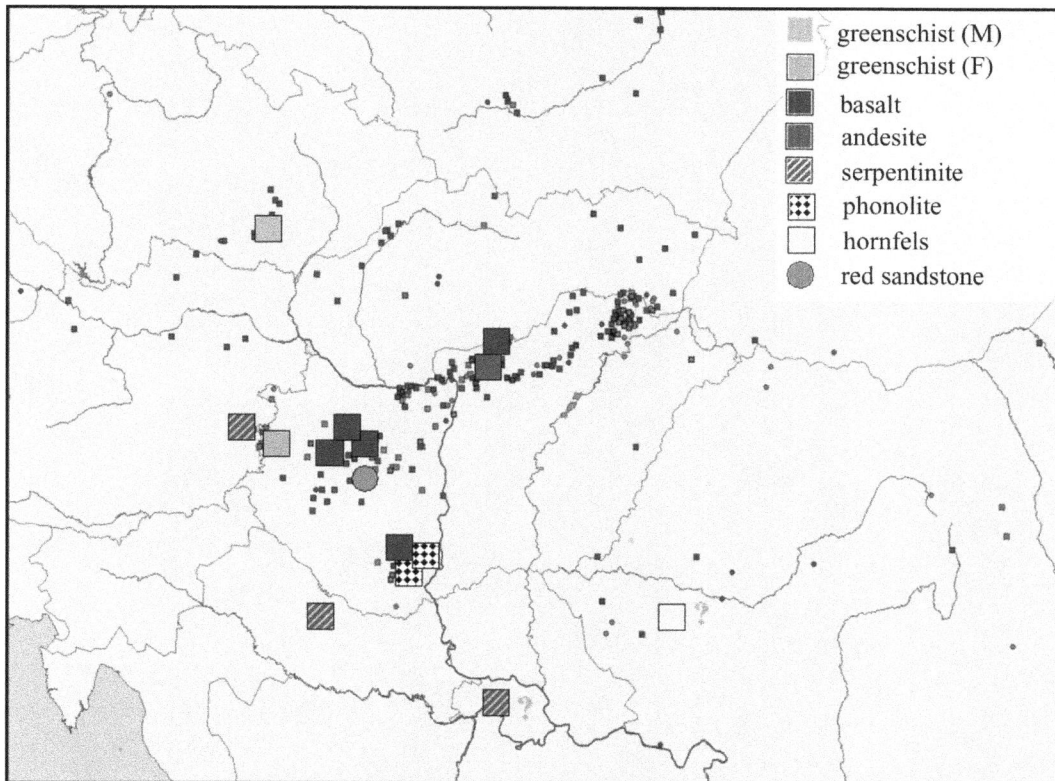

Fig. 6.2. Raw material stock for Neolithic polished stone artefacts and other lithic utensils in Hungary.

felsitic porphyry, a major constituent of Middle and Early Upper Palaeolithic industries, seemingly lost its importance, and it is present in Holocene assemblages only sporadically and locally, often reworked from Palaeolithic stray find. Rock crystal is no longer a leading item in long distance trade, but there is a strong presence of different varieties of Northern flint, especially in the Late Neolithic and the Copper Age (Biró 1998). Tevel flint, that was seemingly unknown or only locally used in the Palaeolithic, became one of the important constituents of the Transdanubian lithic raw material spectrum (Biró 2003). Flint (=silex) mining is observed on large scale, though very few of them can be associated actually with Early and Early/ Middle Neolithic utilisation. The biggest Hungarian flint quarry, Sümeg, has C-14 dates conforming to its use in the LBC (5.960±95 BP uncal., Bácskay 1986). For Szentgál, we have indirect proofs of utilisation in the form of a mined block of raw material in Early LBC context (Biró 2001). The Tevel Hill quarries at Nagytevel were almost certainly in use during the LBC though we have pottery evidence from Lengyel culture only as yet. Distribution data at the same time confirm its use in LBC as well (Biró 1989, 2003).

Distribution data also suggest that the obsidian and limnic quartzite sources were constantly exploited.

There is, however, no dated evidence for the use of mining features in respect of these commodities.

Lithic resources for polished stone tools have only recently been investigated in detail. The most popular raw material kinds are seemingly greenschist and basalt, with occasional long distance elements like serpentinite, greenschist from the Bohemian and Moravian uplands and hornstone. Nephrite/jadeite appears in exceptionally rare instances. In the Eastern part of the country, dark andesite and blueschist were also used. Use of the tephrite and phonolite of the Mecsek Mts. have also been demonstrated, so far only from the Late Neolithic onwards (Biró et al. 2001). The investigation of quernstones and polishers is a developing new field within Hungarian petroarchaeology. Recent results indicate, that typically local resources of sandstone and volcanites were used. Larger transport can be supposed for highly conspicuous raw materials like Permian red sandstone from the Balaton highlands (Szakmány–Nagy 2005) (Fig. 6.2.)

THE SITES INVESTIGATED

Early Neolithic lithic assemblages (better to say, Early Neolithic and Middle Neolithic assemblages together;

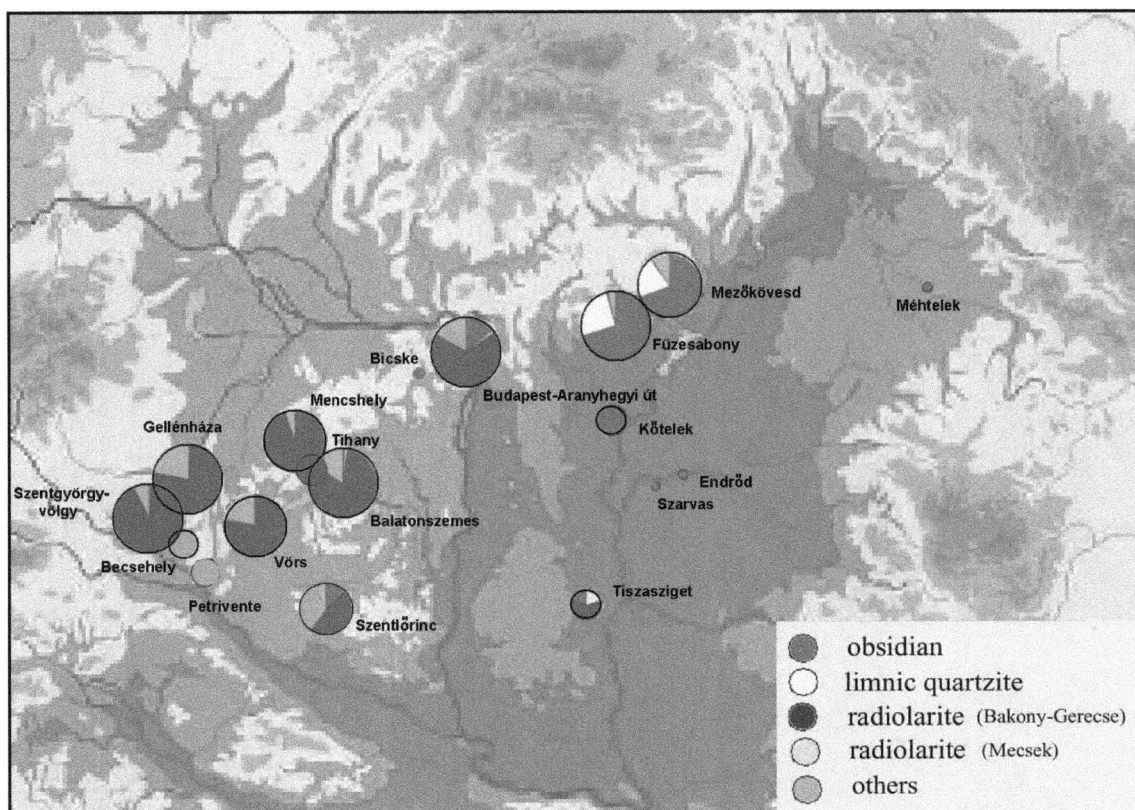

Fig. 6.3. Map of the lithic assemblages investigated.

from Körös culture to Bükk/Zseliz cultures formed the basis of the university doctoral dissertation of E. Bácskay. The summary of results were published in English in the series Dissertationes Archaeologicae (Bácskay 1976). This publication can be considered a landmark in the study of Holocene ('pottery period') lithic assemblages in Hungary. Formerly, the concept of lithic assemblages was mainly confined to Palaeolithic assemblages, with very few notable exceptions, mainly from younger periods like the Lengyel Culture or the Early and Middle Copper Age (Wosinszky 1893, Dobosi 1968, Kutzián 1963, 1972 Patay 1976). The discovery of the rich lithic assemblages of Early Neolithic age from Méhtelek and Bicske (Starnini 1993, 1995 Chapman 1987), respectively, attracted international attention mainly, same as the localities Szarvas and Endrőd (Kaczanowska et al. 1981, Starnini-Szakmány 1998). The next important step in the recognition of the Early Neolithic lithic evidence was the conference organised by J. Kozłowski in Kraków, 1985 published in the periodical Archaeologia Interregionalis (Kozłowski-Kozłowski ed. 1987). In the meantime, new sites became known and the level of knowledge on sources proper surpassed the simplistic level 'obsidian/silex', due to systematical collection of the sources and foundation of the comparative raw

material collection of the HNM. This gave a new dimension to lithic studies. The most recent comprehensive study on Early Neolithic lithic assemblages was compiled in 2002 (Biró 2002)

The sites considered in this study comprise all the important Early Neolithic (Early Middle Neolithic) sites from which I have personal information on raw material provenance (Fig. 6.3). Most of them were excavated and studied recently, some of them published in summaries (Mezőkövesd, Budapest-Aranyhegyi út, Szentlőrinc Biró 1987, Biró 1998, Biró 2001, 2002), some in details (Gellénháza, Szentgyörgyvölgy, Füzesabony). Some of the key sites are currently investigated, especially the localities along the new M7 highway in Somogy and Zala counties, respectively (Balatonszárszó-Bagódomb, Becsehely, Petrivente). Both typological and raw material analysis were performed on all lithic assemblages; for the scope of the present meeting, implications of the raw material aspect will be preferentially considered.

The raw material group distribution of the assemblages studies are summarised on Table 6.1. Technological type group distribution is added on Table 6.2. For a better visual understanding of the data, the same values

6.1. Raw material group distribution of the lithic assemblages investigated

Site name	obsidian	limno-quartzite	transdanubian radiolarite	mecsek radiolarite	northern flint	southern flint	others	total pieces
Balatonszemes	3	2	210				40	255
Budapest-Aranyhegyi út	13	1	61	0	6		9	90
Füzesabony	660	241	5		1		35	942
Gellénháza		1	334	1			95	431
Mencshely			818		2		45	865
Mezőkövesd	623	202	2		5		68	900
Szentgyörgyvölgy		1	658	1			50	710
Szentlőrinc	2		7	5			1	15
Tihany			7					7
Tiszasziget	1		3			1		5
Vörs			96	1			27	124
Kötelek	20							20

6.2. Type group distribution of the lithic assemblages investigated

Site name	raw material	core	flake	blade	retouched tool	polished tool	others	total pieces
Balatonszemes	1	18	116	48	34	4	34	255
Budapest-Aranyhegyi út	0	8	42	20	15	4	1	90
Füzesabony	4	28	265	387	224	26	8	942
Gellénháza	3	33	195	75	44	10	71	431
Mencshely	5	138	434	190	71	3	24	865
Mezőkövesd	8	17	327	278	203	23	44	900
Szentgyörgyvölgy	5	52	383	111	114	7	38	710
Szentlőrinc			4	8	2	1		15
Tihany		1	1	3	2			7
Tiszasziget		2	2	0	1			5
Vörs	3	8	32	19	35	2	25	124

are plotted on pie diagrams (Fig. 6.4) and 3D bar plots (Fig. 6.5). The data are arranged in decreasing values of Group III (Transdanubian Radiolarite) and increasing values of Group I (Obsidian).

LONG DISTANCE IMPORTS ON THE SITES INVESTIGATED

In the study period, none of the important source areas are known to be populated permanently. The settlements were typically further than the range of one day's walking distance from the geological source; the supply area extended for the better quality sources from 50 to 200 km from the source proper.

Long distance goods are considered here basically in two ways: in terms of absolute distance from the source, exceeding 200 kms, or cross-cultural items, passing apparent 'political' boundaries or major natural boundaries. The distances are calculated by modern road finding software (www.viamichelin.com). This solution is considered more realistic, than taking simply geometrical distances because of communication feasibility. It is biased sometimes for big traffic centres; in such cases "shortest distance" calculations were forced.

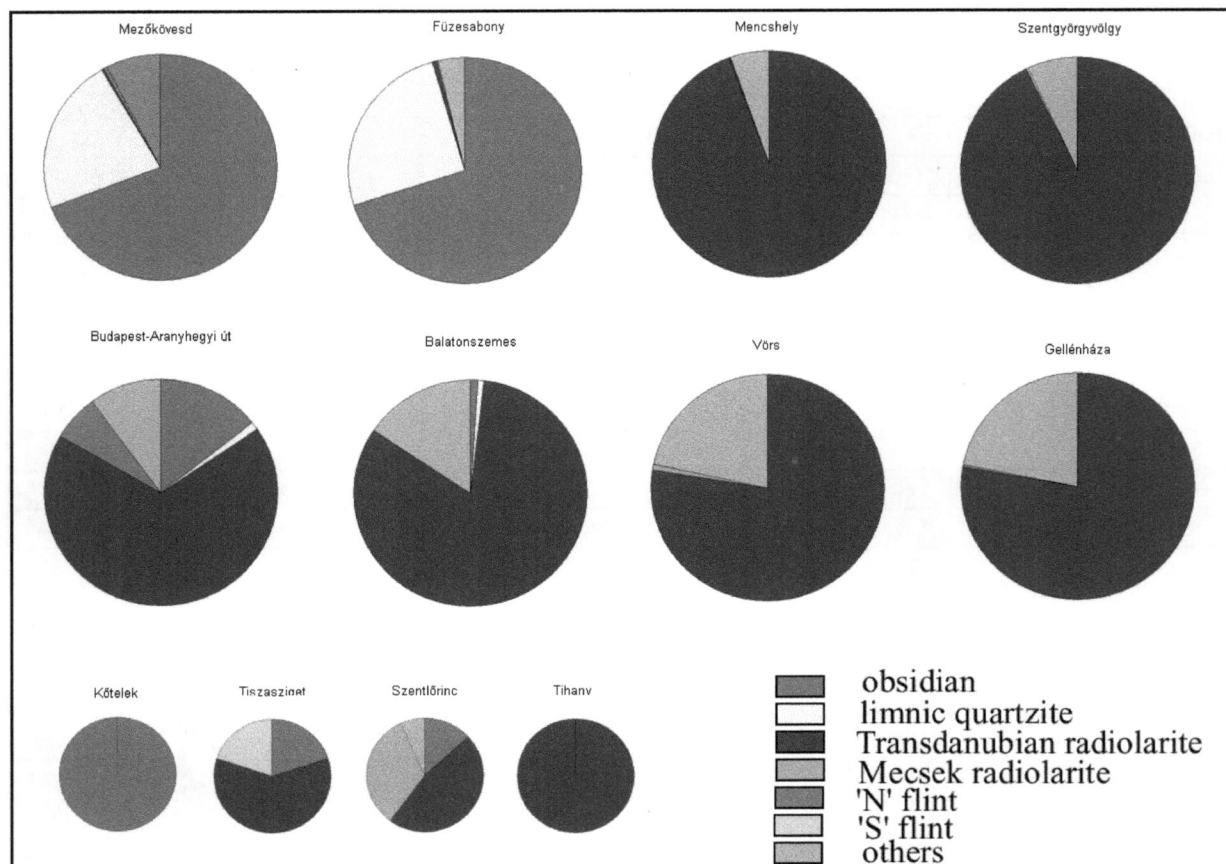

Fig. 6.4. Pie diagrams on the raw material type groups of the lithic assemblages investigated.

Balatonszemes (N=255)

Long distance import: 6 pieces, 2.3 %

Obsidian: 3 pieces (distance from source: 406 km, coming 'across' Danube)

Blue (Carpathian?) radiolarite: 1 piece (distance from source: 342 km, coming 'across' Danube)

nephrite?: 1 piece (min. distance from source: 474 km)

serpentinite: 1 piece (distance from source: 207 km)

Budapest-Aranyhegyi út (N=90)

Long distance import: 20 pieces, 22 %

Obsidian (C1): 12 pieces (distance from source: 270 km, coming 'across' Danube)

Obsidian (C2T): 1 pieces (distance from source: 235 km, coming 'across' Danube)

Jurassic Craców flint: 4+2 pieces (distance from source: 419 km, coming 'across' Carpathians)

Moravian greenschist 1 (distance from source: 324 km),

Füzesabony (N=942):

Long distance import 7 pieces, 0.7 %

Szentgál radiolarite: 3+1 pieces (distance from source: 255 km, coming 'across' Danube)

Other Transdanubian radiolarite: 1 piece (Gerecse radiolarite, distance from source: 177 km, coming 'across' Danube)

Prut flint: 1 piece (distance from source: 716 km, coming 'across' Carpathians)

Moravian greenschist 1+1 (distance from source: 443 km,),

Banat hornstone (distance from source: 380 km)

Gellénháza (N=431, EN, EN+ features)

Long distance import 7 pieces, 0.7 %

Moravian greenschist 1+1 (distance from source: 443 km,)

Slavonski Brod radiolarite ? (distance from source: 329 km,)

Mencshely (N=865)

Long distance import: 2 pieces (0.2 %)

Jurassic Craców flint: 1 piece (distance from source: 564 km, coming 'across' Carpathians)

+ 1 indet. flint: 1 piece

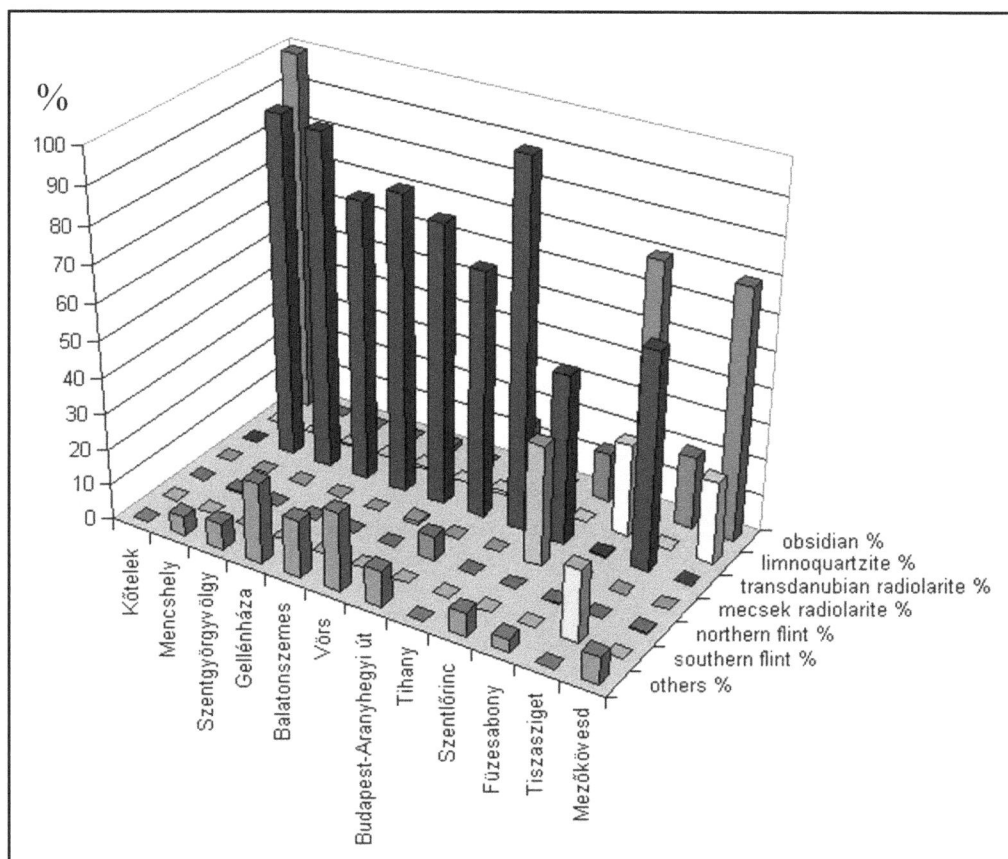

Fig. 6.5. 3D bar plots on the raw material type groups of the lithic assemblages investigated.

Mezőkövesd (N=900)
Long distance import: 12 pieces (1.3 %)
Szentgál radiolarite: 1 piece (distance from source: 269 km, coming 'across' Danube)
Other Transdanubian radiolarite: 1 piece (distance from source: 269 km, coming 'across' Danube)
Jurassic Craców flint: 1+2 pieces (distance from source: 439 km, coming 'across' Carpathians)
Volhynian flint: 2 pieces (distance from source: 639 km, coming 'across' Carpathians)
Moravian greenschist 3+2 (distance from source: 458 km,),

Szentgyörgyvölgy (N=900)
Long distance import: 12 pieces (1.3 %)
Moravian greenschist 3 pieces (distance from source: km,)
serpentinite: 3 pieces (distance from source: km)
Slavonski Brod radiolarite ? (distance from source: 311 km)

Szentlőrinc (N=15)
Long distance import: 10 pieces (66 %)

Szentgál radiolarite: 7 pieces (distance from source: 203 km,)
Obsidian: 2 pieces (distance from source: 517 km, coming 'across' Danube)
greenish metamorphic rock (?) : 1 piece

Tihany (N=7)
Long distance import: 0 pieces

Tiszasziget (N=5)
Long distance import: 5 pieces (100 %)
Szentgál radiolarite: 3 pieces (distance from source: 266 km, coming 'across' Danube)
Obsidian: 1 piece (distance from source: 214 km)
Central Banat flint : 1 piece (distance from source: ~ 200 km)

Vörs (N=124)
Long distance import: 0 pieces

Kőtelek (N=20)
Long distance import: 20 pieces (100 %)
Obsidian: 20 pieces (distance from source: 204 km)

The percentages are a bit misleading for sites in the middle of the Alföld (Great Hungarian Plains), because there the nearest sources of raw material are outside the range of 100 kms. For Kőtelek, obsidian can be just considered the regional supply. For Tiszasziget, there are more options and larger distances involved. The sites located close to important raw material source regions, nevertheless, tend to have a locally based supply (e.g., Mencshely). In the case of some raw materials, the exact source is difficult to locate, in such cases a likely minimum distance is given.

One of the most important recent observations concerning provenance data was locating Lessini-flint at the Neolithic site Petrivente, one of the locations of current rescue excavations. The distances involved is approximately 562 km; however, without the detailed archaeological analysis of the site, it is not possible to tell whether these finds belong to the Early Neolithic horizon or later periods.

SITES INVESTIGATED IN DETAILS

Lithic analyses of complex settlements is dependent on the details of data collection. Lots of valuable information can be collected on the basis of 'bulk' analysis of stone tools from the site, but the complete wealth of information can only be unfolded using the results of stratigraphy, fine relative/absolute dating of the features and strata observed during excavation. The author is most grateful for archaeologist colleagues sharing the details of their research for a fine-tuned lithic analysis of large assemblages. Recently, the detailed analysis of three major Early Neolithic sites could be accomplished, that of Gellénháza-Városrét, Szentgyörgyvölgy-Pityer and Füzesabony-Gubakút. Only the first of these, Gellénháza has been published as yet (Biró–Simon 2003), the others are currently in press (Biró in press a, b). At Szentgyörgyvölgy, it was possible to investigate, apart from the connections of the site on regional level, intra-site distribution of lithics by settlement features. All of the excavation features were attributed to Oldest LBC (Contemporary to Late Starčevo from, e.g., Vörs), therefore the rich assemblage is the most complete lithic evidence for this period to the West of the Danube. All forms, noted typical for the early horizon (trapezes, segments, flake side-scrapers, wedges, burins and borers) are present. Raw material pieces are absent and cores scarce. The variety of forms seems a feature typical for the earliest LBC materials; dominance of flake base forms support Starčevo tradition. The raw material spectrum is absolutely Bakony- (Szentgál-) based, with very few other elements. Appearance of probably southern grey flint was only noted in a few (uncertain) cases; similar direction of contact is suggested by alien radiolarites

(?), also known in one or two pieces and, probably, serpentinite. The Northern, North-Eastern (Bakony) direction of contact is further supported by the presence of Permian red sandstone, basalt and one piece of Tevel flint. Long distance elements are few, probably greenschist (from Bohemian massive?) and serpentinite can be considered here.

At Gellénháza, features were divided, partly shared with more recent Neolithic cultures, basically classical LBC. Intra-site distribution of lithics were investigated as well as the changes between Starčevo and LBC lithics in terms of provenance and typological composition. More than half of the 1414 items from Gellénháza can be attributed to Starčevo culture with considerable certainty. With this amount, Gellénháza is undoubtedly the richest site of this culture uncovered so far in Hungary in respect of lithic material. The chipped stone tool industry is microlithic and flake-based. The ratio of flakes and chips is high (45 %), about half of the retouched tools were made on flake. The cores are typically irregular and microlithic, most of them core remnants only. The overall type-groups from Gellénháza suggest that there was local tool-production and mainly re-sharpening on the site in the period of the Starčevo culture, raw material reached the site typically in the form of cores. The characteristic tool types were mainly simple retouched flakes and blades. Especially in the mixed material, borers and burins are fairly common. Trapezes, segments and points are not numerous but seemingly characteristic elements of the early horizon. The lack of end-scrapers (scrapers in general) and truncated pieces which are dominant elements of the total industry is certainly a distinctive feature of the Starčevo lithic industry.

The raw material composition of the site shows a convincing dominance of Szentgál radiolarite and other more general radiolarite types of the Transdanubian Mid-Mountains. The presence of radiolarite from so far unknown (southern?) origin cannot be excluded. Sandstone is another important component: possibly, red sandstone of the Balaton highlands and other (local?) variants. In the mixed Starčevo material, basalt and greenschist are also important component. The overall impression on the lithic industry does not change much in the later periods. Some general tendencies we can observe are the increase in laminarisation, and variation in the raw material spectrum, mainly the appearance of Tevel flint and a spectacular increase in the use of the Úrkút-Eplény variety of radiolarite.

Füzesabony-Gubakút offered the unique possibility to study the lithic industry in fine chronological details. Due to careful documentation and series of C-14 dates from the key features, 5 distinct chronological phases could be established, ranging from 5.600 to 5.200 BC

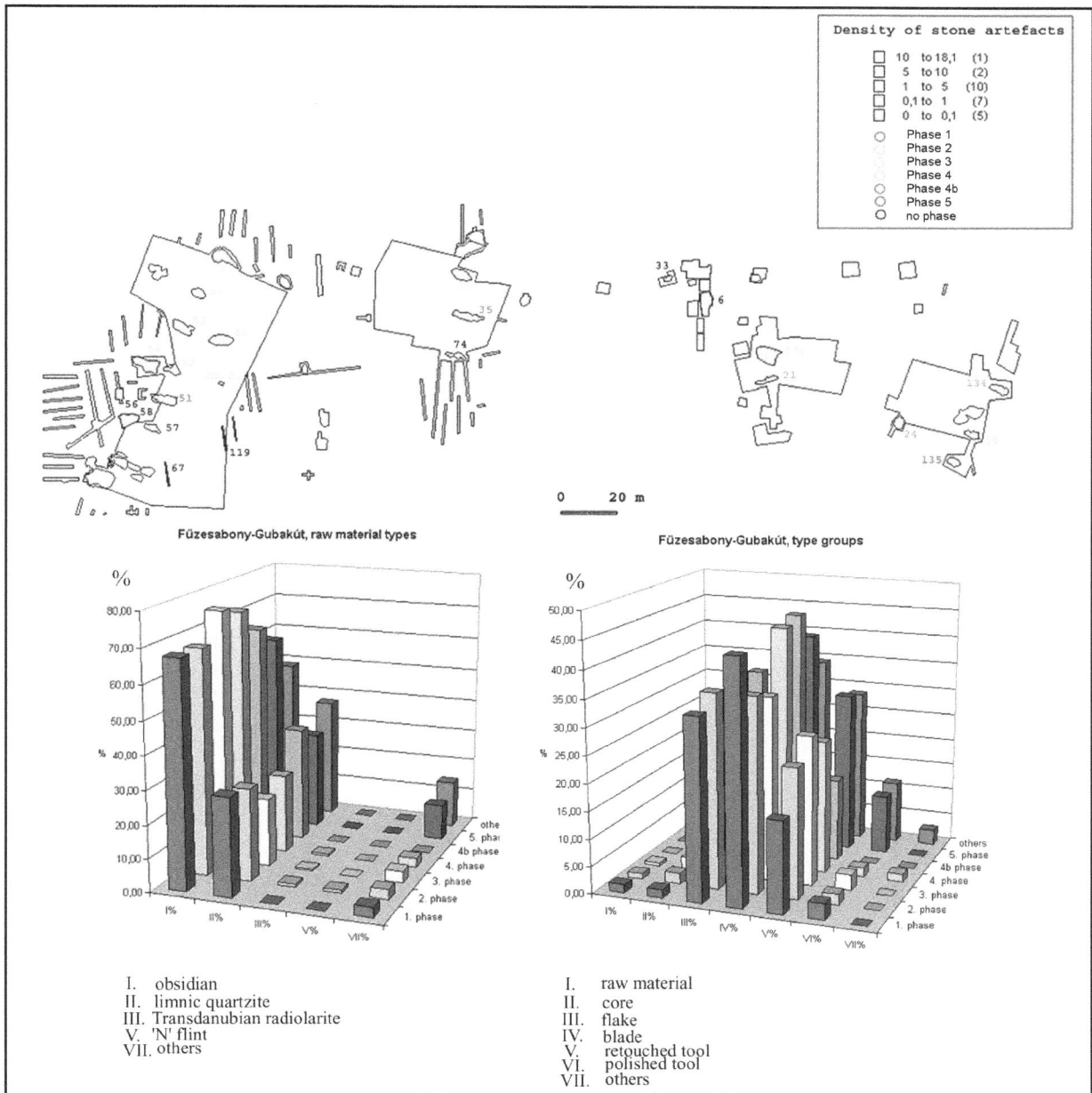

Density of stone artefacts

□	10 to 18,1	(1)
□	5 to 10	(2)
□	1 to 5	(10)
□	0,1 to 1	(7)
□	0 to 0,1	(5)
○	Phase 1	
	Phase 2	
	Phase 3	
	Phase 4	
○	Phase 4b	
○	Phase 5	
○	no phase	

0   20 m

Füzesabony-Gubakút, raw material types

Füzesabony-Gubakút, type groups

I.   obsidian
II. limnic quartzite
III. Transdanubian radiolarite
V.   'N' flint
VII. others

I.   raw material
II. core
III. flake
IV. blade
V.   retouched tool
VI. polished tool
VII. others

Fig. 6.6. Füzesabony-Gubakút. Typological and raw material provenance data by chronological phases.

(Domboróczki 2005, Domboróczki in press). Intra-site analysis of the lithic finds was possible with treating both typological and raw material provenance data separately by chronological phases (Fig. 6.6).

Aspects of changes in type distribution, choice of raw materials and changes in dimensions were considered. The overall impression on the industry is similar for all phases. The type group distribution on the site is fairly consequent; a blade-based, typical settlement material with high number of retouched tools and very few raw materials and cores. There is a little decrease in phase 4 for retouched tools (in favour of less elaborate pieces, notably blades and cores). Most of the polished stone tools were also registered from Phase 4 as well as features and strayfinds not classified into phases. The most frequent tool types, simple retouched blades occur most in phases 3 and 4: it means, phase 1-2 and 5 have more elaborate tools. There is an interesting shift in phase 4b: whereas in all other phases, truncated pieces surpass end-scrapers, in this phase the number of end-scrapers is relatively high. There is a peak of burins in the 2nd phase. The most characteristic element, i.e., trapeze is distributed fairly evenly in all phases.

The most convincing change in the lithic industry during the existence of the Füzesabony settlement is in the choice of raw materials. The industry is comprised basically of obsidian and limnic quartzite, both of them in statistically relevant quantities. It can be stated that following a moderately high obsidian use in the first phase the peak of obsidian use is reached in the periods 3 and 4 of the site, yielding the bulk of the total stone quantity but also the maximum of obsidian used. In phases 4b and 5, the use of obsidian is gradually decreasing - pointing towards the typical MN assemblages of the AVK (Alföld LBC). This trend was already pointed at in a large scale, i.e., obsidian use is very strong at the Early Neolithic and EN/MN assemblages in Eastern Hungary; obsidian is used practically for everything, irrespective of optimisation. The only exception from under this rule is sickle gloss, that is preferentially seen on silex: however, it can also be a result of sickle gloss being hardly visible on obsidian.

The local elements are best seen in the case of Egerbakta type silicite. This raw material is present, though in small quantities, throughout all the phases. The changes are irrelevant as the overall quantity of this material is less than 1,5% of the total industry. Local andesite and gabbro are also evenly distributed in subordinate quantities. Transdanubian radiolarites occur in phase 2-4 (altogether 4 pieces), the single Prut silex is known from phase 2, greenschist is known from phases 3-4 and hornfels from phase 4 and 5, respectively. As they are 1-2 pieces at the maximum, we cannot speak about tendencies and regularities because the occurrence of these single pieces can be also accidental.

In respect of dimensions, all the phases yielded data very close to each other. Most of the differences observed can be attributed to the presence or absence of polished stone tools which are more bulky and rise the average values of, e.g., pieces not attributed to individual chronological phases. The length/width ratio is also fairly constant; phase 4b appears a little bit more elongated (blade-like) than the rest.

By the raw material, obsidian tools in general are smaller than limnic quartzite; however, not much smaller. The items in the first phase are a little bit longer, but still the dimensions are fairly consistent by raw material type groups. Variation occurs mainly at the individual pieces again.

OVERALL TENDENCIES

The Early Neolithic (Early Middle Neolithic) sites are typically based on a sound regional supply, that means in the Eastern part of Hungary Obsidian/Limnic Quartzite dominated industries. Ratio of obsidian is surprisingly high at the EN-EMN settlements: typically, over 70 % (in some small assemblages, as much as 100 %). Compared to Palaeolithic and relatively recent assemblages (from Bükk culture and younger), the ratio of obsidian never reached this high amount. It can be justly supposed that obsidian was one of the motivating factors for the Northern expansion of the Körös culture (especially, the Szatmár group), whether they performed direct expeditions to the sources or were in exchange relations with the source area and its potential inhabitants, mediated by other agents. The obsidian sources were most probably largely exploited during the existence of the Bükk culture, when seemingly a closer regional control was exercised around the sources. The ratio of obsidian decreased gradually towards the Middle Neolithic, in favour of limnic quartzite. Working limnic quartzite is certainly more difficult than that of obsidian; however, the resulting tool is less brittle and more lasting. In the Bükk and Tiszadob cultures, the processing of limnic quartzite reached its perfection, typically on the sites lying close to the source areas (Boldogkőváralja, Vértes 1965; Hejce, Felsővadász etc.)

In Transdanubia, the most important raw material is obviously radiolarite. Most popular and important macroscopic variety is Szentgál radiolarite, occurring typically around the eponym site Szentgál-Tűzköveshegy. The characteristic cherry-red, brownish-red radiolarite comes forth in smaller quantities in other parts of the Transdanubian Mid-Mountains as well. Recent studies on Croatian assemblages and localities close to the Slovenian/Croatian/Hungarian border have demonstrated to possible interection of red radiolarite from the South (possibly, from the region of Slavonski Brod). The exact contribution of the Southern elements in the regional supply is one of the key issues to be studied in lithic provenancing studies of our region.

Other macroscopic varieties of radiolarite also contribute to the Early Neolithic raw material spectrum, mainly Úrkút-Eplény (yellow) and Hárskút (brown) types. Mecsek radiolarite is rather underrepresented, probably because we do not really have sites of EN age with essential lithic assemblages from the environs as yet. Therefore, it is very difficult to estimate the contribution of southern radiolarites (dark blue, dark red). Their presence is indicated by the evidence of Croatian data (http://www.ace.hu/igcp442/croatia.html). Radiolarite is mainly complemented by varieties of grey flint, partly Tevel flint, partly, on the SW parts of the country, grey silex varieties of southern, south-western origin, not properly assigned to source areas as yet.

CONCLUSIONS

The main features are: overwhelming use of high quality local resources (obsidian to the East of the Danube, Transdanubian (Szentgál) radiolarite to the West of the Danube; presence of Southern elements (both from the direction of the Balkans and the Adriatic cost), long distance contacts in the polished stone tool kit and use of local/regional resources for other stone utensils, quernstones and grinders.

The rational and highly developed raw material utilisation structure denotes a sound knowledge of available resources, indicating contacts with the territories around the sources themselves the population of which is hardly known as yet.

References

BÁCSKAY, E. (1976) - *Early Neolithic Chipped Stone Implements in Hungary.* Dissertationes Archaeologicae Budapest, ELTE 4 p. 1-110, I-XVIII. Tábla.

BÁCSKAY, E. (1986) - State of affairs at Sümeg. In: Biró ed. 1986 Biró, K.T. ed., International Conference on Flint Mining and Lithic Raw Material Identification in the Carpathian Basin, Sümeg 1986 (1) Budapest KMI Rota 1986 p. 11-25.

BÁCSKAY, E. – BIRÓ, K.T. (1983) - Függelék. Kőtelek Huszársarok 8. gödör kőeszközanyaga *Archaeológiai Értesítő* 110 Budapest p. 192, fig. 25.

BÁCSKAY, E. – SIMÁN, K. (1987) - Some remarks on chipped stone industries of the earliest Neolithic populations in present Hungary. *Archaeologia Interregionalis* 240 p. 107-130.

BÁNFFY, E. (2004) - *The 6th Millennium BC Boundary in Western Transdanubia and its role in the Central European Neolithic Transition (The Szentgyörgyvölgy-Pityerdomb settlement)* Varia Archaeologica Hungarica 15 Budapest MTA Régészeti Intézete p. 1-451.

BIRÓ, K.T. (1987): Chipped stone industry of the Linearband Pottery Culture in Hungary. *Archaeologia Interregionalis* 240 p. 131-167.

BIRÓ, K.T. (1989) - A Kup-egyesi neolit lelőhely kőeszközei / From stone artifacts of neolithic place of occurrence of Kup-Egyes. *Veszprémi Történelmi Tár* 2 Veszprém Megyei Múzeumi Igazgatóság p. 34-41.

BIRÓ, K.T. (1998) - *Lithic implements and the circulation of raw materials in the Great Hungarian Plain during the Late Neolithic Period.* Magyar Nemzeti Múzeum Budapest p. 1-350.

BIRÓ, K.T. (2000) - Kőeszközök a bronzkorban. (Steingeratschaften aus der Bronzezeit). *Komárom-Esztergom Megyei Múzeumok Közleményei* Tata 7 p. 237-252.

BIRÓ, K.T. (2001) - Lithic materials from the Early Neolithic in Hungary. *From the mesolithic to the neolithic. International Conference*, 1996 Szolnok. p. 89-100.

BIRÓ, K.T. (2001) - The "ham" of Bagódomb. *In: Draşovean ed., Festschrift für Gheorghe Lazarovici* Timisoara p. 91-122.

BIRÓ, K.T. (2002) - Advances in the study of Early Neolithic lithic materials in Hungary. *Antaeus* 25 p. 119-168.

BIRÓ, K.T. (2003) - Tevel flint: a special constituent of the Central European LBC lithic inventories. In: Burnez-Lanotte, ed., Production and Management of Lithic Materials in the European Linearbandkeramik. UISPP Liege, Colloque 9.3 *BAR International Series* 1200 Oxford p. 11-17.

BIRÓ, K.T. – SIMON, K.H. (2003) - Lithic material of the Starčevo culture at Gellénháza-Városrét. In: Jerem-Raczky eds., *Morgenrot der Kulturen. Frühe Etappen der Menschheitsgesichte in Mittel- und Südosteuropa.* Festschrift für Nándor Kalicz zum 75. Geburstag. Archaeolingua Budapest p. 115-126

BIRÓ, K.T. – SZAKMÁNY, Gy. (2000) - Current state of research on Hungarian Neolithic polished stone artefacts 26 *Krystalinikum* Brno p. 21-37.

BIRÓ, K.T. – DOBOSI, T.V. (1991) - *LITOTHECA - Comparative Raw Material Collection of the Hungarian National Museum* – Budapest, Magyar Nemzeti Múzeum 1991 p. 1-268.

BIRÓ et al. (2000) - T. Biró, Katalin-T. Dobosi, Viola-Schléder, Zsolt, *LITOTHECA - Comparative Raw Material Collection of the Hungarian National Museum.* Vol. II. – Budapest, Magyar Nemzeti Múzeum p. 1-320.

BIRÓ et al. (2001) - Biró, Katalin T.-Szakmány, György-Schléder, Zsolt, Neolithic Phonolite mine and workshop complex in Hungary. *Slovak Geological Magazine* Bratislava Geological Survey of Slovak Republic 7/4 p. 345-350.

BIRÓ et al. (2004) - T. Biró K.-Scharek P.-Szakmány Gy. Towards an atlas of prehistoric (non-metallic) raw materials in the Carpathian Basin. In: Actes UISPP XIV Section 2. Archeometry BAR International Series 1270 Oxford 2004 57-60.

BIRÓ, K.T. in press (a) - The lithic finds from Szentgyörgyvölgy-Pityerdomb. In press for *Antaeus.*

BIRÓ, K.T. in press (b) - Lithic finds from Füzesabony-Gubakút. In press for site monograph.

BIRÓ *et al.* in press: - Biró, Katalin T., Dobosi, Viola T., Markó, András, Methods of lithic raw material characterisation and raw material origins in the Palaeolithic. State of art in Hungary. In press for UISPP C-16.

BOGNÁR-KUTZIÁN, I. (1963) - *The Copper Age Cemetery of Tiszapolgár-Basatanya.* Archaeologia Hungarica 42, Budapest 1963.

BOGNÁR-KUTZIÁN, I. (1972) - *The Early Copper Age Tiszapolgár-Culture.* Archaeologia Hungarica 48, Budapest 1972.

CHAPMAN, J. (1987) - Technological and stylistic analysis of the early Neolithic chipped stone assemblage from Méhtelek, Hungary. In: Biró ed. 1987, *International Conference on Flint Mining and Lithic Raw Material Identification in the Carpathian Basin,* Sümeg 1986 (2). Budapest KMI 1987 31-52.

CSONGRÁDI-BALOGH, É (1993) - Rézkori, bronzkori pattintott kőeszközök Pest megyében és a Dunától K-re eső területeken (Tipológiai és statisztikai feldolgozás). [Copper Age and Bronze Age chipped stone tools in Pest county and east of the Danube] University doctoral thesis Budapest 1993.

DOBOSI, V. (1968) - Kupferzeitliche Silexgeräte aus Ungarn. *Acta Archaeologica Carpathica* 10 Kraków 1968 p. 271-285.

DOMBORÓCZKI, L. (2005) - Radiocarbon data from Neolithic archaeological sites in Heves County (North-Eastern Hungary) *Agria, Egri Dobó István Vármúzeum Évkönyve* 39/1 Eger p. 5-76.

DOMBORÓCZKI, L. in press -A Füzesabony-gubakúti településtörténeti modell [Settlement History Model of Füzesabony-Gubakút] *Agria, Egri Dobó István Vármúzeum Évkönyve* (2006).

HORVÁTH, T. (2005) - A vatyai kultúra településeinek kőanyaga. Komplex régészeti és petrográfiai feldolgozás. [Lithic material of the Vatya culture]. PhD dissertation, Budapest 2004.

HOVORKA, D. (2000) - New interdisciplinary/intersectorial scientific IGCP/UNESCO Nr. 442 Project: "Raw materials of the Neolithic/Aenewolithic polished stone artefacts: their migration paths in Europe" approved. *Archeologické Rozlhedy* 52 Praha 2000 p. 114-122.

KACZANOWSKA *et al.* (1981) - Kaczanowska, Malgorzata-Kozłowski, J. K.-Makkay, János, Flint hoard from Endrőd, site 39, Hungary (Körös culture) *Acta Archaeologica Carpathica* 21 Kraków 1981 p. 105-117.

KALICZ, N. (1990) - *Frühneolithische Siedlungsfunde aus Südwestungarn.* IPH 4, Budapest, Magyar Nemzeti Múzeum p. 1-164.

KALICZ, N. (1995) - Die älteste transdanubische (mitteleuropäische) Linienbandkeramik. Aspekte zu Ursprung, Chronologie und Beziehungen *Acta Archaeologica Academiae Scientiarum Hungaricae* 47 Budapest 1995 p. 23-59.

KERTÉSZ, R. (2003) - The Mesolithic: towards a production economy (III. The Palaeolithic and Mesolithic) MRE Budapest NKÖM-Teleki Alapítvány p. 91-95.

KOZŁOWSKI, J. K. – KOZŁOWSKI, S. K. eds. (1987) - New in Stone Age Archaeology. *Archaeologia Interregionalis* 230 Warsaw-Krakow University press 1987 p. 1-210.

ORAVECZ, H. – JÓZSA, S. (2005) - A Magyar Nemzeti Múzeum újkőkori és rézkori csiszolt kőeszközeinek régészeti és kőzettani vizsgálata / Archaeological and petrographic investigation of polished stone tools ... *Archeometriai Műhely / Archaeometry Workshop* 2/1 Budapest Magyar Nemzeti Múzeum p. 23-47.

PATAY, P. (1976) - Les matières premières lithiques de l'âge du cuivre en Hongrie. *Acta Archaeologica Carpathica* 16 Kraków p. 229-238.

PÉTERDI *et al.* in press - Péterdi, B., Horváth, T. and Szakmány, Gy., Petrographical Investigation of Late Copper Age Stone Tools from Balatonőszöd (Temetői dűlő), Western Hungary. *36th ISA Conference Proceedings,* in press.

SCHLÉDER, Zs. – BIRÓ, K.T. (1999) – Petroarchaeological studies on polished stone artifacts from Baranya county, Hungary. *A Janus Pannonius Múzeum Évkönyve* 43 Pécs p. 75-101.

STARNINI, E. (1993) - Typological and technological analyses of the Körös culture chipped, polished and ground stone assemblages of Méhtelek-Nádasd (North-Eastern Hungary). *Atti. Soc. Preist. Prost. Trieste* p. 29-96.

STARNINI, E. (1996) -The Stone assemblage from Bicske-Galagonyás and its connections with the Vinča Culture. In: *Vinča – 1995* p. 93-104.

STARNINI, E. – SZAKMÁNY (1998) - The lithic industry of the Neolithic sites of Szarvas and Endrőd (South-Eastern Hungary): techno-typological and archaeometrical aspects. *Acta Archaeologica Academiae Scientiarum Hungaricae* 50 Budapest p. 279-342.

SÜMEGI, P. – KERTÉSZ, R. (2001) – Palaeogeographic characteristics of the Carpathian Basin - an ecological trap during the Early Neolithic? In: Kertész--Makkay eds. 2001 Kertész, R.--Makkay, J. eds., *From the mesolithic to the neolithic.* Int. Conference, Szolnok. Budapest, Archaeolingua p. 405-415.

SZAKMÁNY, Gy. (1996) - Results of the petrographycal analysis of the ground and polished stone assemblage. In: Makkay, J.-Starnini, E.-Tulok, M.: Excavations at Bicske-Galagonyás (part III.). The notenkopf and Sopot-Bicske. *Societa per la Preistoria e Protostoria della Regione Friuli-Venezia Giulia, Quaderno Trieste* 6 1996 224-241.

SZAKMÁNY, Gy. – KASZTOVSZKY, Zs. (2001) - Greenschist-amphibolite schist Neolithic polished stone tools in Hungary. *Slovak Geological Magazine* 7/4 Bratislava Dionyz Stúr Publishers 2001 430-431.

SZAKMÁNY, Gy. – NAGY, B. (2005) - Balatonlelle - Felső-Gamász lelőhelyről előkerült késő rézkori vörös homokkő őrlőkövek petrográfiai vizsgálatának eredményei / Results of petrographical analysis of red sandstone grinders from the Late Copper Age site Balatonlelle - Felső-Gamász. *Archeometriai Műhely / Archaeometry Workshop* Budapest, Magyar Nemzeti Múzeum 2/3 p. 13-21.

VISY et al. eds. (2003) Visy Zsolt--Nagy Mihály--B. Kiss Zsuzsa, eds. *Hungarian Archaeology at the turn of the Millennium.* Budapest NKÖM-Teleki Alapítvány 2003 1-482.

VÉRTES L. (1965) - The depot of silex blades from Boldogkőváralja. *Acta Archaeologica Academiae Scientiarum Hungaricae* 17 Budapest p. 128-136.

WOSINSZKY, M. (1893) - A lengyeli telep csiszolt kőeszközei s azok készítési módja. *Archaeológiai Értesítő* 13 Budapest p. 193-198.

NEOLITHISATION OF THE UPPER TISZA BASIN

Janusz Krzysztof KOZŁOWSKI

Institute of Archaeology, Jagiellonian University, Gołębia 11, 31-007 Kraków, Poland,
kozlowsk@argo.hist.uj.edu.pl

Marek NOWAK

Institute of Archaeology, Jagiellonian University, Gołębia 11, 31-007 Kraków, Poland,
mniauj@interia.pl

Abstract: The material and chronological data indicate that the earliest Neolithic settlement in the Upper Tisza Basin appeared in the 56 Century BC and was set up by groups of the late Körös/Criş Culture tradition migrating from outside. The starting point of this movement was the middle Tisza Basin and a territory of Transylvania. Because there are no unquestionable traces of Late Mesolithic occupation, we can hardly talk about local hunter-gatherer populations share in the neolithisation of the territory under discussion. Neither does the technology of stone processing point to local Neolithisation, as it is related to the Early Neolithic traditions of the Great Hungarian Plain. The further development of Neolithic followed a course that was independent of the model characteristic for Alföld (i.e. smooth transformation between Körös and AVK, with transitional phenomena like Méhtelek and Szatmár) but it was obviously set in global Eastern Linear stylistics.
Key-words: *Upper Tisza Basin, palaeoenvironment, Late Mesolithic, First Neolithic, Neolithisation*

Résumé : Les données matérielles et chronologiques indiquent que le plus ancien habitat Néolithique dans le basin supérieur de la Tisza apparait au 56-ème siècle BC; cet habitat est représenté par les groupes allogènes appartenant à la tradition de Kőrös-Criş. Le point de départ de ces groupes était le basin moyen de la Tisza et le territoire de la Transilvanie. Manque de traces des habitats du Mésolithique récent sur ce terrritoire ne permet pas de supposer que dans le processus de la Néolithisation ont participé les groupes de chasseurs-cueilleurs indigènes. Egalement les industries lithiques du premier Néolithique ne montrent pas de traces d'impact de traditions locales pré-Néolithiques. Le développement ultérieur du Néolithique a suivi le modèle independant de la Grande Plaine Hongroise, où nous observons une évolution graduelle entre Körös et la ceramique linéaire (AVK) avec phases de transition (comme Méhtelek et Szatmár). Néanmoins, le basin supérieur de la Tisza entre, dans cette période, dans la zone stylistique du Linéaire oriental.
Mots-clés: *Bassin supérieur de la Tisza, paléoenvironnement, Mésolithique récent, premier Néolithique, néolithisation.*

INTRODUCTION

The beginnings of the Neolithic in the Balkan Peninsula (excluding Greece) and the Carpathian Basin are connected with an archaeological complex called Starčevo-Körös-Criş or the First Temperate Neolithic (FTN) in more contemporary literature (Bailey 2000: 39-152; Whittle 1996: 37-72). This phenomenon emerged at about 6.300/6.200 BC, south of the Lower Danube as well as in Strymon/Struma and Axios/ Vardar Basins (Bojadjev *et al.* 1993; Görsdorf & Bojadziev 1996; Nikolova 1998; Stefanova 1996; 1998; Todorova & Vajsov 1993), but it spread significantly northward later (Biagi & Spataro 2005; Budja 2001; Tringham 2000; Whittle *et al.* 2002; Zvelebil & Lillie 2000: 68-72). Criş-Körös branch of FTN appeared in the region of middle Tisza, northern Transylvania and Moldova around 5.800/5.700 BC (Biagi & Spataro 2005: 36; Dergachev *et al.* 1991; Hertelendi *et al.* 1995; Horvàth & Hertelendi 1994; Lazarovici & Maxim 1995: Mantu 1998; 1999; Maxim 1999; Whittle *et al.* 2002). More western wing of the FTN, in other words Starčevo culture, appeared in the region of Balaton lake approximately at 5.500/5.400

BC (Bánffy 2000; 2004a; 2004b; 2005a; 2006: 130-134; Kalicz *et al.* 1998). The aforementioned regions constituted the northernmost zone of the FTN settlement. The First Neolithic in more northern areas of the Carpathian Basin is reflected by another archaeological phenomenon, called Linear Complex, consisting of Linear Band Pottery culture (LBK) (Bánffy 2000; 2004a; 2004b; Gronenborn 1999; Kaczanowska & Kozłowski 2003; Kalicz 1995; Lenneis 2001; Lenneis & Stadler 2002) and Eastern Linear Pottery culture called also Alföld Linear Pottery Culture (*Alföldi Vonaldiszes Kerámia* - AVK) (Kalicz & Makkay 1977; Kozłowski (ed.) 1997; Šiška 1989). It is widely known that the first stage of neolithisation in Central Europe, between Paris Basin and Western Ukraine, took place due to the spectacular expansion of LBK. Such a vast expansion did not distinguish AVK and this unit covered much smaller territory than LBK, i.e. Tisza Basin and Transylvania in general. On the other hand, paradoxically it was more diversified in the space and time. This fact makes the question of AVK origins at least equally complicated and controversial as in the case of LBK. The role of possible Transcarpathain contacts in

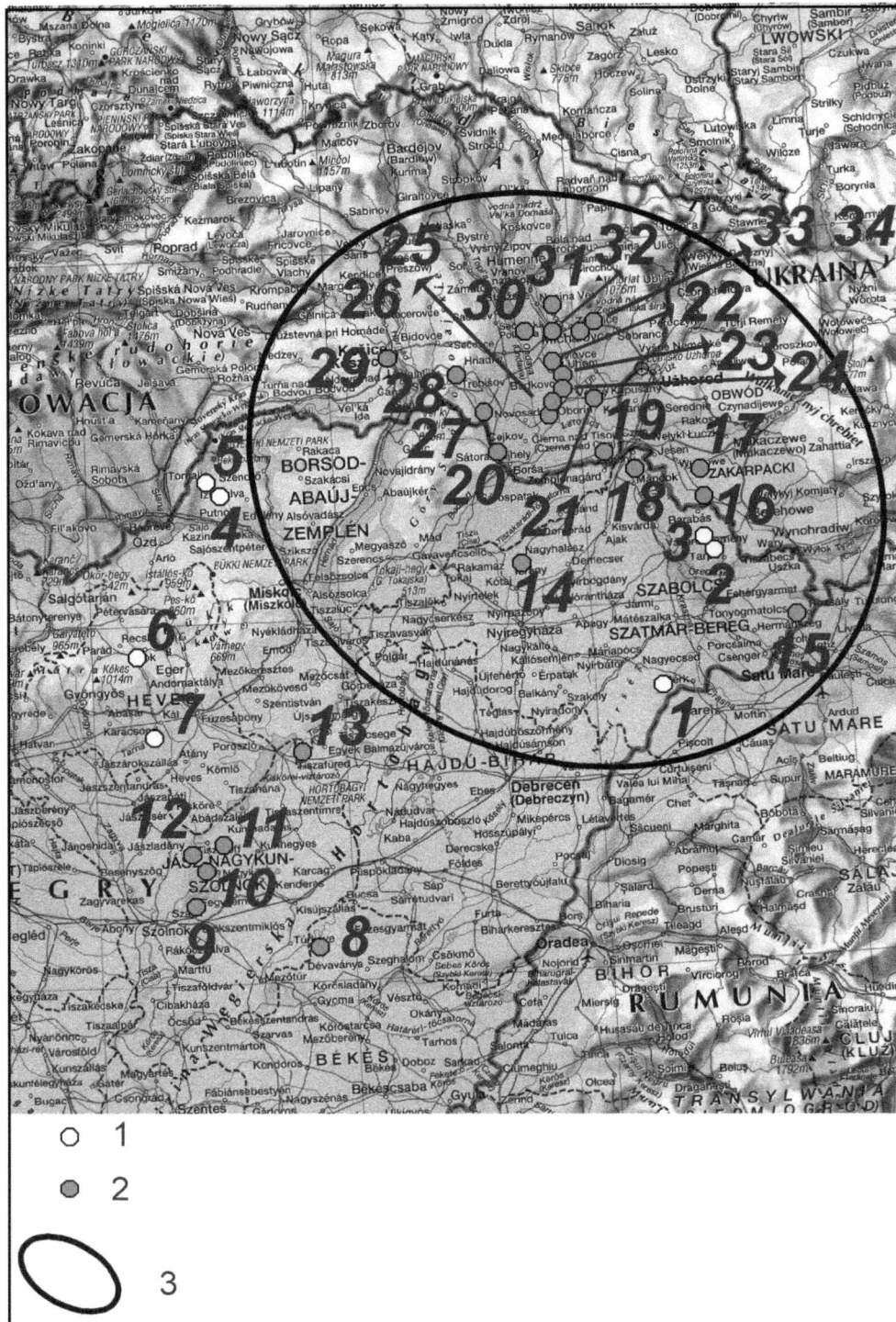

Fig. 7.1. North-eastern part of the Carpathian Basin.
1 – palaeoenvironmental sites, 2 – First Neolithic sites mentioned in the text, 3 – extent of the study area.(1. Bátorlieget, 2. Csaroda-Báb-tava, 3. Csaroda-Nyíres-tó, 4. Kelemér-Kis-Mohos-tó, 5. Kelemér-Nagy-Mohos-tó, 6. Tarnabod, 7. Sirok, 8. Ecsegfalva, 9. Szajol-Felsőföld, 10. Nagykörü-Cooperative-Orchard, 11. Tiszagyenda-Garaholom, 12. Kőtelek-Huszársarok, 13. Tiszaszölos-Domaháza, 14. Ibrány, 15. Méhtelek-Nadas, 16. Zastavne-Mala Hora, 17. Rivne I, 18. Tiszabezdéd-Sevapa, 19. Veľké Trakany, 20. Bara, 21. Veľké Kapušany, 22. Žbince, 23. Slavcovce, 24. Zemplinské Kopčany, 25. Malé Raškovce, 26. Veľké Raškovce, 27. Lastovce, 28. Kuzmice, 29. Košice-Červený rak, 30. Moravany, 31. Zbudza, 32. Michalovce, 33. Malé Zalužice, 34. Lúčky.)

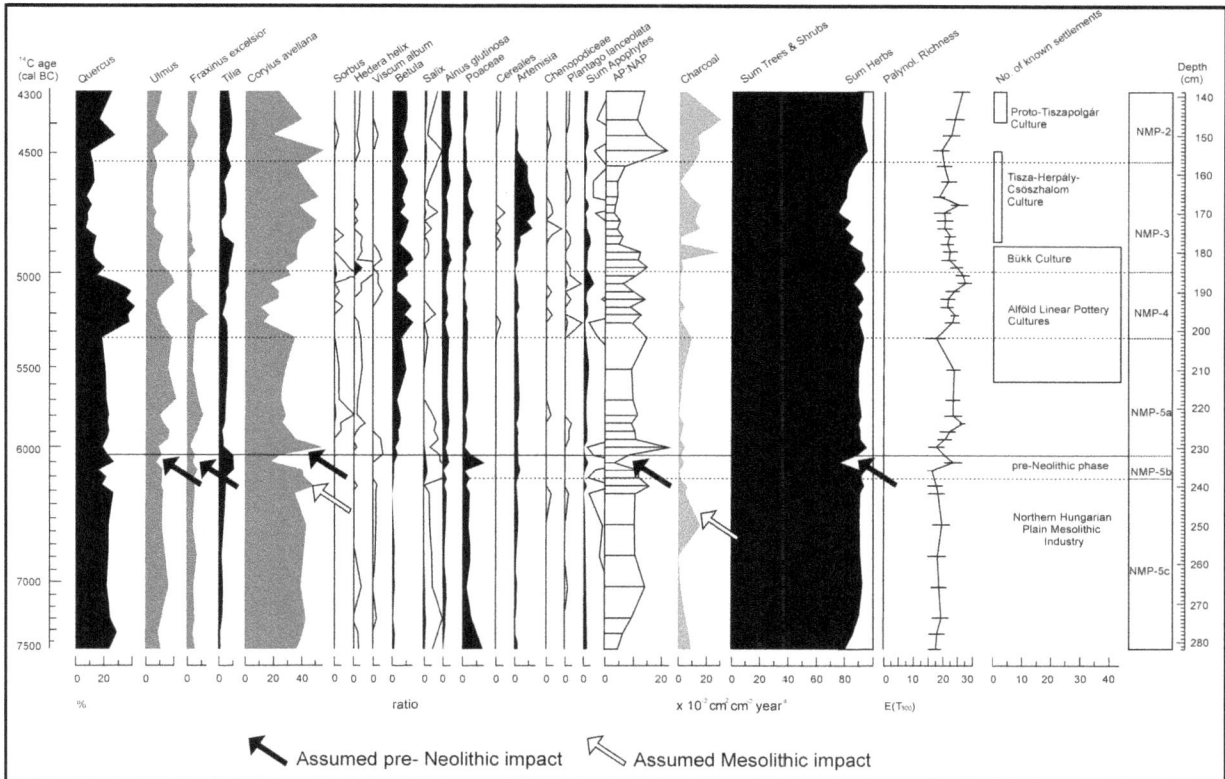

Fig. 7.2. Late Mesolithic and Neolithic environment and supposed Mesolithic and pre-Neolithic impact on environment as reflected in the pollen profile from Kelemér-Nagy-Mohos-tó (after Sümegi 2005a).

genesis and development of the AVK is another specific question. Certainly, there are also issues important for our understanding of neolithisation of the Upper Tisza Basin such us: environmental constraints, relations between indigenous and foreign populations as well as a scale of necessary adaptations to new cultural and natural circumstances that are similar to LBK circumstances.

ENVIRONMENT

The area under discussion constitutes the north-easternmost part of the Great Hungarian Plain including the Eastern Slovakian Lowland and Transcarpathian Ukraine (Fig. 7.1). Therefore the alluvial, plain landscape makes the prevailing part of the region. However there are also other landscapes. We betoken the mountain ranges adjoining the alluvial plains, like the Slanské vrchy – Zempléni-hegység range (with maximum height 1092 m a.s.l.) and Vyhorlat Mts. (with a maximum altitude 1076 m a.s.l.), small intramontane basins like Košice Basin, the hilly lands (*pahorkatina* in Slovak, at an elevation between 150 and 300 m a.s.l.), and flat elevations called tables (*tabula* in Slovak, at an elevation of 100-150 m). There

have been also low-lying marshy areas, with a subsidence tendency, for instance in a place of present-day water reservoir Zemplínska šírava.

Summing up, the North-Eastern part of the Carpathian Basin is by no means a uniform area and this situation is very similar to the ecological differentiation (mosaic) which is typical for more southern parts of Alföld, what is highly emphasised by Pal Sümegi in his recent works (2003; 2004a: 122-126; 2004b: 336-337; 2005a; Sümegi *et al.* 1998; Sümegi & Kertész 2001). We could even suppose that such an ecological mosaic within North-Eastern Alföld was more clear-cut for human perception than in its central and southern areas due to greater relative altitudes.

The break of the Late Glacial and Holocene periods marked the opening of significant change of ecological conditions in the Carpathian Basin. By 8500 BC the communities of the mixed deciduous woodlands type (with oak, ash, elm, lime, hazel and – from latter date onwards – beech, and hornbeam) had replaced the coniferous forests (Fig. 7.2) (Sümegi 2005a: 16-17; Sümegi & Gulyás (eds.) 2004: 164-166, 307-312; Sümegi *et al.* 1998: 187-188). However, on the northern fringes of the Carpathian Basin that transformation had finally finished later, that is by *ca.* 7.000 BC (Braun *et al.* 2005: 25, 33; Gardner 1999; 2005: 93; Juhász 2005a: 42; 2005b: 48-9; Sümegi & Gulyás (eds.) 2004: 314). In the higher areas these mixed deciduous forest were probably dense whereas they took more open shape near the rivers (perhaps similar to so called gallery forests). There were also patches of steppe and forest-steppe vegetation (Gardner 2005: 97-98, 103; Krippel 1986: 160-164; Sümegi 2005a: 19-20; 2005b; Sümegi *et al.* 2005; Sümegi & Gulyás (eds.) 2004: 172, 314-317). If we take into account data from Bátorlieget, it is easily visible that after 6.000 BC there have been some decrease of deciduous trees (although relatively moderate in case of oak, elm and alder as well as hazel) and simultaneous increase of grasses and an aquatic species (Sümegi & Gulyás (eds.) 2004: 167-168, 313; Willis *et al.* 1995: 33, 41, 44). The results of charcoal analyses conducted at the early AVK site at Moravany, Eastern Slovakia, by Maria Lityńska-Zając, Magdalena Moskal and Ernestina Badal confirm the predominance of deciduous trees in the second half of the sixth millennium BC (Kozłowski *et al.* 2003: 139; Kalicki *et al.* 2005: 203; Moskal *et al.* 2007).

Similarly to the central and southern Tisza Basin, the recent river courses were established in consequence of the regulation of the river beds in the second half of 19th century. Before mid-nineteenth century AD their courses were as a rule extremely unstable. In fact, there was not usually a single course; for example the Ondava river was an anastomosing river, divided into at least several meandering branches as it can be seen in historical records (Harbuľova (ed.) 2002). Besides, the whole alluvial plain was flooded to a significant degree almost every spring, not to mention more serious floods that hit the plain every few years (Chapman 1997: 143-145; Harčar 1997: 8-9; Kosse 1979: 70, 80-1; Shiel 1997). This fact is also evident and based on historical data (Šoltésová (ed.) 2006: 25-26); for example the original names of Moravany village (Murva/Morva/Moroua – which in Eastern Slovak dialect describes a wet and boggy area) and the18[th]-century Moravany's coat-of-arms (Harbuľova (ed.) 2002).

The same phenomena took place in prehistoric periods. For instance, sections and borings across the Ondava flood plain demonstrate the older meandering belts, located much closer to the eastern slope of the valley (Kalicki *et al.* 2004; 2005: 194-195). Besides, the profiles with three buried soils occur at the bottom of the valley. The middle fossil soils were dated in the Topľa river valley at 4.720±300 BP and in the Ondava river valley at 4.200±900 BP (Baňacký *et al.* 1987).

Having considered available pollen, archaeobotanical, geological and geomorphologic data we attempted to reconstruct environmental conditions during the Atlantic period in the Eastern Slovakian Lowland (Kalicki *et al.* 2007; Nowak 1997). Four main geoecological zones were discerned and a mountain zone (Zemplínske vrchy range) that formally does not constitute a part of the Eastern Slovakian Lowland:

A. Plains ('Rovina'). The largest area (*ca.* 100 m a.s.l.) with a very unstable river network, waterlogged, flooded every year. Old river channels already existed or were formed in the Atlantic period. The plains are, as they used to be, further divided into four main ecological sub-types:

A1 – Marshy depressions. Covered by open forests; alder communities with abundant grass-perennials and fern vegetation. In practice alluvial soils are the only type of soils.

A2 – Recent aggradational terraces and plains, possibly medium-elevated terraces and alluvial cones. Covered by open forests; predominance of alder communities with rich grass-perennials and fern vegetation; on some medium-elevated terraces there could have been enclaves of mixed oak forests. The treeless enclaves were present in some places. Alluvial soils and brown forest soils are typical in some areas.

A3 – Terraces and periglacial cones. Covered by mixed oak forests; brown soils are the most typical.

A4 – Aggradational plains, low terraces, cones with sandy covers, dunes and sandy loess. In higher terrains the vegetation consisted of mixed oak forests, in lower terrains of sparse forest, Communities of psammophytes were present on sands. Soils were, just as they are now, strongly varied: in lower-lying areas alluvial soils developed, on sands there were regisoils, brown forest soil types, and possibly, occasionally chernozems.

B. Tables ('Tabula'). A slightly higher terrains with flat surface (100-150 m a.s.l.) covered by mixed oak forests similar to the present-day xerophilous and sub-xerophilous oak woods (sub-type B1). In addition to oak, these communities were composed of elm, lime, ash, maple, hornbeam and hazel. Around the edges of the plateaux, treeless enclaves occurred, i.e. the landscape could have been a forest-steppe zone (sub-type B2). Soils were mainly brown forest soils and chernozems at the edge of the plateaux in the forest-steppe.

C. Hill lands ('Pahorkatina'). A higher area (between 150 and 300 m a.s.l.) with more or less hilly landscape covered by mixed oak forests, similar to present-day xerophilous and sub-xerophilous oak

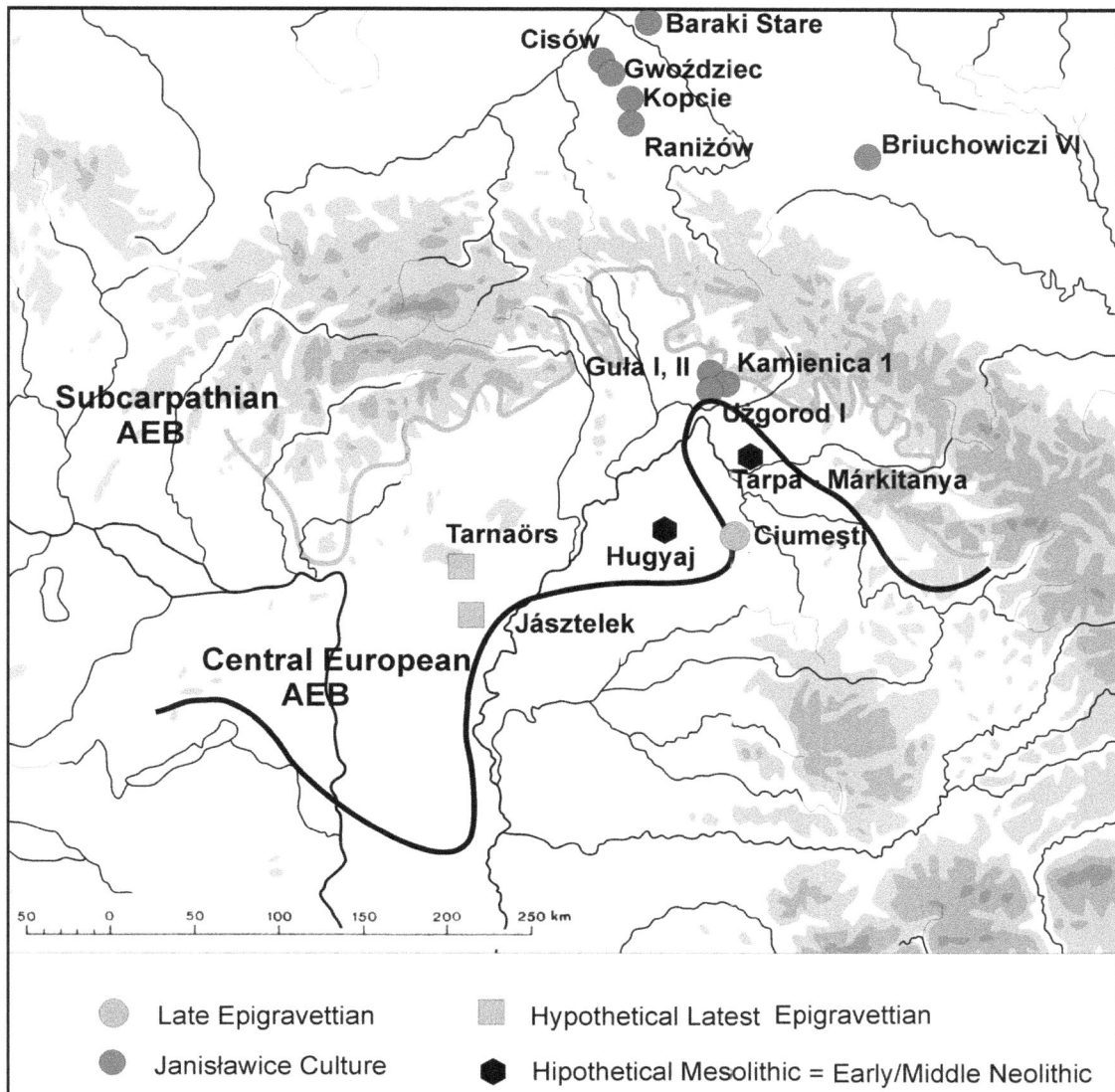

Fig. 7.3. Location of Late Mesolithic sites discussed in the text. Courses of Central European and Subcarpathian Agro-Ecological Barriers (acc. to Kertész & Sümegi 2001; Sümegi & Kertész 2001; Sümegi 2004a).

woods. Ash, elm, maple, lime (?) and hazel were also typical. Brown forest soils predominated.

D. The highest, denudated parts of the hill regions of submontane type covered by oak forests with some hornbeam. Brown forest soils predominated.

M. Mountain zone - the Zemplínske vrchy range with the highest point 469 m a.s.l (Rozhľadňa).

We would like to emphasise that the areas of some tables (Malčicka, Inačovska, Zavadzka), as well as some other forms (some single hills in the southern part of the Lowland) constituted a kind of ecological islands when compared to the low-lying plains.

THE LATE MESOLITHIC IN THE NORTH-EASTERN PART OF THE CARPATHIAN BASIN

The question of the Late Mesolithic has been the subject of many controversies (Kertész 2002; Kozłowski 2005). Although various attempts were made at increasing the number of Late Mesolithic sites in the Upper Tisza Basin and in the interfluve of the Tisza and the Danube, the number of sites that provided Late Mesolithic diagnostic forms is small (Fig. 7.3); there are no homogeneous sites with radiometric dates among them.

In the entire north-east part of the Carpathian Basin we can ascribe only one site in north-western Romania i.e.

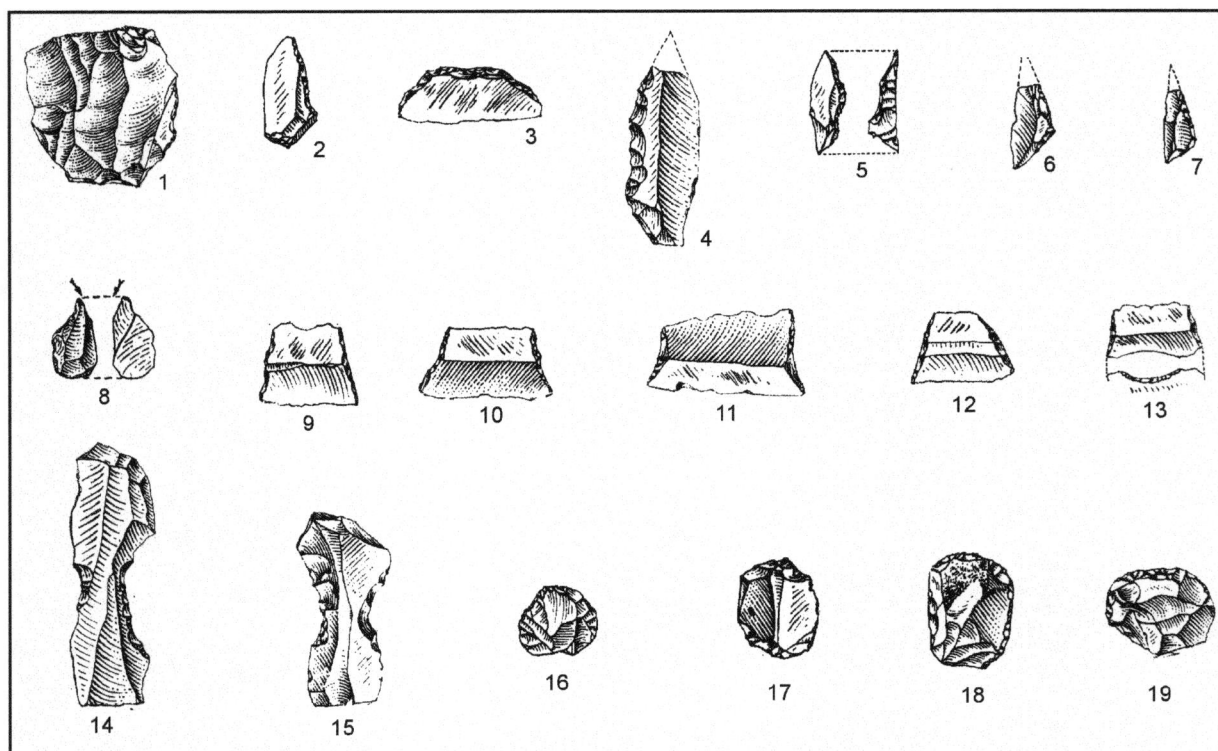

Fig. 7.4. Chipped lithics from Late Mesolithic site at Ciumeşti (after Paunescu 1964; 1970).
1. Core, 2-5. arched backed blades, 6-7. triangles, 8. microburin, 9-13. trapezes,
14-15. notched blades, 16-19. short end-scrapers.

Ciumeşti II (Paşune) in the region of Satu Mare (Păunescu 1964; 1970), and several sites in Transcarpathian Ukraine to the Late Mesolithic, with all certainty (Kamienica I and Užgorod I, belong to unquestionable sites and the doubtful sites are Guta I, Guta II, Srednieye II and III – Matskevoy 1991), whose dating was based on typology, and absolute dates were obtained from none of them.

The industry at the site of Ciumeşti II (Fig. 7.4) was often ascribed to the same group together with the industries of the Pontic (Black Sea steppes) zone, represented in Romania by the sites of Erbiceni and Ripiceni (Păunescu 1970). From our point of view, this diagnosis is incorrect: two Moldavian sites are characterised by the presence of pencil-like cores and blanks which were obtained from them; this technique was not known at Ciumeşti where blades were less regular, obtained from single-platform cores with broad, flat flaking surfaces. Trapezes are present both at Ciumeşti as well as in the assemblages of the Pontic zone, constituting an inter-cultural element and a diagnostic form of the Late Mesolithic. At Ciumeşti symmetrical and asymmetrical specimens of trapezes account for about 20% of all retouched tools (Fig. 7.4: 9-13). The blades with lateral notches (Fig. 7.4: 14-15),

which are described as *lames etranglées*, can also be ascribed to the inter-cultural Late Mesolithic elements.

However, besides these inter-cultural elements Ciumeşti II provided forms typical of the Epigravettian tradition of the Balkan-Danubian zone such as microlithic arched and straight backed blades (Fig. 7.4: 2-5), microlithic convex truncations and scalene triangles (Fig. 7.4: 6-7). Short end-scrapers represent the same tradition (Fig. 7.4: 16-19). The presence of microburin technique (Fig. 7.4: 8) used for the production of triangles and possibly also trapezes is significantly relevant. Unfortunately, these typological elements do not allow to date precisely the materials from Ciumeşti II. We can merely define their age as Atlantic, Late Mesolithic.

The materials from Transcarpathian Ukraine belong to the entirely different cultural tradition. The relatively rich materials from the site of Kamienica 1 held together within the Janisławice culture (Kozłowski 2001): blades were obtained from single- and double-platform cores that are characterised by careful preparation of the back and sides, and also platforms which were often rejuvenated by detaching tablets (Fig. 7.5: 1-6). Blade blanks were used chiefly in the

82

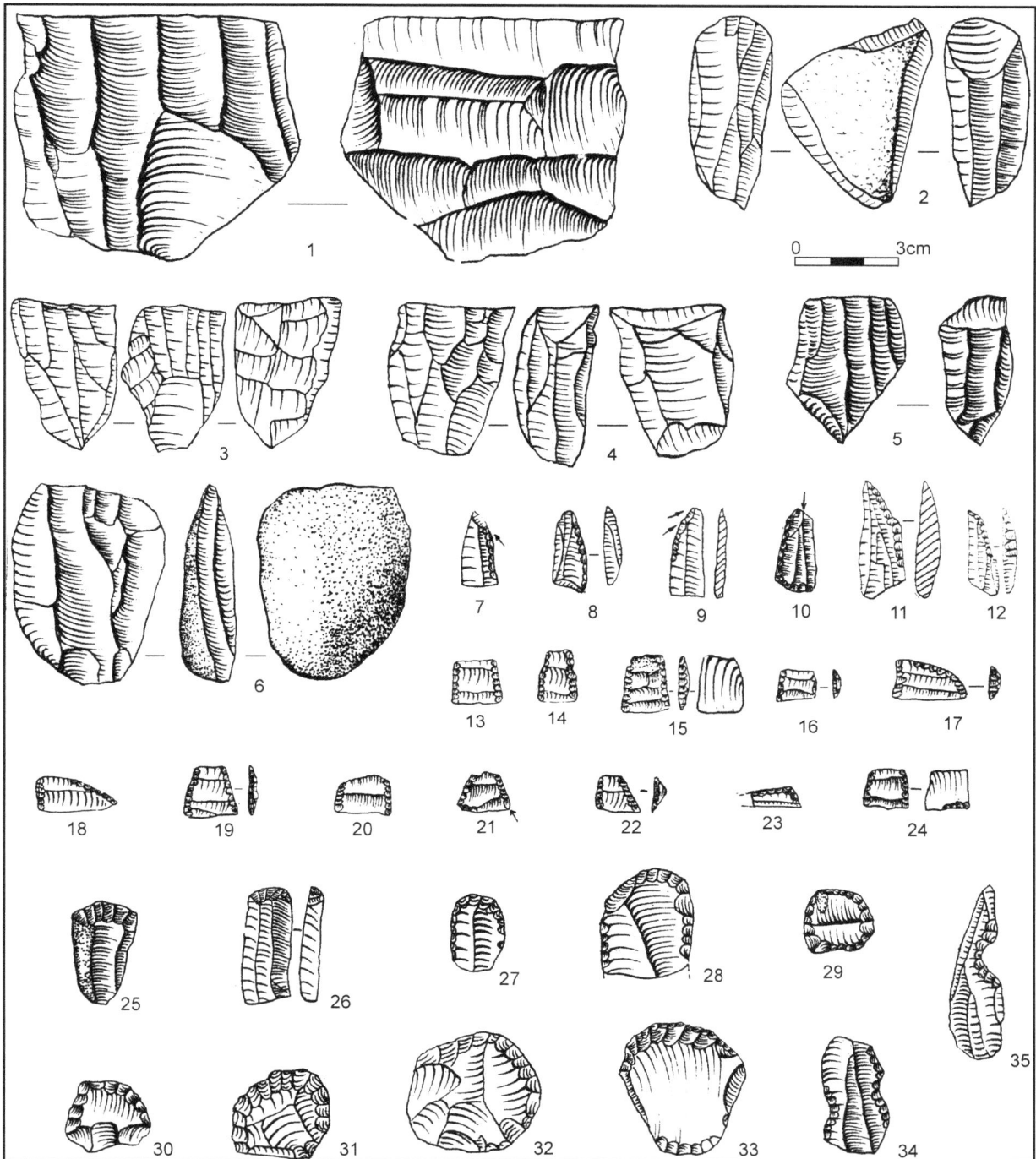

Fig. 7.5. Chipped lithics from Late Mesolithic site at Kamienica 1 (after Matskevoy *et al.* 1983). (1-6. Cores, 7-10. Janisławice points, 11-12. oblique truncations, 13-24. trapezes, 25-33. end-scrapers, 34-35. notched blades.)

production of the typical Janisławice points – backed pieces or truncations with the tip shaped by a microburin blow in the form of *piquant-trièdre* (Fig. 7.5: 7-10). There were also various types of trapezes (asymmetrical and symmetrical) (Fig. 7.5: 13-24), Montbani blades with notches, numerous end-scrapers (Fig. 7.5: 25-33), flake side-scrapers, perforators and burins. The site of Kamienica 1 is a sub-surface site (in the Bt level of Holocene podzol soil), situated on the low terrace of the Už river. The site is probably the palimpsest of repeated occupational events – when we consider the extent of the site (480 square m) and the number of artefacts (3.700) (Matskevoy *et al.* 1983).

The Janisławice culture occupied *inter alia* the territories in the Upper Vistula and San basins as well as the territory between the Bug and the middle Dneper (Zalizniak 1998, fig. 63). Basically, (with the exception of Briuchowiczi and Diliatina) Janisławician sites are absent in the Upper Dnester basin. For this reason the presence of Janisławician assemblages in Transcarpathian Ukraine is undoubtedly the effect of the diffusion of population groups of this culture from south-eastern Poland (where there are relatively numerous, large assemblages of this unit e.g. Baraki Stare, Raniżów, Jawornik-Czarna, Gwoździec and others – Libera & Talar 1990; Talar 1966; Wąs 2002). The links between both regions are confirmed by the presence of imports of Transcarpathian raw materials.

So far the chronology of the Janisławice culture has been based on several dates from Poland which, reaching the beginning of the sixth millennium BC (Dęby 29 in Kujavia), concentrate in the fifth millennium BC (Kozłowski 1989). Thus, it does not seem likely that the appearance of the Janisławice culture in the Upper Tisza Basin had taken place before the first Neolithic settlement in that territory. In all likelihood the Janisławician groups reached the Upper Tisza Basin just after the First Neolithic. Other Mesolithic sites in Transcarpathian Ukraine, ascribed by L. Matskevoy (2001) to the Niezviska-Oselivka culture (such as e.g. Kamienica V, Mukachevo IX) contain the predominantly elements of the Upper or Late Palaeolithic industries with backed pieces (see: Matskevoy 2001, fig. 2:28), possibly with posterior Neolithic additions.

Another controversial issue is the presence of an alleged Late Mesolithic settlement in north-eastern Hungary. In this context two sites are mentioned: Tarpa-Márkitanya – in the region of Tiszahat (Dobosi 1983) and Hugyaj (Dobosi 1972).

In the case of the site of Tarpa-Márkitanya Dobosi's claim is based on patination (which led her to diagnose Upper Palaeolithic artefacts) and on typology (which she (mis-) used to separate Mesolithic artefacts: "hohe hobelartige Kratzer, winzige Klingen, Mikrolithen" – Dobosi 1983: 18). The examination of the collection at the National Museum in Budapest (kindly placed at our disposal by Dr. Dobosi) revealed, however, that the entire material from all the settlement loci (A–E; excuding locus B) contains Neolithic ceramics which could be ascribed to the Szatmár group. All the settlement points provided single-platform blade-flake or flake cores (these cores are probably described as "Hobelartige Kratzer" by V. Dobosi) (Fig. 7.6: 1-6). Corresponding debitage products were also present.

The only tools were: flake end-scrapers (Fig. 7.6: 7-9) and a convex truncations on a bladelet (Fig. 7.6: 11).

At locus B, which is the only site where ceramics had not occured, there were a large flake end-scraper (Fig. 7.6: 10), a blade detached after the crested blade, a tablet, a flake core with changed orientation. Such a set is far from sufficient to document the Mesolithic age of this site. The entirety of material fuses to the framework of the lithic industry of the Eastern Linear Pottery Complex – which is also supported by the raw material composition (limnoquartzites and obsidian).

Regretfully, we were not able to verify the pieces of information about the alleged Mesolithic nature of the site of Hugyaj as the finds from the site have been lost.

The most surprising thesis is proposed by E. Bánffy (2005b: 207) on the basis of hypothetical traces of an anthropogenic impact on the vegetation in the region of Csaroda in the period between the seventh and sixth millennia BC. Bánffy assumes the presence of Mesolithic groups in this territory 'irrespective of which tool making tradition they followed'. Furthermore, in her work she states that 'Mesolithic finds similar to ones from Csaroda (which) have been reported from Hugyaj and Tárpa' (*ibid.*: 208). So far – in any case – Tarpa lithic finds should be ascribed to the Early Neolithic (just as, in all likelihood, the hypothetical anthropogenic impact in the palynological profile at Csaroda – Juhász 2005c).

The aforementioned idea that links some changes in pollen spectra with activities of Mesolithic hunter-gatherers in northern areas of the Carpathian Basin has been also expressed by other authors (e. g. Juhász 2004). P. Sümegi (2005a: 21) claims that the formation of the 'mosaic-like woodland environment' in the northern part of the Carpathian Basin was the effect of pre-Neolithic 'human activity' by putative Late Mesolithic population. According to Sümegi, intensive gathering of hazel, using shoots and foliage of ash and linden saplings for animal fodder belong to the effects of that activity. Locally, the deforestation took place by fire registered as 'smaller or greater micro-charcoal peaks' (*ibid.*: 22).

Sümegi's claims are based on over-interpretation of pollen diagrams from the eastern Hungarian sites such as Kelemér-Nagy-Mohos-tó (*ibid.*: 18) which show the pre-Neolithic oscillations in the frequency of hazel, lime, ash-tree, oak, elm, drop of trees & shrubs index (AP) and an increase in grasses (Fig. 7.2). However, the degree of resolution of the radiometric dating of these events in the pollen diagrams and also the allegedly anthropogenic cause of the foregoing oscillations are disputable questions.

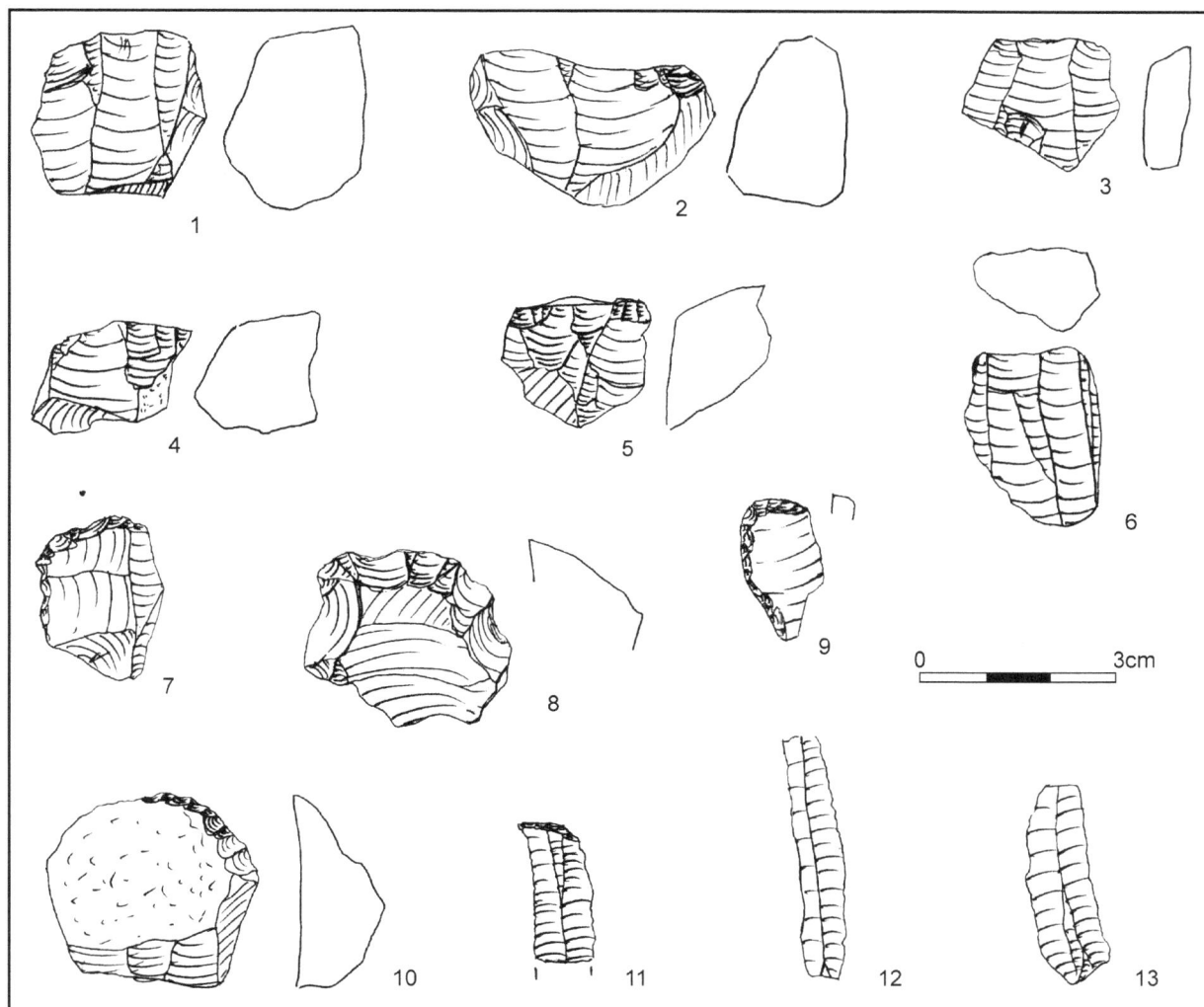

Fig. 7.6. Chipped lithics from Tarpa-Márkitanya (after Dobosi 1983).
1-6. Cores, 7-10. end-scrapers, 11. retouched truncation, 12-13. blades.

The supposed participation of man in the formation of mosaic of environments, which is typical of the transition between the seventh and sixth millennia BC (Sümegi & Gulyás (eds.) 2004: 171-172, is also disputable. In that period, the presence of steppe-forest patches has been confirmed – among others – by palaeomalacological data from the northern part of the Carpathian Basin. This, however, should be explained by the general climatic tendencies (the overlapping of boreal, the oceanic, steppe-forest climatic zones and the Mediterranean influence), and the varied relief landscape, hydrological conditions notably oscillations of ground water level- and the occurrence of residual loess culmination with specific soil conditions (Raczky *et al.* in press). The southern boundary of this zone demarcates the so-called lowland agro-ecological barrier in the Tisza Basin, whereas its northern boundary is the Sub-Carpathian agro-ecological boundary (Kértesz & Sümegi 2001) (Fig. 7.3). These two boundaries are vital for the adaptation of the Early Neolithic subsistence economy to the conditions in the northern part of the Carpathian Basin and, subsequently, for the introduction of Neolithic settlement into the Carpathian zone.

CHRONO-CULTURAL SETTING OF THE FIRST NEOLITHIC IN THE NORTH-EASTERN PART OF THE CARPATHIAN BASIN

As regards the absolute chronology of the First Neolithic in Upper Tisza Basin we have two sets of radiocarbon dates at our disposal. The first, i. e. three dates from Méhtelek generally point at 58, 57 and 56 centuries BC (Titov 1980: 112). Over 30 dates from four sites in the Eastern Slovakian Lowland make

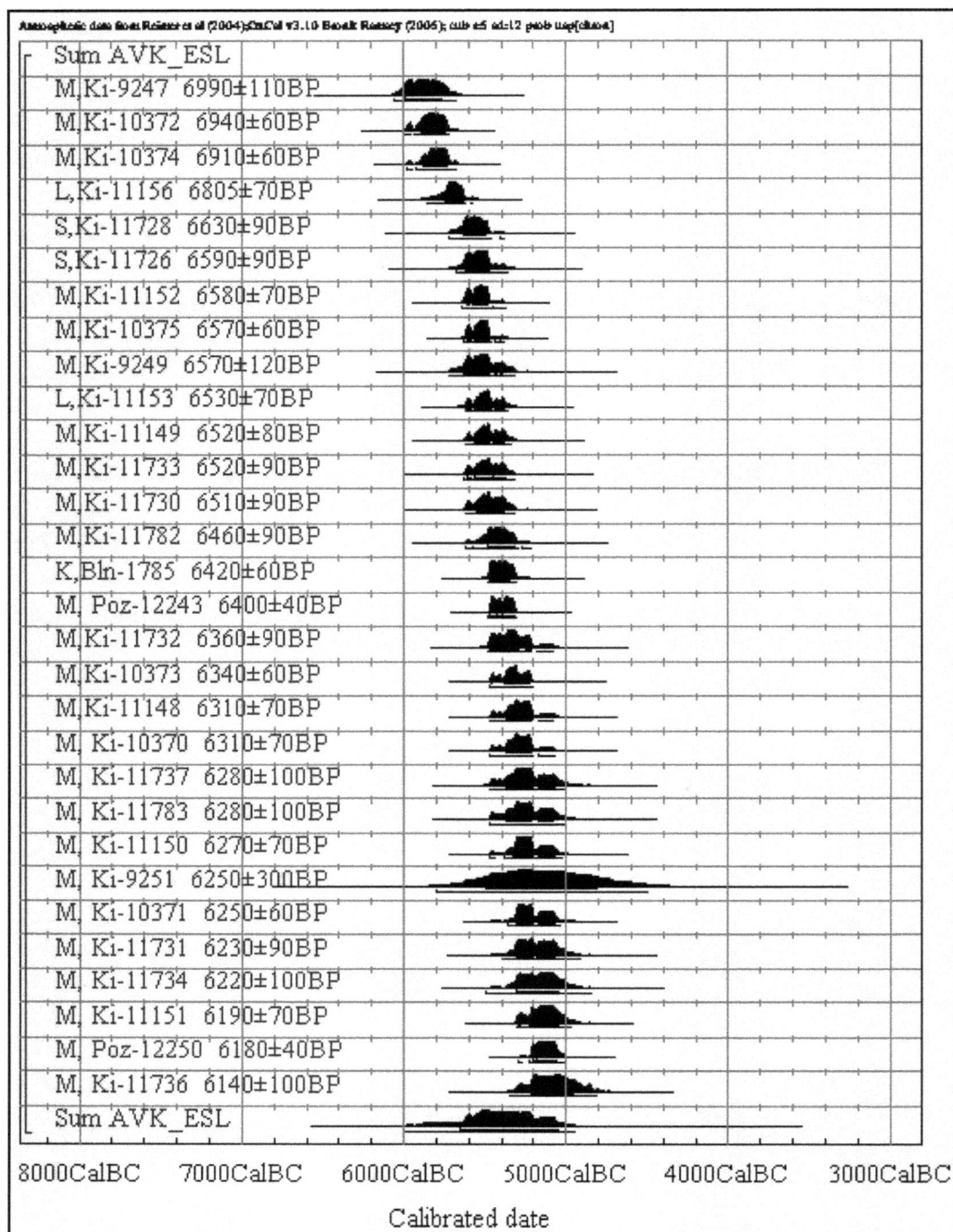

Fig. 7.7. Radiocarbon dates from First Neolithic context in Eastern Slovakian Lowland.
(L – Lúčky; K – Zemplinské Kopčany; M – Moravany; S – Slavkovce)

the second set (Fig. 7.7). All of them – except for one date from Kopčany (Šiška 1989) – have been obtained recently during joint research project conducted by Institute of Archaeology, Jagiellonian University and Faculty of Philosphy, Prešov University (Kozłowski *et al.* 2003; Kalicki *et al.* 2004; 2007). The simple sum of all these dates gives the range of 6.000-5.950 BC for two sigma probability and of 5.650-5.050 BC for one sigma probability. The first range is totally impossible to acknowledge in reference to the beginning of the Neolithic. The second one is more probable, although in our opinion the date of 5.650 BC seems to be still

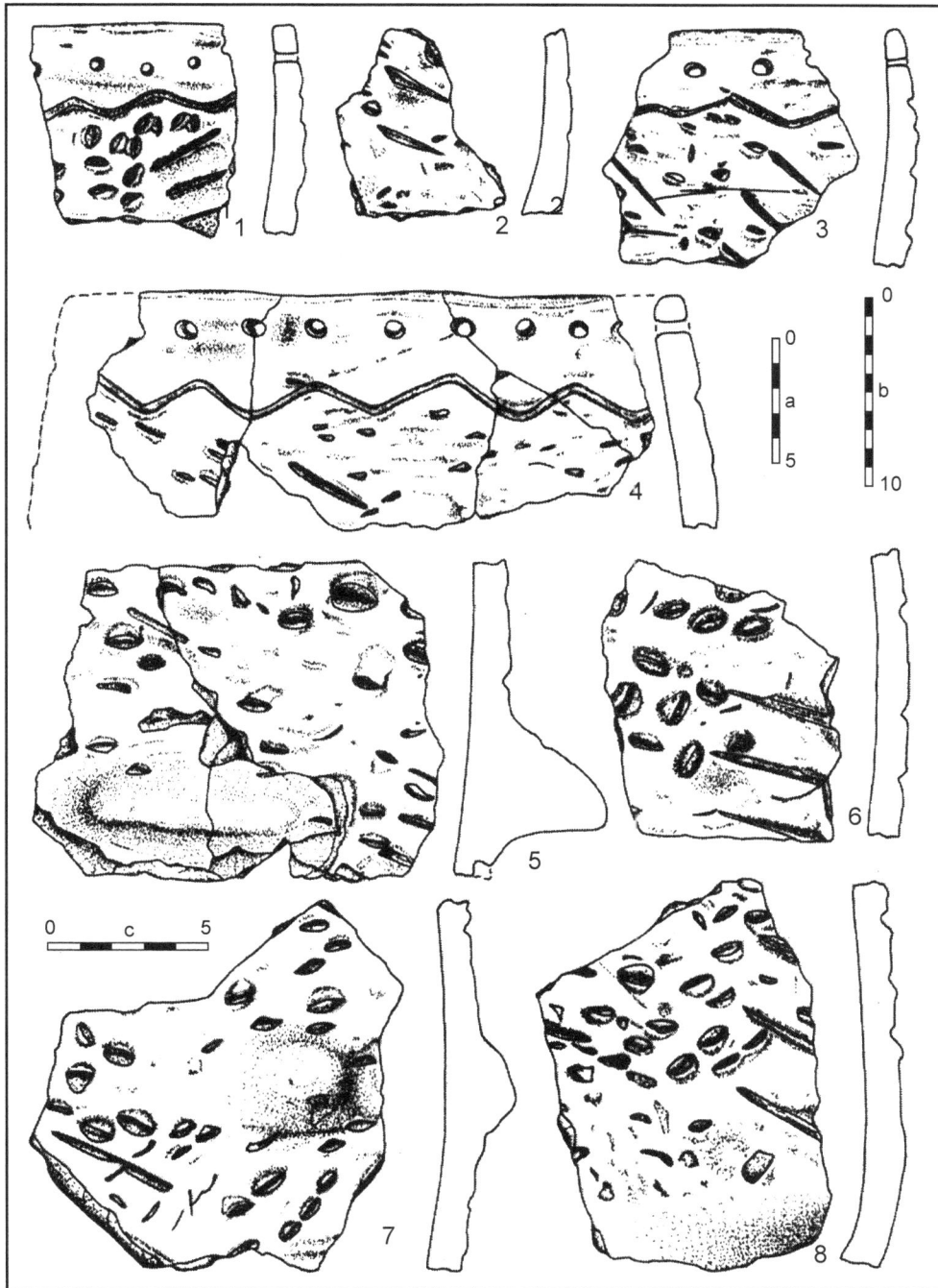

Fig. 7.8. Coarse pottery (pots and bag-shaped pots) from First Neolithic site at Slavkovce (after Vizdal 1997).
Scale: a – 1, 4, 5; b – 2, 3, 6, 7, 8.

too early, especially when compared with the dates from neighbouring regions (Horváth & Hertelendi 1994; Hertelendi *et al.* 1995). Another factors like: possible contamination of the dated samples by older charcoal, discovered in clayey layers the anthropogenic pits were dug into, as well as 'old-wood problem' also contribute to our scepticism as regards such an early

dating. In brief, the date of 5.500 BC seems to be the most accurate as to the dawn of the Neolithic in the Eastern Slovakian Lowland.

We reckon that analyses of the First Neolithic pottery from the north-eastern part of the Carpathian Basin suggest this category of material culture cannot provide

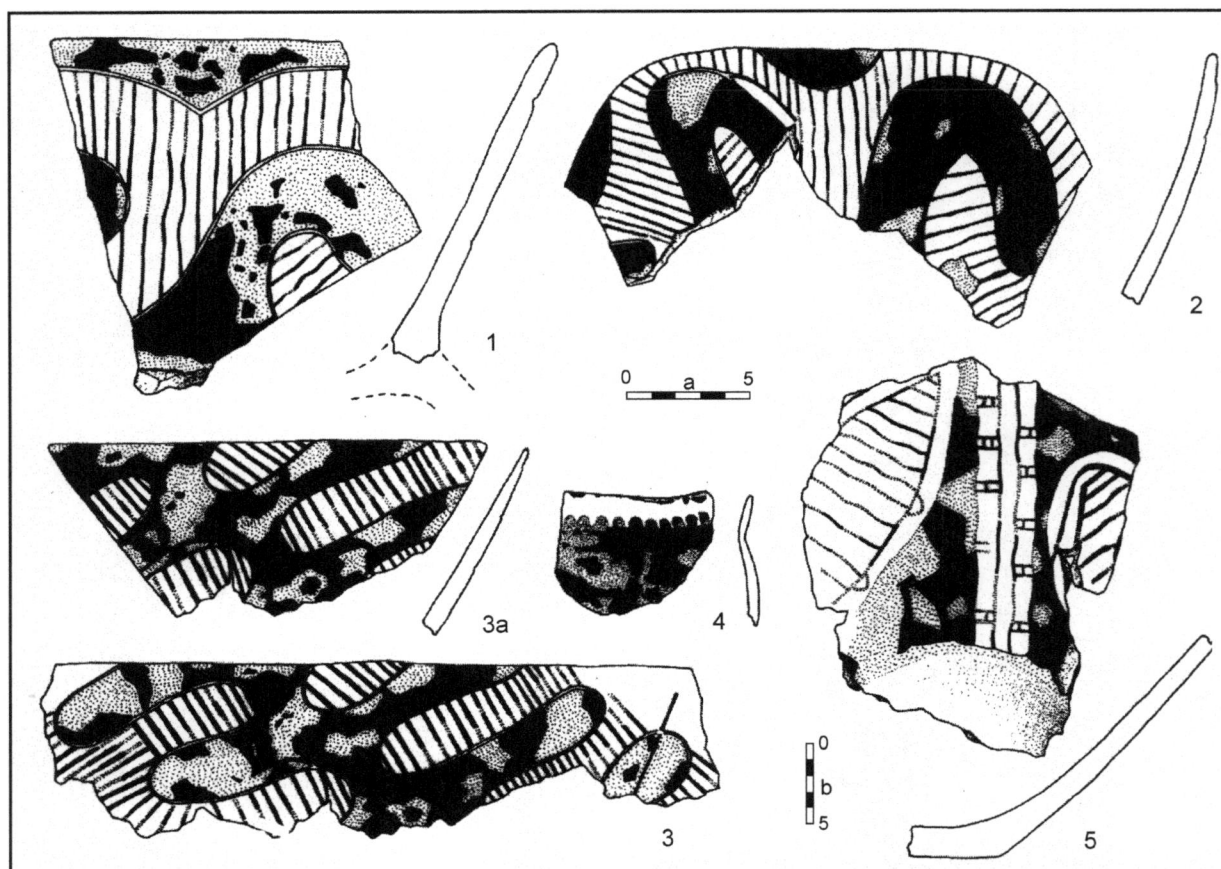

Fig. 7.9. Fine pottery from First Neolithic site at Slavkovce (after Vizdal 1997).
1, 3, 3a. Hollow-pedestalled bowls, 4. vase with low neck, 5. conical bowl.
Scale: a – 4; b – 1, 2, 3, 3a, 5.

us exclusively with unequivocal data referring to the course of neolithisation. The problem steams from the situation that at many Eastern Linear sites among the ceramic finds we can identify specimens with more archaic features (technological, morphological or ornamental) and specimens with younger features. Such a situation there brings about the risk of the subjective selection of certain features and an overestimate of features considered to be typical of one or another culture group. Our intention is not to question the methodology used so far for the distinguishing of taxonomic ("cultural") units and phases, but to point to "exceptions" which – after all – occur regularly and do not correspond to the accepted models. To illustrate this case we felt allowed to mention the pottery from Moravany and Slavkovce (Kaczanowska *et al.* 2002; Vizdal 1997) where according to M. Vizdal archaic, almost Körös-like characteristics are present in the group of coarse-ware vessels (Fig. 7.8), but on the other hand highly developed painted ornamentation (Figs. 7.9, 7.10) suggests younger chronology.

There is clearly visible difference between distribution of Early Linear sites with and without painted pottery and this situation continues to exist during the developed stage of AVK (Potushniak 1997; Raczky & Anders 2003). The high frequency of painted ornamentation seems to be typical for more eastern part of AVK; consequently some authors (like M. Potushniak – 1997: 37-39) have shared the opinion that a quite separate archaeological unit called Painted Pottery Culture should be distinguished here. Certainly, we could discuss this matter continuously. Actually, it depends on individual understanding of such a term as the archaeological culture. Anyway, it is our belief that this phenomenon reflects the real existence of at least two long-lasting communication spheres amongst AVK societies. We presume that the roots of eastern one, i.e. painted pottery communication sphere, should be sought in Transylvania. In other words, Early Linear sites with the painted pottery in Transcarpathian Ukraine, the Eastern Slovakian Lowland, and in the north-easternmost Hungary were linked genetically with Transylvanian Early Neolithic.

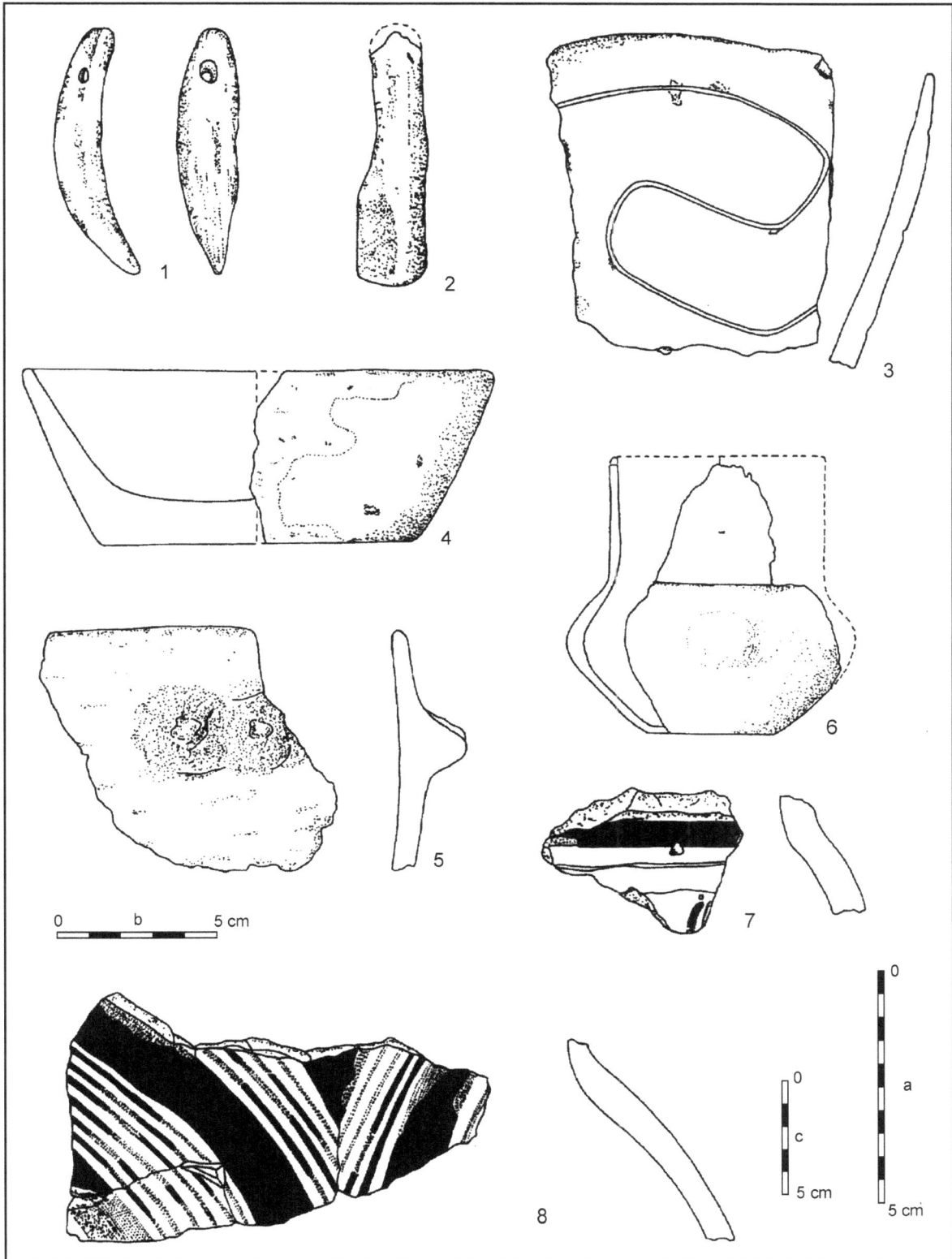

Fig. 7.10. Pottery from First Neolithic site at Moravany (after Kozłowski *et al.* 2003).
1. Pendant in the shape of animal tooth, 2. rod-shaped object (?), 3. hollow-pedestalled or conical bowl,
4. thick-walled bowl ("roasting pan"), 5. pot, 6. vase with collar, 7-8. large, vase-like vessels (?).
Scale: a – 1, 2, 7; b – 3, 5; c – 4, 6, 8.

Some similarities in ceramic technology (e. g. mineral temper) may also support this opinion (Lazarovici, Maxim 1995: 376-377).

LITHIC PRODUCTION OF THE FIRST NEOLITHIC IN THE NORTH-EASTERN PART OF THE CARPATHIAN BASIN

In the Early Neolithic sites in the eastern part of the Carpathian Basin ascribed to the Körös culture we can see a rather radical disappearance of the technological tradition that was typical for the Early Balkan Neolithic. This tradition is registered in the lithic industry of the units with white-painted ceramics as well as in the Starčevo culture. In the Early Balkan Neolithic:

i) Macroblade technology is based on off-site preparation of cores, primarily from "Balkan" flint from north Bulgaria. These cores were reduced mostly on-site, in several episodes, providing blades and core rejuvenation products (sometimes kept for further use, e.g. at Endröd 39 stored in a vessel - Kaczanowska *et al.* 1981). Core discard in that model was minimal; but core caches are recorded occasionally (at Lepenski Vir III – also in a vessel – Srejović 1969). Such taphonomic processes created assemblages where discard of debitage products was fairly small; unretouched blades or blade tools predominate (see: Gatsov 1993, Kaczanowska & Kozłowski 1987). In terms of anthropology this model could mean that specialized workshops functioned, which produced tools to meet the demands of a fairly broad market. In all likelihood goods were supplied by itinerant knappers. This model accounts for the presence of pressure technique of blade production at some sites. In some aspects it resembles lithic goods procurement system, such as we can see at the PPNB sites (the so-called BAI complex – Kozłowski 1999), and – subsequently – in the Eneolithic (Kaczanowska & Kozłowski 2000).

ii) Retouched tools production used mainly lateral retouches to shape retouched blades, less often transversal retouch to form end-scrapers and backed pieces.

iii) As a rule tools are highly curated in this industry what has been confirmed by analyses of reduction cycle of retouched blades and use-wear examinations.

The changes which take place in the lithic industry of the Körös culture communities, especially as it spreads into the north-east part of the Carpathian Basin, first of all are visible in transferring lithic production to the level of an individual household. As a result:

i) The full production cycle: from unworked flint concretions to retouched tools is an on-site activity. Consequently, off-site workshops with specialised knappers have vanished, and raw materials procurement is embedded within everyday activities.

ii) The such effect of production process was that local and meso-local raw materials were worked; in the Upper Tisza Basin these were mainly Carpathian obsidian and limnoquartzite, sometimes radiolarites. Extralocal raw material were rare.

iv) The on-site discard of cores and debitage products is considerable; cores are exploited in a single episode until the final phase. In the majority of cases the knapper did not attempt to preserve such core features as flaking surface convexity, appropriate coring angle, *cintrage*, rejuvenation of core preparation and other parameters that would have enabled to obtain blade blanks until the final phase of reduction.

v) Tools are frequently of expedient types; this is particularly well seen in the case of retouched blades which have marginal retouch and are not retrimmed as they were being used. In terms of typological tradition lateral retouches predominate, indicating clearly the tradition of the Early Neolithic macroblade industries.

Industries with such parameters are typical for the Körös culture sites that are close to the agro-ecological boundary line in the Hungarian Plain: on one side encroaching into the northern part of the Middle Tisza Basin (Nagykörü-Cooperative-Orchard, Tiszaszölos-Domaháza, Tiszagyenda – Garaholom, Kotelek-Felsöfeld, Raczky *et al.* in press), and on the other side entering deep into the Upper Tisza Basin (Méhtelek-Nadas, Tiszabezdéd-Sevapa, Ibrány). The evidence of radiometric chronology of the sites of Nagykörü and Tiszaszölös-Domaháza (5.990–5.620 and 5.850–5.629 BC respectively - Raczky *et al.* in press, Domboróczki 2005) tells us that this process had taken place relatively early.

The lithic tradition in the period between *ca.* 5.750 to 5.500 BC is recorded supremely by the rich assemblage from Méhtelek (Fig. 7.11) (Kalicz & Makkay 1977; Kozłowski 2001; Starnini 1993; 1994; 2001). This assemblage still retained the traditional features of the Balkan macroblade tradition: the occasional use of Balkan flint for the production of large blades (Starnini 2001, fig. 2:1), and the presence of rare blades and blade tools from Balkan flint (Fig. 7.11: 1-3) (Starnini 2001, fig. 3:9), quantitative domination of blade tools with marginal retouch (up to 30% of all tools – Kozłowski 2001: 249). At the same time, all the aforementioned characteristics of the Körös culture

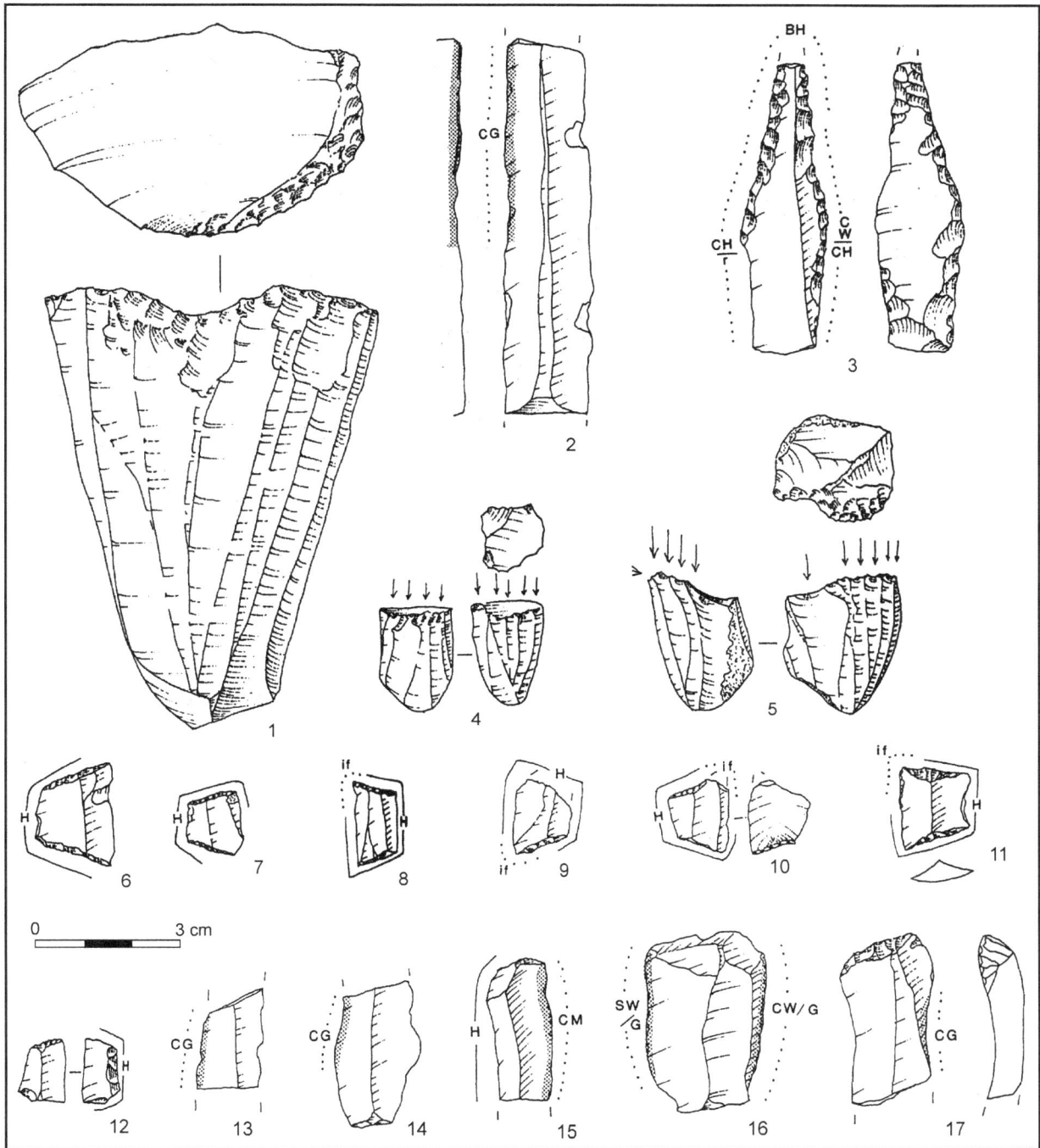

Fig. 7.11. Chipped lithics from First Neolithic site at Méhtelek-Nadas (after Starnini 1993; 1994; 2001). (1. Blade core, 2. sickle blade, 3. perforator, 4-5. bladelet cores, 6-12. trapezes, 13-16. sickle blades, 17. end-scraper. 1-3: Balkan flint, 4-17: obsidian and limnoquarzite.)

cultural tradition can also be seen, namely: on-site production of medium and small blades (mainly from obsidian and limnoquartzite) from single-platform sub-conical cores with prepared platforms (Fig. 7.11: 4), a large proportion of debitage products discarded on the site, the use of unretouched blades that were often broken off or fractured to be used as sickle inserts (Karanovo type sickles) (Fig. 7.11: 13-16). Moreover, the ratio of end-scrapers and truncations (10–20%) is larger than in the Early Balkan Neolithic. The presence of retouched flakes is also noteworthy. Numerous trapezes (Fig. 7.11: 6-12), that are typologically varied;

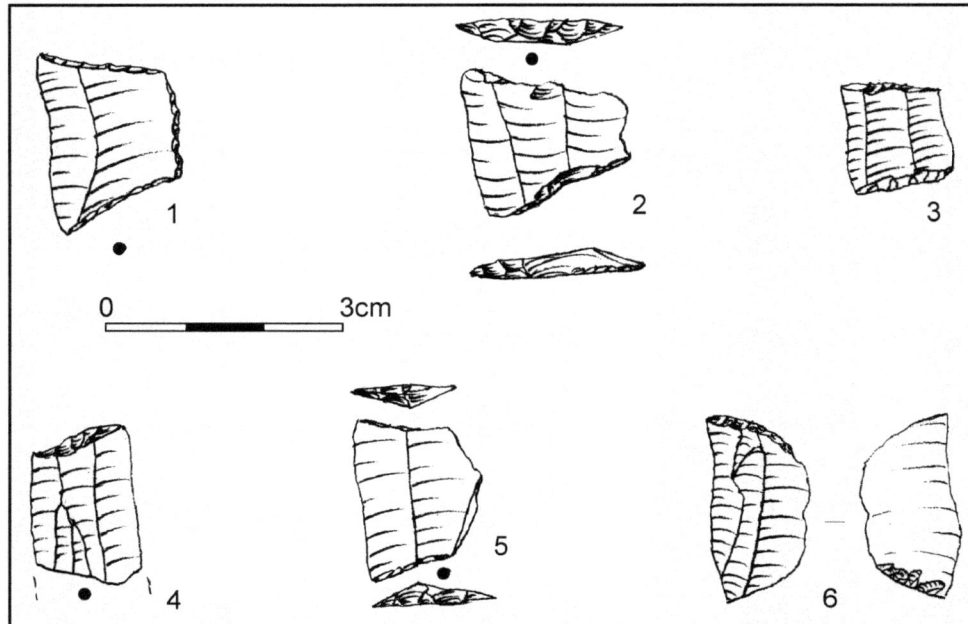

Fig. 7.12. Obsidian trapezes from First Neolithic site at Zastavne – Mala Hora.

symmetrical, simple, with alternate retouch, trapezes with three retouched sides, are the specific element of the lithic industry. As far as technique is concerned these trapezes do not show the use of microburin technique but retouch was made on breaks or fractures, sometimes removing the bulb. For this reason we are not able to regard them as representing the Late Mesolithic tradition but – just as in other First Neolithic assemblages – as an independent invention related most probably to the growing role of hunting in the north-east part of the Carpathian Basin in the Early Neolithic. This function is documented by frequent occurrence of impact fractures.

One of the northernmost Körös culture sites is Zastavne-Mala Hora (first of all hut 3/82 – Potushniak 1992). At this site elements of the Early Balkan Neolithic tradition in the chipped stone industry are not so apparent. Among raw materials obsidian is most important (90%), a small component of local andesites was used (first of all, for the production of flake tools) and some chalcedony. Medium-size blades (2.5 – 4.0 cm) were detached from flat, single-platform cores with broad flaking surfaces without preparation (except for butts). Just as at Méhtelek the largest group among tools are blades with marginal retouch (often notched, discontinuous); they are accompanied by single end-scrapers, and fine perforators. Numerous trapezes (Fig. 7.12) in variety of shapes also occur (symmetrical, asymmetrical, with three retouched sides, even with convex, alternately retouched truncations). All the trapezes were made on segments of broken blades, by

– sometimes – removing bulbs by proximal retouch. Similar features are exhibited by other, located the mostly northward and east Körös culture sites.

Summing up we can say that as the Körös culture comes interchangeably to the agro-ecological boundary in the north-eastern part of the Carpathian Basin essential changes take place in the approach to the lithic production both in the techno-typological aspect as well as in the organization of the production and its position in the socio-economic system. These changes correlate well with the fast adaptation of the economy to new ecological conditions. Moreover, these changes were stimulated by induced modifications in the ideology and beliefs, but they were, first of all, the effect of internal developmental dynamics of the Körös culture itself. No evidence exists to be obvious that the changes should have been adopted from Mesolithic communities, especially as Mesolithic settlement in that area was sparse.

The lithic production tradition that was created in the northern peripheries of the Körös culture played a vital role in the formation of industries of the Eastern Linear Pottery culture. Typical industries of this stage are recorded at the Eastern Slovakian Plain, such as Slav-kovce (Kozłowski 2001; Kaczanowska & Kozłowski 1997) and Moravany (Kozłowski et al. 2003; Kalicki et al. 2005). At these sites we record all the characteristic features which appeared in the Körös culture industries close to the agro-ecological boundary zone. The most important ones are listed below:

i) A full cycle of on-site production based on bladelet/bladelet-flake technology. Mainly single-platform blade cores were used with preparation restricted to the platform.

ii) All debitage products remained at the site and each household cluster had its own workshop (including a pit for production waste). Waste pits could contain as many as 1.600 artefacts, among them more than 50 cores, more than 1.100 flakes and chips and up to 350 unretouched blades and 150 tools for example at Moravany (feature 2/99).

iii) The most important raw materials were obsidian (mainly Carpathian obsidian 2) and limnoquartzite, also from the Zemplin-Prešov Plateau and the Slanské Mountains. Raw materials from the territories northward appear sporadically, namely: Carpathian radiolarite, occasionally Trans-Carpathian raw materials (e.g. at Moravany a trapeze made of chocolate flint). Such raw materials could be the evidence of contacts with the LBK groups in south-east Poland (for example: the site of Gwoździec near Tarnów where – in turn – a trapeze made from limnoquartzite was found). The role of the Janisławice culture is also possible in the trade of Trans-Carpathian raw materials especially as obsidian appears at Janislawician sites in southern Poland (Szeliga 2002).

iv) The structure of retouched implements shows typical predominance of blades with lateral retouch; end-scrapers, retouched flakes are less numerous.

In some early Linear assemblages the presence of backed bladelets – although in small quantities – was also recorded. They appear at Moravany (Kozłowski *et al.* 2003, fig. 7:6), Slavkovce (Kaczanowska & Kozłowski 1997, Pl. VI–11,3) and Zbudza (*ibid.*:, Pl. VI–19,14). At Zbudza a scalene triangle was also discovered (*ibid.* Pl. VI–20,16). The sporadic occurrence of these microliths suggests that – after the emergence of Linear ceramics – contacts with the Mesolithic groups could have existed. They need not have taken place in the Carpathian Basin, but north of the Carpathians where in the second half of the sixth millennium BC – or even in the first half of the fifth millennium BC – many groups of Mesolithic population occupied the areas beyond the loess territories settled by the LBK groups.

SETTLEMENT AND ECONOMY

The analyses of environmental context of the First Neolithic sites conducted for the Eastern Slovakian Lowland show that there were three main types of their location (Figs. 7.13, 7.14).

1) The first type is connected with hill lands, but the plains were also important when a larger area around two sites was considered.

2) In the second type, the proportion of tables is significant, but plains are prevailing, therefore, we could call it a transitional (plain/table) type.

3) The third type, in practice, can be called a plain type, as almost only plains are present around the sites.

It must be said that locations of the first and second types – but especially of the first type – are rather unusual when we take into account the previous state of knowledge about the settlement pattern of first farmers in Carpathian Basin (e. g. Chapman 1994; 1997; Gillings 1997; Shiel 1997; Sümegi 2004b). In other words, it should be emphasised that there are sites in the Eastern Slovakian Lowland that have relatively high locations or lie at least close to higher areas. As regards some sites, they have more or less the same access to two types of environment, that is to plains as well as tables or hill lands. The observed transitional pattern is confirmed by the results of archaeozoological analyses performed in the case of two sites: Malé Raškovce and Slavkovce (Fig. 7.15) (Godula 1997). They demonstrate that people living there in the mid-sixth millennium BC exploited both the waterlogged, flooded plain and higher terrain (tables), west of their settlements. When everything is considered, it seems interesting that at least some of the earliest Neolithic groups exploited not only plains but also higher environmental zones. These phenomena appear to be a kind of adaptation to slightly different geo-ecological conditions than those in the central and southern Great Hungarian Plain.

A scarcity of archaeobotanical and archaeozoological data from First Neolithic context in North-East Carpathian Basin does not allow to draw any reliable conclusion as to relations between domesticated and wild food although most of available research (Fig. 7.16) suggest predominance of domesticated ("traditional") food (Bartosiewicz 2005; Bogaard 2004: 53; 2005: 182-3; Craig *et al.* 2005; Moskal *et al.* 2007; Raczky *et al.* in press). Interestingly enough, the frequency of wild animals seems to be higher in many later archaeological units (Gál 2005: 149-54; Vörös 1994), similarly to many post-LBK units in more Central Europe.

Pollen spectra could be other source of information about prehistoric economy and settlement. Traces of the First Neolithic populations activity in north-eastern part of Carpathian Basin are a bit ambiguous though. They are not connected only with evident deforestation, appearance of *Cereal* pollen and other taxa typical

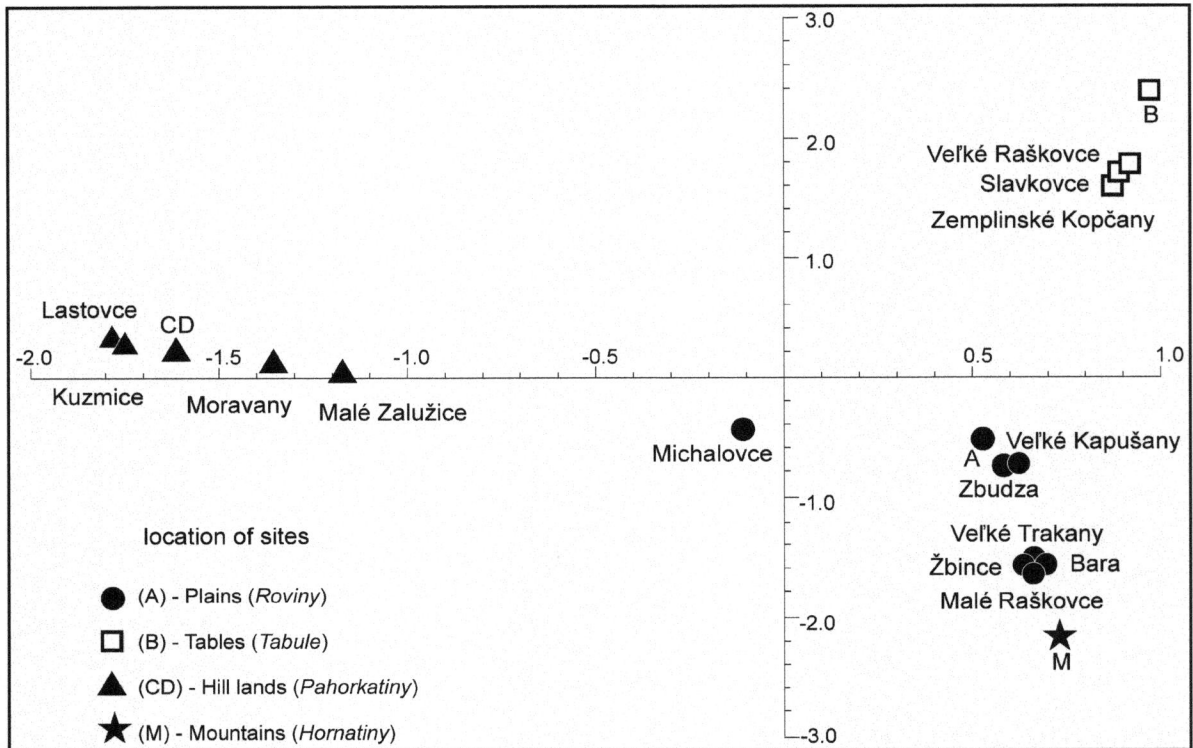

Fig. 7.13. Environmental context of the First Neolithic sites in Eastern Slovakian Lowland -
correspondence analysis of the 1 km "catchment areas".

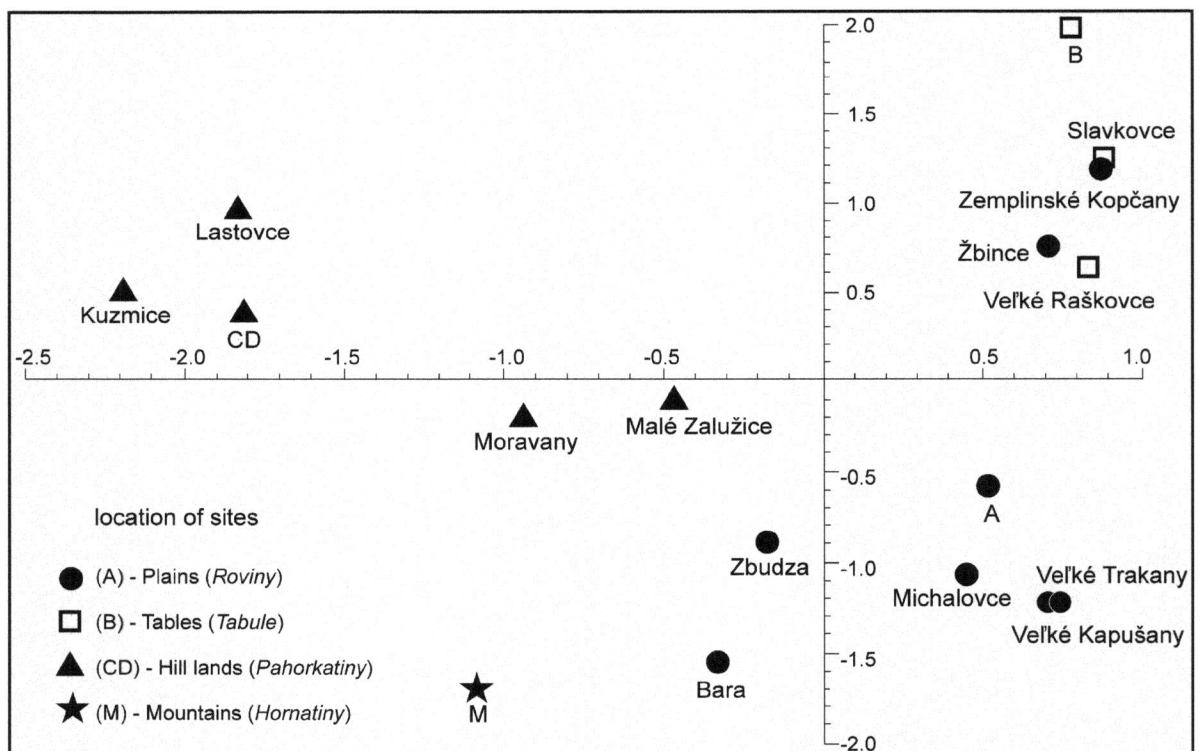

Fig. 7.14. Environmental context of the First Neolithic sites in Eastern Slovakian Lowland -
correspondence analysis of the 5 km "catchment areas".

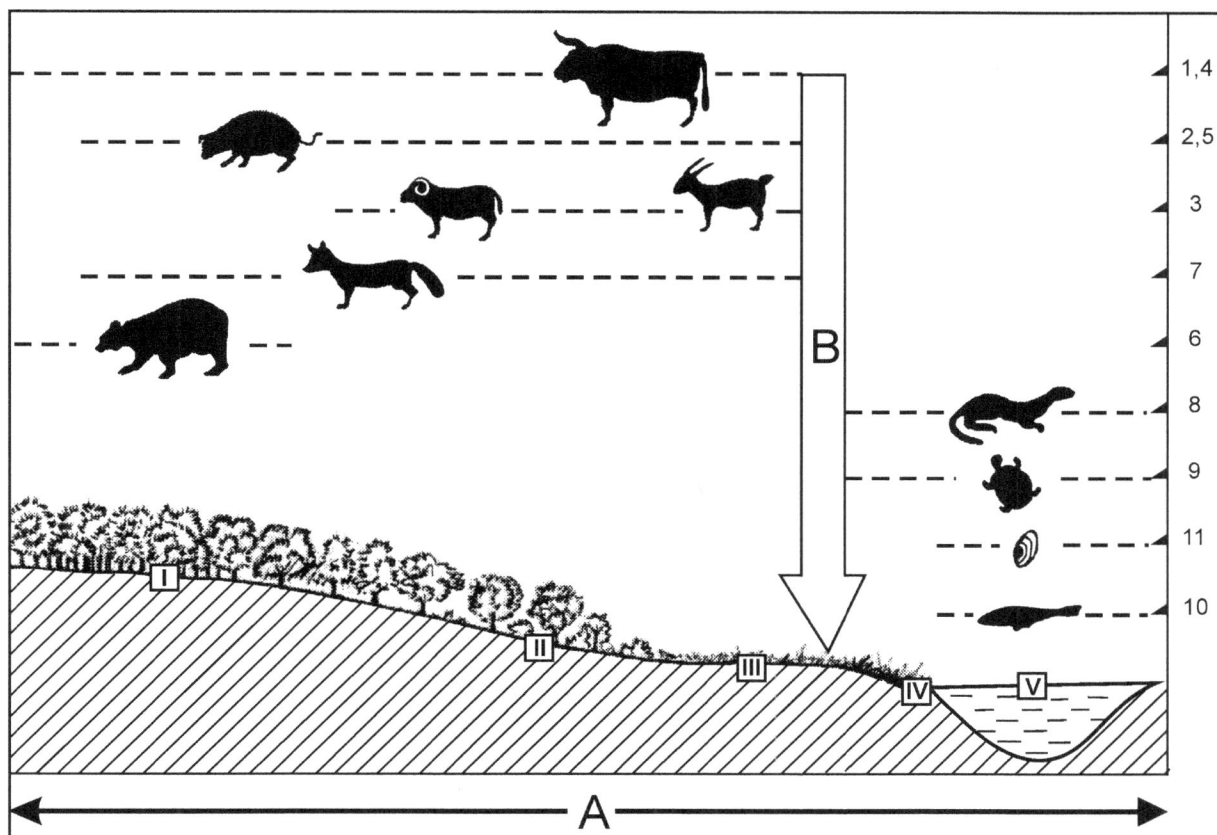

Fig. 7.15. The model of the location of First Neolithic sites at Malé Raškovce and Slavkovce
and their "site territory" indicated by characteristic animal species identified on these sites.
I – extended wood, II – open wood and bush, III – open steppe, IV – marsh, V – water (after Godula 1997).

for agro-pastoral economy (like for instance *Plantago lanceolata*). There are still situations that include floristic transformations either exclusively (Kis-Mohos-Tó - Juhász 2005a: 43, Willis *et al.* 1998, Nagy-Mohos-Tó - Juhász 2005b: 50) or combined with some classical agro-pastoral attributes (Bátorlieget, Báb-tava, Csaroda – Juhász 2005b: 50; Sümegi & Gulyás (eds.) 2004: 325; Willis *et al.* 1995). I. Juhász's interpretation of the former impact points at the stockbreeding activity and coppicing, whereas the latter impacts are considered to reflect the progressive opening of the forest environ-ment.

Similarly, other profiles in northern Hungary (e.g. Tarnabod – Gardner 2005) do not exhibit the degradation of plant cover or erosional processes related to Neolithic economy. Such a situation can at least partially be accounted for by the fact that naturally open land, suitable for agriculture, did not require the clearance prior to tending land.

Some results of palaeogeographical research around Early Linear settlement at Moravany (with agriculture

activity proved by archaeobotany – Fig. 7.16) across the Šarkan valley also suggest the lack of major human influence on environment in the First Neolithic period (Kalicki *et al.* 2004; 2005; 2007). The bottom of the valley is filled with 3-metre thick silts containing numerous charcoals and vegetational macroremnants. Some layers with a sandy-gravel admixture could be distinguished inside this silty member. These deposits, on different levels, reflected the channel changes during the filling of the valley. Radiocarbon dating helped us to establish the aftermath of events caused by climatic fluctuations and human impact. Four AMS-radiocarbon datings (Poz-10271: 146.4±-0.3 pMC; Poz-10272: 250±35 BP; Poz-10273: 145±35 BP; Poz-10274: 154.2± -0.3 pMC) indicate that the alluvia of the valley are much younger than Neolithic. In other words, there are no traces of the activity of Neolithic people. It was a deep valley with a perennial creek for most of the Holocene (this inference resolves the problem of water supply for the Neolithic settlement). The filling processes began in the Little Ice Age, most probably after the Maunder minimum (1675-1715 AD).

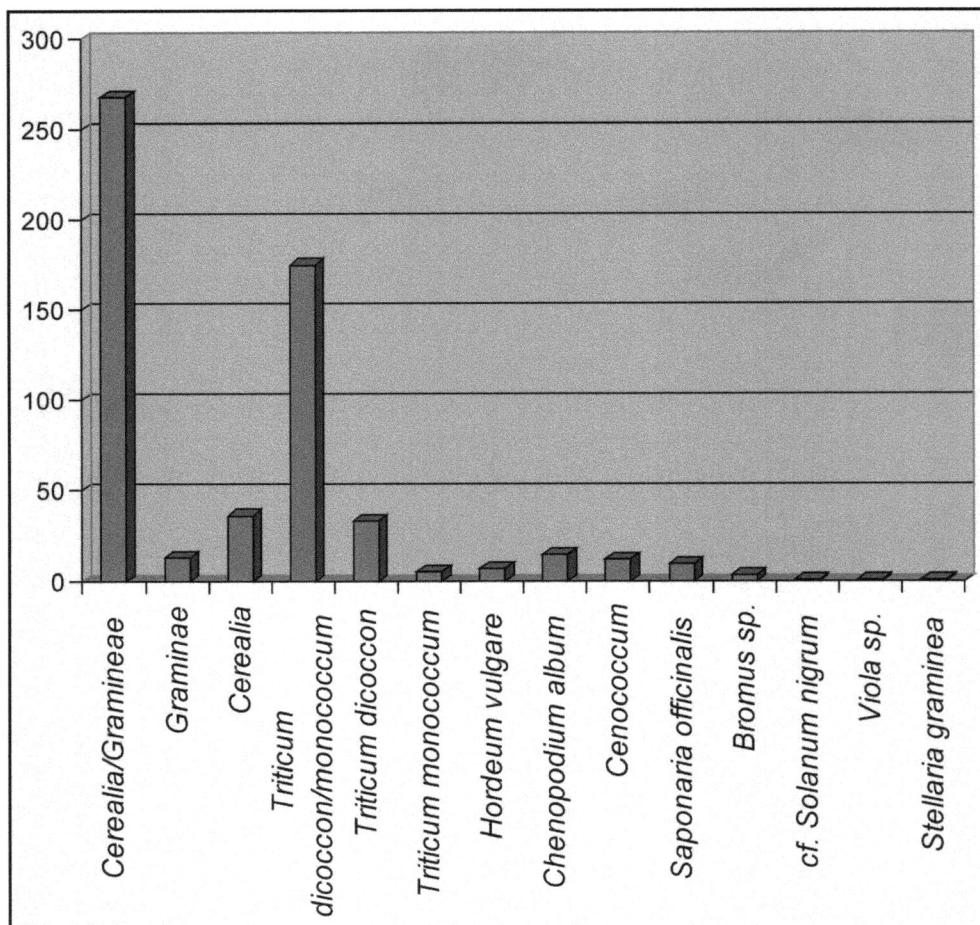

Fig. 7.16. Moravany. A summary diagram depicting results of archaeobotanical analyses of wet-sieved samples from anthropogenic features and plant imprints on daub (by M. Lityńska-Zając)

CONCLUSION

In the context of the Neolithisation of the Upper Tisza Basin three points of utmost importance should be mentioned: i) similarities between pottery of the Earliest AVK in the Eastern Slovakian Lowland and Zastavne/Rivne I assemblages as well as the pottery of the Transylvanian Criş/Körös culture; ii) traces of the Körös (FTN) advances in chipped lithic industries of the Earliest AVK in the area under consideration (Kaczanowska & Kozłowski 1997; Kozłowski et al. 2003); iii) the scarcity of Mesolithic sites in the Eastern Slovakian Lowland, iv) predominance of 'domesticated food' in the First Neolithic of the Carpathian Basin.

Putting together these pieces of evidence, we reckon that the origin of the Neolithic in the Upper Tisza Basin could be viewed as a three-stage process (Fig. 7.17).

1. Before *ca.* 5.700 BC, the Körös/Criş culture had existed in the southern and central part of the Great Hungarian Plain and possibly some Late Mesolithic groups in its northern part.

2. A migration of Körös/Criş people to Transcarpathian Ukraine took place *ca.* 5.700 BC; as a result the Méhtelek and Zastavne/Rivne I assemblages appeared there.

3. *Ca.* 5.550 BC the further migration from Transcarpathian Ukraine to the Eastern Slovakian Lowland occurred and the Kopčany Group came into being. Either at the same time or slightly later, the Szatmár group emerged in northern Alföld, due to the Körös/Criş movement towards the upper Tisza Basin. Perhaps the earliest Neolithic settlement in the Košice Basin (Košice-Červený rak) is also an outcome of the latter movement.

There is no evident proof that local Mesolithic populations participated in the proposed scenario of

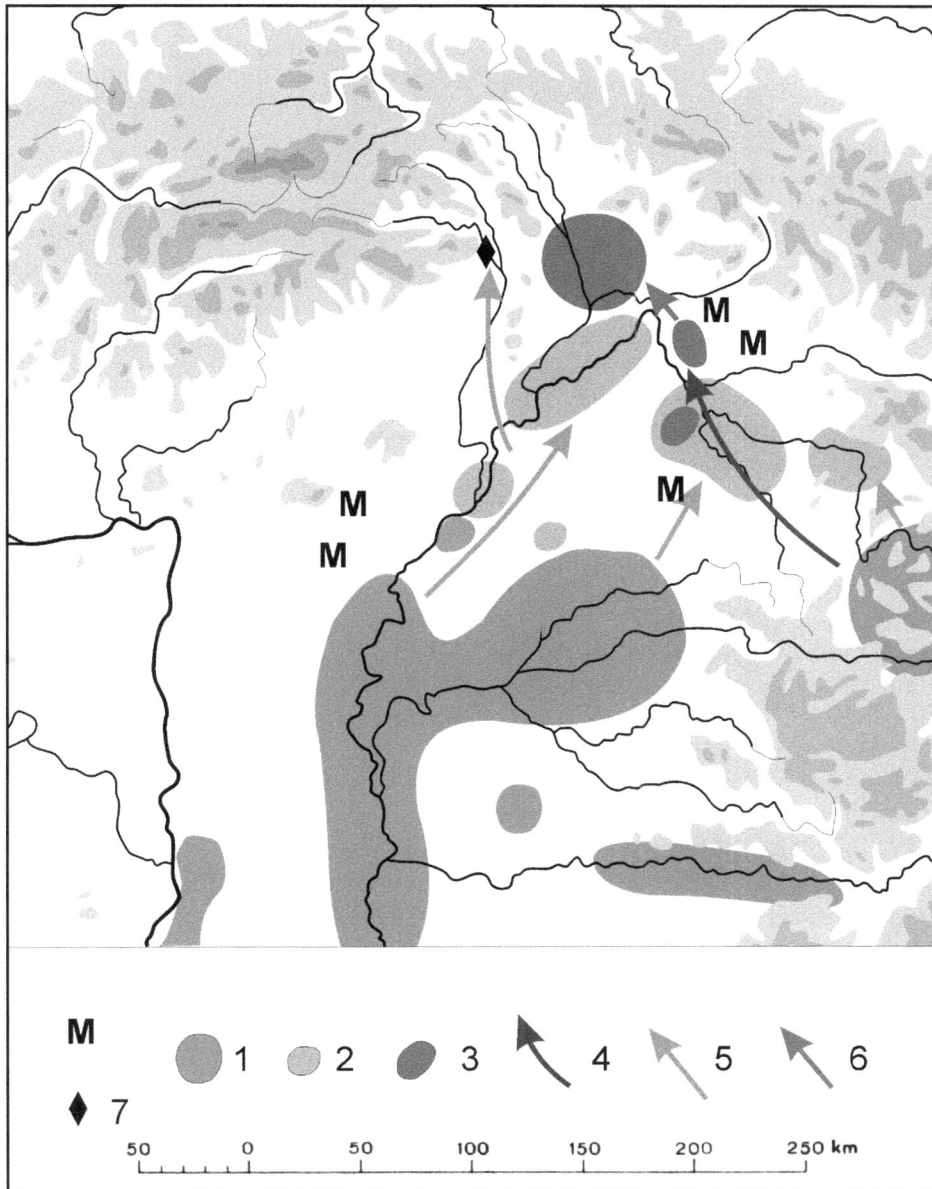

Fig. 7. 17. Neolithisation of the Upper Tisza Basin – a model (see explanation in the text).
M – Late Mesolithic; 1 – Körös-Criş; 2 – Szatmár; 3 – Méhtelek, Zastavne/Rivne, Kopčany;
4 – movement *ca*. 5.700 BC; 5, 6 – movements *ca*. 5.550 BC; 7 - Košice-Červený rak.

neolithisation. On the other hand, we presume that the very convincing model of forager – farmer (Mesolithic – Neolithic) coexistence in the mosaic-like environment, postulated recently by Pal Sümegi (Raczky *et al*. in press; Sümegi 2003: 56-8; 2004a: 122-6), can be also implemented in the area under consideration in the Linear period. Consequently participation of indige-nous foragers in Neolithisation could have taken place simultaneously with further development of AVK and perhaps of later archaeological units.

References

BAILEY, D. W. (2000) *Balkan Prehistory. Exclusion, Incorporation and Identity*. London: Routledge.

BAŇACKÝ, V., VASS, D., KALIČIAK, M., REMŠIK, A. & POSPIŠIL, L. (1987) *Vysvetlivky ku geologickej mape severnej časti Vychoslovenskej Nížiny v mierke 1:50.000*. Bratislava.

BÁNFFY, E. (2000) The Late Starčevo and the Earliest Linear Pottery groups in western Transdanubia. *Documenta Praehistorica*, 27: pp. 173-187.

BÁNFFY, E. (2004a) *The 6th Millennium BC Boundary in Western Transdanubia and its Role in the Central European Neolithic Transition (the Szentgyörgyvölgy-Pityerdomb Settlement)*. Budapest: Archaeological Institute of the Hungarian Academy of Sciences.

BÁNFFY, E. (2004b) Advances in the research of the Neolithic transition in the Carpathian Basin. In LUKES, A. & ZVELEBIL, M., eds. *LBK Dialogues. Studies in the formation of the Linear Pottery Culture*. Oxford: BAR Publishing, pp. 49-71. (BAR International Series; 1304).

BÁNFFY, E. (2005a) Mesolithic-Neolithic contacts as reflected in ritual finds. *Documenta Praehistorica*, 32: pp. 73-86.

BÁNFFY, E. (2005b) The Csaroda area during the Mesolithic, the Neolithic and the Copper Age. In GÁL, E., JUHÁSZ, I. & SÜMEGI, P., eds. *Environmental Archaeology in North-Eastern Hungary*. Budapest: Archaeological Institute of the Hungarian Academy of Sciences, pp. 207-221.

BÁNFFY, E. (2006) Eastern, Central, and Western Hungary – variations of Neolithisation models. *Documenta Praehistorica*, 33: pp. 125-142.

BARTOSIEWICZ, L. (2005) Plain talk: animals, environment and culture in the Neolithic of the Carpathian Basin and adjacent areas. In BAILEY, D., WHITTLE, A. & CUMMINGS, V., eds. *(Un)settling the Neolithic*. Oxford: Oxbow, pp. 51-63.

BIAGI, P. & SPATARO, M. (2005) New observations on the radiocarbon chronology of the Starčevo-Criş and Körös cultures. In NIKOLOVA, L. & HIGGINS, J., eds. *Prehistoric Archaeology & Anthropological Theory and Education*, pp. 35-52. (RPRP 6-7).

BOGAARD, A. (2004) The nature of early farming in Central and South-East Europe. *Documenta Praehistorica*, 31: pp. 49-58.

BOGAARD, A. (2005) 'Garden agriculture' and the nature of early farming in Europe and the Near East. *World Archaeology*, 37: pp. 177-196.

BOJADJEV, J., DIMOV, T. & TODOROVA, H. (1993) Les Balkans Orientaux. In KOZŁOWSKI, J. K., ed. *Atlas du Néolithique européen, vol. 1. L'Europe orientale*. Liège: Université de Liège, pp. 61-110 (Études et Recherches Archéologiques de l'Université de Liège; 45).

BRAUN, M., SÜMEGI, P., TÓTH, A., WILLIS, K. J., SZALÓKI, I., MARGITAI, Z. & SOMOGYI, A. (2005) Reconstruction of long-term environmental changes at Kelemér-Kis-Mohos-Tó. In GÁL, E., JUHÁSZ, I. & SÜMEGI, P., eds. *Environmental Archaeology in North-Eastern Hungary*. Budapest: Archaeological Institute of the Hungarian Academy of Sciences, pp. 25-38.

BUDJA, M. (2001) The transition to farming in Southeast Europe: perspectives from pottery. *Documenta Praehistorica*, 28: pp. 27-47.

CHAPMAN, J. (1994) Social power in the early farming communities of Eastern Hungary - Perspectives from the Upper Tisza region. *Jósa András Múzeum Évkönyve*, 36: pp. 79-101.

CHAPMAN, J. (1997) Places as timemarks – the social constructions of prehistoric landscapes in Eastern Hungary. In CHAPMAN, J. & DOLUKHANOV, P., eds. *Landscapes in Flux. Central and Eastern Europe in Antiquity*. Oxford: Oxbow, pp. 137-162.

CRAIG, O. E., CHAPMAN, J., HERON, C., WILLIS, L. H., BARTOSIEWICZ, L., TAYLOR, G., WHITTLE, A. & COLLINS, M. (2005) Did the first farmers of central and eastern Europe produce dairy foods? *Antiquity*, 79: pp. 882-894.

DERGACHEV, V., SHERATT, A. & LARINA, O. (1991) Recent results of Neolithic research in Moldavia. *Oxford Journal of Archaeology*, 10: pp. 1-17.

DOMBORÓCZKI, L. (2005) A Körös-Kultúra északi elterjedési határának problematikája Tiszaszölös-Domaháza-Pusztán végzett ásatás eredményeinek fényében. *Archeometriai Mühely*, 2005/2: pp. 5-15.

DOBOSI, V. (1972) Mesolitische Fundorte in Ungarn. *Alba Regia*, 12: pp. 39-60.

DOBOSI, V. (1983) Ásatas Tarpa-Márki tanyán. *Communicationes Archaeologicae Hungariae*, 1983: pp. 5-18.

GÁL, E. (2005) Animal remains from archaeological excavations in north-eastern Hungary. In GÁL, E., JUHÁSZ, I. & SÜMEGI, P., eds. *Environmental Archaeology in North-Eastern Hungary*. Budapest: Archaeological Institute of the Hungarian Academy of Sciences, pp. 139-174.

GARDNER, A. (1999) The ecology of Neolithic environmental impacts - ree-evaluation of existing theory using case studies from Hungary & Slovenia. *Documenta Praehistorica*, 26: pp. 163-183.

GARDNER, A. (2005) Natural environment or human impact? A palaeoecological study of two contrasting sites in North-Eastern Hungary. In GÁL, E., JUHÁSZ, I. & SÜMEGI, P., eds. *Environmental Archaeology in North-Eastern Hungary*. Budapest: Archaeological Institute of the Hungarian Academy of Sciences, pp. 87-106.

GATSOV, I. (1993) *Neolithic Chipped Stone Industries from Western Bulgaria*. Kraków: Uniwersytet Jagielloński.

GILLINGS, M. (1997) Spatial organisation in the Tisza flood plain: dynamic landscapes and GIS. In CHAPMAN, J. & DOLUKHANOV, P., eds. *Landscapes in Flux. Central and Eastern Europe in Antiquity*. Oxford: Oxbow, pp. 163-179.

GODULA, G. (1997) Animal remains from the Early Neolithic sites in eastern Slovakia. In KOZŁOWSKI, J. K. ed. *The Early Linear Pottery Culture in Eastern Slovakia*. Kraków: Polska Akademia Umiejętności, pp. 259-266.

GÖRSDORF, J. & BOJADZIEV, J. (1996) Zur absoluten Chronologie der bulgarischen Urgeschichte. *Eurasia Antiqua*, 2: 105-173.

GRONENBORN, D. (1999) A variation on a basic theme: the transition to farming in southern Central Europe. *Journal of World Prehistory*, 13: pp. 123-210.

HARBUĽOVA, Ľ. (ed.). (2002) *Dejiny Obce Moravany*. Michalovce.

HARČAR, J. (1997) The East Slovakian Lowland: general physical and geographical characteristics. In KOZŁOWSKI, J. K. ed. *The Early Linear Pottery Culture in Eastern Slovakia*. Kraków: Polska Akademia Umiejętności, pp. 7-14.

HERTELENDI, E., KALICZ, N., RACZKY, P., HORVÀTH, F., VERES, M., SVINGOR, E., FUTÓ, I. & BARTOSIEWICZ, L. (1995) Re-evaluation of the Neolithic in eastern Hungary based on calibrated radiocarbon dates. *Radiocarbon*, 37: pp. 239-244.

HORVÀTH, F., HERTELENDI, E. (1994) Contribution to the ^{14}C based absolute chronology of the Early and Middle Neolithic Tisza region. *Jósa András Múzeum Évkönyve*, 36: pp. 111-135.

JUHÁSZ, I. (2004) Palynological evidence of preneolithization in South-West Tarnsdanubia. *Antaeus*, 27: pp. 213-225.

JUHÁSZ, I. (2005a) An overview of the palaeobotanical data from Keler-Kis-Mohos-Tó, In GÁL, E., JUHÁSZ, I. & SÜMEGI, P., eds. *Environmental Archaeology in North-Eastern Hungary*. Budapest: Archaeological Institute of the Hungarian Academy of Sciences, pp. 39-45.

JUHÁSZ, I. (2005b) Comparison and correlation of the pollen sequences concerning the Holocene environmental history of the Mohos lakes at Kelemér. In GÁL, E., JUHÁSZ, I. & SÜMEGI, P., eds. *Environmental Archaeology in North-Eastern Hungary*. Budapest: Archaeological Institute of the Hungarian Academy of Sciences, pp. 47-53.

JUHÁSZ, I. (2005c) Detecting anthropogenic impacts in the palaeobotanical samples from Csaroda-Nyíres-Tó. In GÁL, E., JUHÁSZ, I. & SÜMEGI, P., eds. *Environmental Archaeology in North-Eastern Hungary*. Budapest: Archaeological Institute of the Hungarian Academy of Sciences, pp. 55-66.

KACZANOWSKA, M., KAMINSKA, L., KOZŁOWSKI, J. K., NOWAK, M. & VIZDAL, M. (2002) Badania wykopaliskowe na wczesnoneolitycznej osadzie w miejscowości Moravany na wschodniej Słowacji w latach 1998-2001. *Materiały i Sprawozdania Rzeszowskiego Ośrodka Archeologicznego*, 23: pp. 173-199.

KACZANOWSKA, M. & KOZŁOWSKI, J. K. (1987) Barbotino (Starčevo-Körös) and Linear Complex: evolution or independent development of lithic industries? *Arheološki Radove i Rasprave*, 10: pp. 25-52.

KACZANOWSKA, M. & KOZŁOWSKI, J. K. (1997) Lithic industries, In KOZŁOWSKI, J. K. ed. *The Early Linear Pottery Culture in Eastern Slovakia*. Kraków: Polska Akademia Umiejętności, pp. 177-254.

KACZANOWSKA, M. & KOZŁOWSKI, J. K. (2000) Neolithic vs Eneolithic lithic raw material procurement, technology and exchange in Eastern Central Europe In: *Uzdarje Dragoslavu Srejovicu*, Beograd, 221-234.

KACZANOWSKA, M. & KOZŁOWSKI, J. K. (2003) Origins of the Linear Pottery Complex and the Neolithic transition in Central Europe. In AMMERMAN, A. J. & BIAGI, P., eds. *The Widening Harvest: the Neolithic Transition in Europe. Looking Back, Looking Forward*. Boston: Archaeological Institute of America, 227-248.

KACZANOWSKA, M., KOZŁOWSKI, J. K. & MAKKAY, J. (1981) Flint hoard from Endröd, site 39, Hangary. *Acta Archaeologica Carpathica*, 21: pp. 105-117.

KALICKI, T., KOZŁOWSKI, J. K., NOWAK, M. & VIZDAL, M. (2005) A settlement of the Early Eastern Linear Pottery Culture at Moravany (Eastern Slovakia): palaeogeographical and archaeological perspective. In GÁL, E., JUHÁSZ, I. & SÜMEGI, P., eds. *Environmental Archaeology in North-Eastern Hungary*. Budapest: Archaeological Institute of the Hungarian Academy of Sciences, pp. 187-207.

KALICKI, T., NOWAK, M. & VIZDAL, M. (2004) Geomorphology and palaeogeography of Early Neolithic site at Moravany (Eastern Slovakia). *Geomorphologica Slovaca*, 4: pp. 62-69.

99

KALICKI, T., NOWAK, M., VIZDAL, M. & LITVINYUK, G. I. (2007) Early Neolithic settlement pattern and its influence on morphology in Eastern Slovakian Lowland. *in press*.

KALICZ, N. (1995) Die Älteste Transdanubische (Mitteleuropäische) Linienbandkeramik. Aspekte zu Ursprung, Chronologie und Beziehungen. *Acta Archaeologica Academiae Scientiarum Hungaricae*, 47: pp. 23-59.

KALICZ, N. & MAKKAY, J. (1977) *Die Linienbandkeramik in der Grossen Ungarischen Tiefebene*. Budapest: Akadémiai Kiadó.

KALICZ, N., VIRÁG, Z. M. & BIRÓ K. T. (1998) The northern periphery of the Early Neolithic Starčevo culture in south-western Hungary: a case study of an excavation at Lake Balaton. *Documenta Prehistorica*, 25: pp. 151-189.

KERTÉSZ, R. (2002) Mesolithic hunter-gaterers in the north-western part of the Great Hungarian Plain. *Preahistoria*, 3 pp. 281-304.

KERTÉSZ, R. & SÜMEGI, P. (2001) Theories, critiques and a model: Why did the expansion of the Körös-Starčevo culture stop in the centre of the Carpathian Basin? In KERTÉSZ, R. & MAKKAY, J., eds. *From the Mesolithic to the Neolithic. Proceedings of the International Archaeological Conference held in the Damjanich Museum of Szolnok, September 22-27, 1996.* Budapest: Archaeolingua, pp. 225-246.

KOSSE, K. (1979) *Settlement Ecology of the Körös and Linear Pottery Cultures in Hungary.* Oxford: BAR Publishing. (BAR Int. Series; 64).

KOZŁOWSKI, J. K. (2001) Evolution of the lithic industries of the Eastern Linear Pottery Culture, In KERTÈSZ, R. & MAKKAY, J., eds. *From the Mesolithic to the Neolithic. Proceedings of the International Archaeological Conference held in the Damjanich Museum of Szolnok, September 22-27, 1996.* Budapest: Archaeolingua, pp. 247-260.

KOZŁOWSKI, J. K. (2005) Remarks on the Mesolithic in the northern part of the Carpathian Basin. In GÁL, E., JUHÁSZ, I. & SÜMEGI, P., eds. *Environmental Archaeology in North-Eastern Hungary*. Budapest: Archaeological Institute of the Hungarian Academy of Sciences, pp. 175-186.

KOZŁOWSKI, J. K., ed. (1997) *The Early Linear Pottery Culture in Eastern Slovakia.* Kraków: Polska Akademia Umiejętności.

KOZŁOWSKI, J. K., NOWAK, M. & VIZDAL, M. (2003) A settlement of the Early Eastern Linear Pottery culture at Moravany (Eastern Slovakia) within the context of the Neolithisation of the Upper Tisza Basin. In JEREM, E. & RACZKY, P.,

eds. *Morgenrot der Kulturen. Frühe Etappen der Menschheitsgeschichte in Mittel- und Südost-europa.* Budapest: Archaeolingua, pp. 127-145.

KOZŁOWSKI, S. K. (1989) *Mesolithic in Poland. A New Approach.* Warszawa; Wydawnictwo UW, 252 pp.

KOZŁOWSKI, S. K. (1999) *The Eastern Wing of the Fertile Crescent: Late Prehistory of Greater Mesopotamian Lithic Industries.* Oxford: BAR Publishing (BAR International Series; 760).

KOZŁOWSKI, S. K. (2001) Eco-Cultural/stylistic zonation of the Mesolithic/Epipalaeolithic in Central Europe. In KERTESZ R. & MAKKAY, J., eds. *From the Mesolithic to the Neolithic. Proceedings of the International Archaeological Conference held in the Damjanich Museum of Szolnok, September 22-27, 1996.* Budapest: Archaeolingua, pp. 247-260.

KRIPPEL, E. (1986) *Postglacialny vyvoj vegetacie Slovenska.* Bratislava: Veda.

LAZAROVICI, G. & MAXIM, Z. (1995) *Gura Baciului.* Cluj-Napoca (Biblioteca Musei Napocensis; 11).

LENNEIS, E. (2001) The beginning of the Neolithic in Austria - a report about recent and current investigations. *Documenta Praehistorica*, 28: pp. 99-116.

LENNEIS, E. & STADLER, P. (2002) ^{14}C-Daten und Seriation altbandkeramischer Inventare. *Archeologické rozhledy*, 54: pp. 191-201.

LIBERA, J. & TALAR, A. (1990) Osadnictwo kultury janisławickiej w Gwoździcu, stan. 9, gm. Bojanów, woj. Tarnobrzeg, w świetle badań 1966-1967. *Sprawozdania Archeologiczne*, 42: pp. 9-68.

MANTU, C-M. (1998) Absolute chronology of Neolithic cultures in Romania and relations with the Aegeo-Anatolian world. In OTTE, M., ed. *Préhistoire d'Anatolie. Genèse de deux mondes.* Liège. pp. 159-173. (Études et Recherches Archéologiques de l'Université de Liège; 85).

MANTU, C-M. (1999) The absolute chronology of the Romanian Neolithic and Aeneolithic/Chalcolithic periods. In EVIN, J., OBERLIN, CH., DAUGAS, J-P. & SALLES, J-F., eds. *[14]C et Archéologie. 3éme Congrés International, Lyon 6-10 avril 1998.* Mémoires de la Société Préhistorique Française 26, pp. 225-32.

MATSKEVOY, L. G. (1991) *Mezolit Zapadnoj Ukrainy.* Kiev: Naukova Dumka.

MATSKEVOY, L. G. (2001) Miezolit krajniego zapada Ukrainy. In KERTÉSZ, R. & MAKKAY, J., eds. *From the Mesolithic to the Neolithic.*

Proceedings of the International Archaeological Conference held in the Damjanich Museum of Szolnok, September 22-27, 1996. Budapest: Archaeolingua, pp. 313-339.

MATSKEVOY, L. G., ADAMIENKO, O. M., PASZKIEWICZ, G. A. & TATARINOW, K. A. (1983) Prirodnaja srieda i miezolit zapada Ukrainy. *Sovietskaja Archieologia*, 1: pp. 5-29.

MAXIM, Z. (1999) *Neo-Eneoliticul din Transilvania. Date Arheologice şi Matematico-Statistice.* Cluj-Napoca (Bibliotheca Musei Napocensis; 19).

MOSKAL, M., LITYŃSKA-ZAJĄC, M. & BADAL, E. (2007) Charcoal analysis from Neolithic site of Moravany (Slovakia). *in press.*

NIKOLOVA, L. (1998) Neolithic sequence: the upper Stryama valley in western Thrace (with an appendix: radiocarbon dating of the Balkan Neolithic). *Documenta Praehistorica*, 25: 99-131.

NOWAK, M. (1997) Regional settlement patterns of the early phases of the Eastern Linear Pottery Culture in the Eastern Slovakian Lowland. In KOZŁOWSKI, J. K. ed. *The Early Linear Pottery Culture in Eastern Slovakia.* Kraków: Polska Akademia Umiejętności, pp. 15-42.

PĂUNESCU, A. (1964) Cu privire la perioda de sfirsit a epipaleoliticului in nord estul Romainiei siunele persistente ale lui in neoliticul vechi. *SCIV* 15, 3, pp.321-336.

PĂUNESCU, A. (1970) *Evoluţia uneltelor şi armelor de piatra cioplita descoperite pe teritoriul Romaniei.* Bucureşti.

POTUSHNIAK, M. (1992) Do pitania nieolitizacji wierchivia rieki Tisy. *Novi matierialy z archieologii Prikarpatia i Wolyni*, 2: pp. 15-17.

POTUSHNIAK, M. (1997) Some results of research on the Middle Neolithic layer from a multilevel settlement near the village of Zastavne/Zápszony-Kovadomb in the Carpathian Ukraine. *Jósa András Múzeum Évkönyve*, 37-38: pp. 35-50.

RACZKY, P. & ANDERS, A. (2003) The internal relations of the Alföld Linear Pottery culture in Hungary and the characteristics of human representation. In JEREM, E. & RACZKY, P., eds. *Morgenrot der Kulturen. Frühe Etappen der Menschheitsgeschichte in Mittel- und Südosteuropa. Festschrift für Nándor Kalicz zum 75. Geburtstag.* Budapest: Archaeolingua, pp. 155-182.

RACZKY, P., SÜMEGI, P., BARTOSIEWICZ, L., GÁL, E., KACZANOWSKA, M., KOZŁOWSKI, J. K. & ANDERS, A. (*in press*) Ecological barier versus mental marginal zone? Problems of the northernmost Körös culture settlements in the Great Hungarian Plain.

SHIEL, R. S. (1997) Surviving in the Tisza valley – plants' and people's perspectives on the environment. In CHAPMAN, J. & DOLUKHANOV, P., eds. *Landscapes in Flux. Central and Eastern Europe in Antiquity.* Oxford: Oxbow, pp. 181-192.

SREJOVIĆ, D. (1969) *Lepenski Vir. Nova praistorijska kultura u Podunavlju.* Beograd.

STARNINI, E. (1993) Typological and technological analyses of the Körös Culture chipped, polished and ground stone assemblages from Méhtelek-Nádas (north-eastern Hungary). *Atti dell Societá per la Preistoria e Protostoria della Regione Friuli Venezia-Gilulia*, 8: pp. 29-96.

STARNINI, E. (1994) Typological and technological analysis of the Körös culture stone assemblages of Méhtelek-Nadas and Tiszacsege (north-east Hungary). A preliminary report. *Jósa András Múzeum Évkönyve*, 36: 101-111.

STARNINI, E. (2001) The Mesolithic/Neolithic transition in Hungary: the lithic perspective. In KERTÈSZ, R. & MAKKAY, J., eds. *From the Mesolithic to the Neolithic. Proceedings of the International Archaeological Conference held in the Damjanich Museum of Szolnok, September 22-27, 1996.* Budapest: Archaeolingua, pp. 395-404.

STEFANOVA, T. (1996) A comparative analysis of pottery from the "Monochrome Early Neolithic Horizon" and "Karanovo I Horizon" and the problems of the Neolithization of Bulgaria. *Poročilo o raziskovanju paleolitika, neolitika in eneolitika v Sloveniji*, 23: pp. 15-38.

STEFANOVA, T. (1998) On the problem of the Anatolian-Balkan relations during the Early Neolithic in Thrace. *Documenta Praehistorica*, 25: pp. 91-97.

SÜMEGI, P. (2003) Early Neolithic man and riparian environment in the Carpathian Basin. In JEREM, E. & RACZKY, P., eds. *Morgenrot der Kulturen. Frühe Etappen der Menschheitsgeschichte in Mittel- und Südosteuropa. Festschrift für Nándor Kalicz zum 75. Geburtstag.* Budapest: Archaeolingua, pp. 53-60.

SÜMEGI, P. (2004a) Environmental changes under the Neolithisation process in Central Europe: before and after. *Antaeus*, 27: pp. 117-27.

SÜMEGI, P. (2004b) Findings of geoarchaeological and environmental historical investigations at the Körös site of Tiszapüspöki-Karancspart Háromág. *Antaeus*, 27: pp. 307-342.

SÜMEGI, P. (2005a) Pre-Neolithic development in North-Eastern Hungary. In GÁL, E., JUHÁSZ, I. & SÜMEGI, P., eds. *Environmental Archaeology in North-Eastern Hungary.* Budapest: Archaeological Institute of the Hungarian Academy of Sciences, pp. 15-24.

SÜMEGI, P. (2005b) The environmental history of the Jászság. In GÁL, E., JUHÁSZ, I. & SÜMEGI, P., eds. *Environmental Archaeology in North-Eastern Hungary*. Budapest: Archaeological Institute of the Hungarian Academy of Sciences, pp. 107-114.

SÜMEGI, P., BODOR, E. & TÖRÖCSIK, T. (2005) The origins of alkalisation in the Hortobágy region in the light of the palaeoenvironmental studies at Zám-Halasefenék. In GÁL, E., JUHÁSZ, I. & SÜMEGI, P., eds. *Environmental Archaeology in North-Eastern Hungary*. Budapest: Archaeological Institute of the Hungarian Academy of Sciences, pp. 115-126.

SÜMEGI, P. & GULYÁS, S., eds. (2004) *The Geohistory of Bátorlieget Marshland. An Example for the Reconstruction of Late Quaternary Environmental Changes and Past Human Impact from the Northeastern Part of the Carpathian Basin*. Budapest: Archaeolingua.

SÜMEGI, P., HERTELENDI, E., MAGYARI, E. & MOLNÁR, M. (1998) Evolution of the environment in the Carpathian Basin during the last 30.000 BP years and its effects on the ancient habits of the different cultures. In KÖLTÖ, L. & BARTOSIEWICZ, L., eds. *Archaeometrical Research in Hungary II*. Budapest-Kaposvár-Veszprém, pp. 183-197.

SÜMEGI, P. & KERTÉSZ, R. (2001) Palaeographic characteristics of the Carpathian Basin – an ecological trap during the Early Neolithic. In KERTÈSZ, R. & MAKKAY, J., eds. *From the Mesolithic to the Neolithic. Proceedings of the International Archaeological Conference held in the Damjanich Museum of Szolnok, September 22-27, 1996*. Budapest: Archaeolingua, pp. 405-415.

SZELIGA, M. (2002) Stan badan nad napływem obsydianu na ziemie polskie w starszej i środkowej epoce kamienia. In GANCARSKI, J. ed. *Starsza i środkowa epoka kamienia w Karpatach Polskich*. Krosno: Muzeum Podkarpackie, pp.339-358.

ŠIŠKA, S. (1989) *Kultúra s východnou lineárnou keramikou na Slovensku*. Bratislava: Veda.

ŠOLTÉSOVÁ, M., ed. (2006) *Lúčky: História a Súčasnosť*. Lúčky: Obecný úrad Lúčký.

TALAR, A. (1966) Badania powierzchniowe na terenie powiatu niżańskiego. *Sprawozdania Rzeszowskiego Ośrodka Archeologicznego za rok 1965*: pp. 121-124.

TITOV, V. (1980) Rannij i sriednij nieolit vastocznoj Wiengri. In TITOV V. & ERDELY, I., eds. *Archieologia Wiengri: Kamiennyj Viek*. Moskva: Nauka, pp. 73-249.

TODOROVA, H. & VAJSOV, I. (1993) *Novokamennata epocha v Bălgarija. Krajat na sedmosĕsto chiljadoletie predi novata era*. Sofia: Nauka i Izkustvo.

TRINGHAM, R. (2000) Southeastern Europe in the transition to agriculture in Europe: bridge, buffer, or mosaic. In PRICE, T. D., ed. *Europe's First Farmers*: Cambridge...: Cambridge University Press, pp. 19-57

VIZDAL, M. (1997) Pottery finds. In KOZŁOWSKI, J. K. ed. *The Early Linear Pottery Culture in Eastern Slovakia*. Kraków: Polska Akademia Umiejętności, pp. 43-141.

VÖRÖS, I. (1994) Animal husbandry and hunting in the Middle Neolithic settlement at Tiszavasvári-Deékhalmi dűlő (upper Tisza region). *Jósa András Múzeum Evkönyve*, 36: pp. 167-185.

WĄS, M. (2002) Składanki mezolitycznych materiałów krzemiennych kultury janisławickiej ze stanowiska Gowoździec 9, woj. podkarpackie. In MATRASZEK, B. & SAŁACIŃSKI, S., eds. *Krzemień świeciechowski w pradziejach*. Warszawa: Państwowe Muzeum Archeologiczne, pp. 71-88 (Studia nad gospodarką i surowcami krzemiennymi w pradziejach; 4).

WHITTLE, A. (1996) *Neolithic Europe. The Creation of New Worlds*. Cambridge: Cambridge University Press.

WHITTLE, A., BARTOSIEWICZ, L., BORIĆ, D., PETTITT, P. & RICHARDS, M. (2002) In the beginning: new radiocarbon dates for the Early Neolithic in northern Serbia and south-east Hungary. *Antaeus*, 25: pp. 63-117.

WILLIS, K. J., SÜMEGI, P., BRAUN, M. & TÓTH, A. (1995) The late Quaternary environmental history of Bátorlieget, N.E. Hungary. *Palaeogeography, Palaeoclimatology, Palaeoecology*, 118: pp. 25-47.

WILLIS, K. J., SÜMEGI, P., BRAUN, M., BENNETT, K. D. & TÓTH, A. (1998) Prehistoric land degradation in Hungary: who, how and why? *Antiquity* 72: pp. 101-113.

ZALIZNIAK, L. (1998) *Predistorija Ukraini X-V tis.do n.e.* Kiev: Biblioteka Ukraini, 305 pp.

ZVELEBIL, M. & LILLIE, M. (2000) Transition to agriculture in eastern Europe. In PRICE, T. D., ed. *Europe's First Farmers*: Cambridge: Cambridge University Press, pp. 57-93.

PROBLEMS IN READING THE MESOLITHIC–NEOLITHIC RELATIONS IN SOUTH-EASTERN EUROPE

Janusz Krzysztof KOZŁOWSKI

Institute of Archaeology, Jagiellonian University, Gołębia 11, 31-007 Kraków, Poland,
kozlowsk@argo.hist.uj.edu.pl

Marek NOWAK

Institute of Archaeology, Jagiellonian University, Gołębia 11, 31-007 Kraków, Poland,
mniauj@interia.pl

METHODOLOGY

Undoubtedly, the knowledge of Mesolithic/Neolithic interactions especially from the point of view of local relations between pre-Neolithic foragers and allochthonous food producing migrants, calls for interdisciplinary and multiaspectual investigations, extending far beyond the traditional analysis of archaeological sources alone. When proposing the programme of the Symposium we tried to approximate this objective. We have succeeded only partially, first of all, because the present state of archaeological sources and their analyses are inadequate, notably in the Eastern and Central Balkans and in the Middle Danube basin. A multiaspectual approach to the problem of Mesolithic/Neolithic interaction requires that results of a number of disciplines are used and that attention is focused on a variety of aspects of archeological sources.

To achieve our objective we need to make use of the knowledge of biology of interacting populations. Physical anthropology needs to be taken into account, especially:

- anthropological types (Nemeskéri & Szathmáry 1978; Menk & Nemeskéri 1989; Roksandić 2000),

- population structure in terms of age and sex (e.g. Nemeskéri & Szathmáry 1978),

- physical-chemical examinations of bone remains as to the content of elements and stable isotopes indicating the origin of these populations and their diet (Bonsall et al. 1997; 2000; 2004).

Investigations into population variability based on morphology often lead, however, to opposing conclusions. On the other hand, more precise data on population genesis are provided by palaeogenetics – although their applicability for fossil materials is limited and, sometimes, doubtful. Nonetheless, studies on the reconstruction of sequences of ancient DNA, e. g. investigations into N1a haplotypes of the Early Neolithic populations in the Tisza and the Rhein basin (Haak et al. 2005), create fascinating perspectives for the evaluation of relation between the migrating and the local populations – descendants of the pre-Neolithic populations.

Palaeodemography, too, allows to build dynamic models of neolithization processes whose verification by archaeologists requires intensive survey and excavations, perfecting dating methods and critical analysis of sources. Unfortunately, in the Balkans and the Middle Danube Basin few regions where both Mesolithic and Neolithic sites occur have been intensively explored. Among such regions belong the Iron Gate – discussed at the Symposium in several papers (Borić, Mihajlović, Roksandić), south-western Serbia and Montenegro (Mihajlović). Some researchers attempt to include Transdanubia (Banffy, Eichmann, Marton) and Turkish Thrace (Gatsov) among these territories. Regretfully, because critical analysis of sources from surface surveys is insufficient, the attempts at reconstruction of the pre-Neolithic settlement network in Argolide are inadequate (Runnels et al. 2005). Among the territories where an exceptionally complete reconstruction of Late Mesolithic and Neolithic settlement networks was done are the north-west Balkans, especially Istria with the Trieste Karst (Biagi 2001; Biagi & Spataro 2001; Biagi et al. 1993).

From the very definition of the Mesolithic and Neolithic it follows that investigations into subsistence economy, including the study of preserved archaeo-botanical and archaeozoological relics, are of vital importance for the relation between these two formations. This type of sources has been best recognized in the Iron Gate region, while in other regions, discussed at the Symposium, such sources are scarce. These aspects of studies of subsistence economy from Lepenski Vir and Vlasac (Bökönyi 1970; 1974) had been presented earlier, and recently discussed in reference to Lepenski Vir, Padina, Schela Cladovei (Bartosiewicz et al.

2001), summed up by D. Borić (2001) and Bonsall and others (2000).

The object of investigations of interactions in the sphere of material culture are, first of all, lithic artefacts at Mesolithic and Neolithic sites. Analysis of technology and style of production of stone tools allow to trace cultural traditions and mutual influences between the Mesolithic and Neolithic groups (Kozłowski & Kozłowski 1982; 1983; Kozłowski et al. 1994; Kozłowski & Kaczanowska 2006; Radovanović 1996; Mihajlović 2001; 2004 and others). At the same time, analyses of lithic raw materials and studies of raw material procurement systems enable to determine population shifts and inter-group exchange. Unquestionably, next after palaeogenetic studies, investigations into lithic industries provide the most reliable arguments that can verify hypotheses about genetic relations and various types of synchronous inter-group relations. An advantage of lithic artefacts analyses is the widespread presence of these artefacts on all Mesolithic and Neolithic sites.

In the case of bone artefacts, preserved at only some sites, and architecture the situation is different. Architecture as a type of source provided a base for interesting considerations of the origins of dwelling and ceremonial structures in the region of the Iron Gate (Srejović 1972; Radovanović 1996; Borić 2002) and in the Aegean Sea basin (Sampson ed. 2006), though it can also be used for interpretations of social structure (Chapman 1992).

From the perspective of postprocessual archaeology an important role in the process of replacement of foragers by food-producing groups is ascribed to symbolic culture, which is especially well represented in the Lepenski Vir Culture (Srejović 1969; Radovanović 1996; Borić 2001 and others).

ENVIRONMENTAL CHANGES

Environmental changes in the period spanning the Late Glacial/Holocene transition, the Early and Middle Holocene are of vital importance for the Late Mesolithic settlement and the evolution of neolithization of the Balkan zone. Just as in other parts of the Europe, in the Balkan Peninsula and in the Carpathian Basin at the Late Glacial/Holocene boundary the mean annual temperature, the level of humidity, and forest cover gradually increased (Andrič 2001; Feurdean 2005; Jeraj 2002; Lazarova & Bozilova 2001; Tantau et al. 2003; Willis 1994: 774–778; Willis et al. 1998). In most pollen profiles signs of this transformation appear between about 10.600 and 8.800 BC (Willis 1994: 778). On the other hand, the differences between the Late Glacial and the Holocene ecological conditions were not as drastic as in e.g. central Europe (Allen 2003: 368; Culiberg & Šercelj 1996: 698; Willis 1994: 769). Moreover, in the Early and Middle Holocene climatic conditions were milder than they are now. For example, mean annual temperatures are estimated as about 5°C lower than today; similarly, mean winter temperatures were higher. The level of precipitations was similar, and – consequently – humidity conditions were much better (Prentice et al. 1998: 664). The reconstruction of temperature curves in the Early and the Middle Holocene does not show a constant increasing tendency. At least one cooler oscillation should be considered (Allen 2003: 360–366, 370; Feurdean 2005: 443) corresponding, roughly, to 8.2 ka event (Alley & Augustdottir 2005: 1126–1129; Thomas et al. 2007). This oscillation could change (improve, but also disturb) humidity, or even cause disastrous floods. Such floods are suggested to have taken place in, among others, the Iron Gate region where many riverbank sites were abandoned between, about, 8.250 and 7.900 cal BP (Bonsall et al. 2002; different opinion – Borić & Miracle 2004).

The change in the vegetational cover meant not so much the appearance and growing importance of dense forest stands, but – to a large extent – replacement of coniferous forest by mixed deciduous woodland (e.g. Bátorlieget – Willis et al. 1995). However, in some, more northern, territories the proportion of coniferous species remained noticeable (Jeraj 2002; Willis et al. 1995), if not predominant (Juhász 2004: 217). Mixed deciduous woodlands were, often, more open than in Central Europe. The growth in importance of these habitats was first recorded in the south, whereas at the northern outskirts of the Carpathian Basin this process ceased at about 7.000 BC. It was the Early Atlantic period when pollen profiles in the Balkans and in the Carpathian Basin show the maximum level of indices of termophylus oak woodland (Willis 1994: 780–781). This situation differs from the one found today. In the Early and the Middle Holocene, because conditions of humidity were more favourable, "temperate deciduous forests extended into regions that now experience a Mediteranean-type climate, and where the dominant vegetation today is either evergreen/warm mixed forest of (in drier areas) xerophytic woods and scrub" (Prentice at al. 1998: 664). The beginnings of the transformation from temperate to evergreen forest in some territories could have taken place already within the period under discussion, e.g. for the Dalmatian zone such a radical change is dated to about 5.500 BC (Jahns 2002).

In their thesis C. Perlès (2001) and S. Bottema (2003) hold that the spread of dense, shady forest stands in the Early Holocene created extremely unfavourable ecological conditions for the Holocene ungulates. Consequently, conditions that enabled the functioning of hunter-gatherer communities deteriorated drastically. So much so that the territories exploited by hunter-gatherer groups in the Late Glacial had become depopulated. An attractive zone, on the other hand, are to have been large river valleys and the littoral zone, that ensured incomparably richer nutrition and food resources (Bartosiewicz & Bonsall 2005; Bottema 2003: 134; Chapman 1989). Although C. Perlès constructed this scenario for Greece, nevertheless it can easily be extended to other Balkan territories. This scenario, quite convincingly, allows to account for the lack of a greater number of Mesolithic sites in the Balkans.

Existing settlement would have concentrated in relatively small areas, in the valleys of large rivers and along the sea coast. In the effect of extremely dynamic fluvial activity on alluvial plains (Mlekuž 1999; Mlekuž et al. 2006) and erosional processes in the Early and Middle Holocene Mesolithic sites in valleys would have been buried underneath thick layers of sediments, whereas littoral sites would have disappearred in the consequence of sea transgressions and remain unavailable for archeologists.

Unfortunately, this undoubtedly attractive scenario has some weak points. Firstly, the domination of dense, shady, mixed deciduous forests was not a phenomenon restricted only to the Balkans. In central or western Europe tens of thousands of Mesolithic sites have been recorded, although – in all likelihood – in the Early Holocene forest stands in this territory were denser than in the Balkan zone. Secondly, the landscape of the Balkan Peninsula and in the Carpathian Basin during the Early and the Middle Holocene, was, in fact, much more diversified. Certainly, patches of open landscape occurred (which C. Perlès notes too: (2001: 14), but she sees the consequences only for the Neolithic), including forest-steppe and steppe formations (Božilova et al. 1996: 703–706, 727; Howard et al. 2004: 274; Juhász 2004: 218). An example of the presence of open habitats is the expansion of pistachio (*Pistacia lentiscus* and *Pistacia terebinthus*) in Greece between about 8.250 and 7.000 years BC (Willis 1994: 779–780). Because these are the species typical of dry, open woodlands and scrub, in the northern areas of the Balkan zone there must have existed such habitats before, at least, 7.000 BC. Ecological conditions in those habitats must have remained favourable for hunter-gatherer populations. The fairly high degree of continuity between the Late Glacial and the Holocene environments (the higher proportion of AP in pollen profiles is marked as early as about 14.000 BP – Allen 2003: 368; e.g. the AP index in the Late Glacial spectrum from Bátorlieget is more than 50% – Willis et

al. 1995: 40) must also have been a factor favourable to the existence of foragers (see also Bailey 2000: 18-22). To sum up: some Balkan territories, beyond riparian and littoral environments, offered advantageous ecological conditions for the functioning of Mesolithic populations, at least in some phases of the Early Holocene.

Finally, it should be added that the rise of the sea level in the Holocene and, related to this, inundation and disappearance of the extensive and rich littoral zone should have caused the appearance of more numerous Mesolithic sites near the present-day coastline, roughly contemporaneous with younger sea transgressions. Such sites would represent the remains of the population that was forced to retreat from the inundated littoral *oikumene*. However, the present state of research does not allow to distinguish this phase of Mesolithic occupation neither along the Adriatic coast nor in the Aegean or Black Sea zones. Another difficulty are inadequate investigations into the patterns of sea transgressions in the, broadly understood, East Mediterranean zone. The classical example is the problem of the sudden Black Sea transgression that in recent years has been broadly discussed. Publications from the mid-1990s proposed a catastrophic scenario, namely: the lake that existed in the present Black Sea basin – but smaller in area – was flooded by the Mediterranean waters via Bosphorus (Ryan et al. 1997; Ballard et al. 2000). According to the authors, this natural disaster must have taken place within 1 to 2 years and was experienced by the population inhabiting the present Black Sea shelf. Initially, this event was dated to about 7.100 BP. On the other hand, a number of publications, entirely or partially, refute this scenario (Aksu et al. 2002a; 2002b; Görür et al. 2001; Myers et al. 2003) or radically change its chronology (e.g. to 8.400 BP – Major et al. 2006; Ryan et al. 2003). In some of alternative scenarios the existence of an extensive, ecologically attractive, littoral zone is denied (Görür et al. 2001). Thus, the Black Sea transgressions cannot constitute a point of reference for the issues of the Late Mesolithic in the Balkans or – the more so – the problems of neolithization (Dergachey & Dolukhanov 2007).

To sum up, in terms of environmental determinants the density of Mesolithic settlement in the Balkans can be regarded as an open question. Even if we assumed that the hypothesis that acknowledges the low density of Mesolithic settlement is correct it is difficult to explain its causes.

The considerable ecological differentiation of the Balkans has been stressed by several authors (Allen 2003; 360, 367, 372; Andrić 2001; Bottema 2003; Perlès 2001: 16–19; Raczky et al. in press; Sümegi

2003; 2004; Willis 1994: 769–770; Willis *et al.* 1995). In the present volume this differentiation is emphasized by P. Sümegi as well as by J.K. Kozłowski and M. Nowak, as a factor that may have made the neolithization of the Carpathian Basin easier, notably in its stage corresponding to the formation of the LBK and the AVK in the northern regions of the Carpathian Basin. This concept assumes close coexistence of Early Neolithic and Late Mesolithic populations in neighbouring, but separate: i) riparian and ii) Pleistocene loess areas. In the effect of inevitable contacts and interactions some Neolithic attributes were transmitted to Mesolithic groups. It seems that the strongly mosaic landscape of ecological zones could have, indeed, been a vital factor for the advance of neolithization also in other zones of the Carpatian Basin.

In a kind of fractal pattern there existed enclaves with ecological conditions approximating the original, Near East-Anatolian conditions of farming and stock-breeding (Perlès 2001; Raczky *et al.* in press). Possibly, the spread of agricultural formations reflects the search for such enclaves in the situation when most of the new territory offered ecological conditions unlike those of the homeland territories.

CLASSIFICATION OF THE MESOLITHIC IN THE BALKAN-DANUBIAN ZONE

The discussion at the Symposium showed that researchers are in agreement as to the origins of the main Mesolithic units in the Balkans and the Middle Danube Basin, whose roots can be sought in the Epigravettian tradition. Because at the end of the Palaeolithic Epigravettian units were considerably varied, consequently, the Mesolithic in this zone displays certain territorial differentiation. Thus, we can distinguish the Mesolithic with Epigravettian tradition in the Middle Danube Basin (Kertész *et al.* 1994), in the Iron Gate region (Radovanović 1996), in south-western Serbia and Montenegro (Mihajlović 1999; this volume), in the Aegean Sea basin (Kozłowski 2005), and – possibly – also in the eastern Balkans (Gatsov 1982). In the same territories continuation from the Early to the Late Mesolithic although not everywhere well documented is observed.

A specific phenomenon – but, too, rooted in the Epigravettian tradition – are culture sequences in the north-western Balkans where, at the interface between the Early Mesolithic and the Late Mesolithic, the Sauveterrian is replaced by the Castelnovian; the technological change that takes place at this boundary is part of broader, trans-European cultural changes manifested in the appearance of regular blade technique and trapezes. Sauveterrian influences occur,

as well, in the Middle Danube Basin, whereas those of the Castelnovian in the middle-western Balkans (Kozłowski *et al.* 1996; Mihajlović this volume).

But the Balkan-Danubian culture zone remained as well under the influence of units from other territories, thus making the map of the Mesolithic still more intricate. The influence of the Black Sea culture units such as the Grebeniki (Păunescu 1972; S.K. Kozłowski 1989; 2001), occur in the lower Danube basin, extending also to the western Balkans (even as far as Turkish Thrace – Gatsov & Özdögan 1994).

The impact of the western Mesolithic complex, namely: the Beuronian, is limited to only the Middle Danube Basin (S.K. Kozłowski 2001).

CHARACTERIZATION OF THE FIRST NEOLITHIC PHENOMENA IN THE BALKAN ZONE

The beginnings of Neolithic settlement in Greece are dated to the very beginning of the seventh millennium BC (Perlès 2001: 90-93, 99-110; a different view was proposed by Thiessen 2000: 144-147). The earliest Neolithic sites in western, northern and north-eastern Bulgaria as well as in Macedonia (FYROM) are younger by at least 500 years (Biagi & Spataro 2005: 35-36; Görsdorf & Bojadžiev 1996; Nikolova 1998: 117, 128; Stefanova 1996; Todorova 1999) (the first occupation of the site of Hoca Çeşme at the mouth of the Marica river is dated at *ca.* 6.400 BC, but this settlement is more closely related to the specific NW Anatolian Neolithic – Özdögan 1997). For another several hundred years the First Neolithic continued to spread northwards, to the central part of the Great Hungarian Plain (*ca.* 5.800/5.400 BC), to the region of the Balaton Lake (*ca.* 5.500/5.400 BC) and to northern Moldavia (*ca.* 5.600/5.500 BC) (Bánffy 2000; 2004; Biagi & Spataro 2005: 36; Breuning 1987: 106, 108; Dergachev *et al.* 1991: 3; Kalicz *et al.* 1998: 158-181; Mantu 1998: 162, 171; Nikolova 1998: 125-128; Ursulescu 2001: 62-65; Virág & Kalicz 2001; Whittle *et al.* 2002). When we analyse the territorial distribution of the oldest dates we can see that they are considerably dispersed. In between these scattered, earliest traces of the First Neolithic there extend large territories untouched by First Temperate Neolithic. FTN reached these territories later, e.g. the Thrace Plain – one of the most important regions of Neolithic settlement – at the beginning of the sixth millennium BC, some other territories only at about the middle of the sixth millennium BC (e.g. eastern Macedonia – Demoule & Perlès 1993: 366; Nikolova 1998: 117; Roque *et al.* 2002; eastern Thrace – Erdogu 1999; eastern Bulgaria – Boyadijev nd: 3). The data available now do not allow to claim a systematical and gradual expansion to the north.

Chronological and chorological data demonstrate that Neolithic communities appeared at the northern outskirts of the Carpathian Basin at least a thousand years later than in Greece. Regardless the genesis of the FTN or the density of Balkan-Carpathian Late Mesolithic settlement, during such a long period contacts between Neolithic and Mesolithic groups must have been unavoidable, bringing transformations of existing economic-settlement and cultural models (Zvelebil 1998: 16–21; 2001: 6–11).

In 1994 K. Willis and K. Bennett (1994; see also: Willis 1994: 784) published a short paper that summed up the knowledge up till then on palynological evidence of human activity in the Balkans. The authors pointed to the fact that prior to the fifth millennium BC there are no distinct traces of human activity in the territory of the Balkans. In any case, the earliest such traces in the fifth millennium BC are, as a rule, decreased frequency of trees that are replaced by other plants, or some changes in the species composition of plant communities; these changes were not permanent. Willis and Bennet concluded:

> The hypothesis that the Neolithic transition was caused by a surplus and rapidly growing population ... moving northwards and cultivating the land as they went is not supported by these results.

> (Willis & Bennett 1994: 328).

While we concur with this conclusion (extremely valuable), we cannot support the authors' another conclusions:

> This in turn implies that the associated time-transgressive spread of the Indo-European language from the Near East to northern Europe between 8.000 and 6.000 BP ... must also be reconsidered ...

> ... suggests that linguistic evidence alone indicates a later date of around 6.000 BP for the initial development of the Indo-European language. If the spread of the language is associated with the spread of landscape-scale farming activity, then palaeoecological results support this later date

> (ibid.).

The value of changes in the forest species composition is questionable as a means to reflect human activity (Magri 1996). Besides, the authors' conclusion seems to overlook a number of ways of expansion of agro-pastoral economy, other than demic diffusion caused by population explosion (Edwards et al. 1996: 121–

122). And, last but not least, the weakness of pollen analysis itself seems to be ignored (ibid.).

A brief review of recent palynological data (Andrič 2001: 146–156, 162; Bottema 2003; Gardner 1999: 172–175; Jahns 2002; Lazarova & Bozilova 2001; Marinova 2006; Tantau et al. 2003; Willis et al. 1998: 108–109) suggests that there is still a lack of clear, evident traces of human activity that could be identified with the first stage of neolithization of the Balkan zone. This is corroborated, besides, by investigations in the alluvial plains (Moravany, Teleorman – Kalicki et al. 2004; 2005; Howard et al. 2004) where signatures of human activity that would have been linked with the Early Neolithic are absent, as well. It is only the activity of the Vinča complex population groups, and – in the north – the Late Linear and Early Lengyel-Polgar cultures that was sufficiently intensive to have been reflected in environmental evidence. Environmental data suggest that at the very beginning of the Neolithic human activity was territorially limited. This is an important piece of information because aforesaid observations that the onset of the Neolithic in the Balkans was restricted to rather small enclaves dispersed over a large territory, usually associated with larger rivers (Kertész & Sümegi 2001: 410–411), are confirmed.

Another characteristic of the material, settlement and economic situation in seventh and sixth millennia BC is the occurrence of "weak" versions of the Early Neolithic package. For instance, i) ceramics frequently coexists with lithics that differ from the macroblade Early Neolithic industries (layers IX–VIII at Knossos; upper layers at Sidari on Korfu; the assemblage with monochrome ceramics from Vlush (Prendi 1990: 401–402); lithic inventories from the Marmara Sea basin discussed in this volume by Gatsov and Nedelcheva; flake industry at Starčevo Culture sites of Divostin, Banja, Grivac (Bailey 2000: 129-130; Tringham et al. 1988: 205)), ii) at several Early Neolithic sites in Bulgaria wild animals' share is quite substantial (Benecke 2006). A further example of settlement-economic situations of the kind is the Adriatic zone where the importance of agriculture and stock-breeding varies considerably among the Impresso-Cardium ware communities. Certainly, in some cases it had minimal significance (Červena Stijena, Edera, Pupićina), in some others it played a major role (Smiljčić, Tinj, Vizula) (Chapman & Shiel 1993: 76–77; Forenbacher & Miracle 2005: 517-518; Miracle 1997: 57; Mlekuž 2003: 145). A specific feature of the mountainous areas of the Balkan zone is also early appearance of pastoralism (Mlekuž 2005; Dennel 1978).

An example of problems are discussions on the status of the settlement-economic system in the Körös culture in the Great Hungarian Plain (Kosse 1979: 125–132; Barker 1985: 95–97; Bartosiewicz 2005). The presence of elements that are not quite typical in the classical understanding of the Neolithic, is noticeable. The proportion of wild mammals (up to 30%) is relatively high (higher than in "southern" sites); there occur as well remains of fish, molluscs, turtles, water birds (at some settlements features contain refuse layers composed entirely of mollusc shells, fish bones and scales, remains of turtle carapaces and bones of water fowl – Whittle 1996: 67). On the other hand, agriculture – though less well documented – was certainly practiced, possibly as fairly intensive, quasi gardening (Bogaard 2004; Kosse 1979: 128–130). In the same way, some stock-breeding was done (sheep/goat continue to be the dominant species - Barker 1985: 97; Bartosiewicz 2005; Craig *et al.* 2005; Kosse 1979: 131). The Körös culture population seem to have exploited a large variety of food resources, which has also been confirmed by use-wear evidence (Starnini 2001: 401).

Settlement pattern in the Great Hungarian Plain is also remarkable. Numerous Körös culture sites concentrate only along the Tisza and its main tributaries, in distinct clusters (Kosse 1979: 16–125, 148; Sherrat 1982: 303–304; 1983: 23–24, 33), unlike the scattered FTN sites in other areas of the Balkan zone (with the exception of Thessaly). Körös culture sites are situated low, between the terrace and the flood plain, on levee tops or on "islands" in the floodplain. Some sites stretch as much as 800 m along streams; however, these may not have been single settlements as culture layers are thin. The problem of stability of settlements cannot be resolved without further investigations into seasonality of sites. Some researchers believe that the picture of Körös culture settlement in the Great Hungarian Plain documents its mobility (Chapman 1994: 79–80; Sherrat 1983: 23, 33; Whittle 1996: 52–54; 2001: 454–455; but a different view – Kosse 1979: 129) i.e. most settlements would have been short-term camps, whereas within microregional clusters seasonal (?) rotation would have taken place. On the other hand, faunal data from some settlements in south-east Hungary seem to provide evidence to the contrary indicating occupation the whole year round (Bökönyi after Kosse 1979: 128); thus – providing mobility – it was on the scale of several or a dozen or so years, but not seasonal.

Obviously, the question can be posed whether such economy and settlement system were an expression of adaptation to local conditions where multidirectional exploitation of natural resources was more advantageous, or whether this was a reflection of local tradition (read: Mesolithic). These questions were discussed at the Symposium by Gatsov & Nedelcheva, Mihailović, and Marton.

CONCLUSIONS FROM THE SYMPOSIUM

When the Mesolithic/Neolithic interaction is discussed the first problem we have to face is the size of Late Mesolithic populations i.e. those who encountered the earliest Neolithic groups in the Balkans and in the Middle Danube Basin. Except for the Iron Gate region and the eastern coast of the Adriatic, there is, unquestionably, a disproportion in the settlement network density between the Early and the Late Mesolithic. This disproportion is striking in the northeast part of the Aegean Sea basin, the eastern Balkans and the Middle Danube Basin. Is this apparently sparse settlement network in the Late Mesolithic the effect of insufficient research, or does it reflect a real demographic crisis? Providing the demographic crisis is a fact (which seems likely in view of intensification of research in various parts of the discussed territory and the environmental determinants described earlier), what caused this crisis?

Thus, we can deal with cultural Mesolithic/Neolithic interactions only in selected regions that in the Late Mesolithic were densely settled. This is, first of all, the region of the Iron Gate where vital modifications took place in the cultural, social and ideological way of life of the Late Mesolithic foragers. The question is whether the changes and innovations were the consequence of cultural and social integration of local Mesolithic population or a response to extra-local cultural trends, that - in turn - reflected the diffusion of food producing economy from the Near East. However, the basic problem is the model of this diffusion, notably the role of migrant groups and location of their home territories as well as routes of migrations.

At the Symposium several issues were addressed, vital for the problems enumerated above:

- are trapezoidal stone houses with hard limestone plaster floors, stone sculpture, funeral rites uniting the worlds of the living and the dead in the Lepenski Vir cultures the result of convergence, in the conditions of pre-agricultural sedentary way of life, with Pre-Pottery Neolithic communities, or the expression of contacts with PPN units in Anatolia or Cyprus?

- was the expansion of first agriculturalists in the Balkans a single-phase phenomenon related to cultures with white painted pottery, or a multiphase phenomenon (e.g. in the case when white-decorated pottery was preceded by monochrome ceramic phase)? Can a model that assumes pre-pottery diffusion of some traits of Neolithic package – based on the Mesolithic settlement network in e.g. the Aegean Sea Basin - be also considered?

• did the scarcity of Late Mesolithic settlement network indeed make easier – as C. Perlès holds (2001) – fast expansion of the Ceramic Neolithic via Greece and the Central Balkans into the middle Danube basin?

The papers presented at the Symposium emphasize the multi-phase nature of these interactions, confirmed, first of all, by the discoveries of the sites of the typical Ceramic Neolithic in the surroundings of Lepenski Vir. There the Mesolithic and the Pottery Neolithic units must have co-existed for at least 200–300 years. An earlier phase can also be distinguished when Mesolithic groups had acquired prestigious goods from Neolithic groups that had exploited a broader territory than the Mesolithic inhabitants of Lepenski Vir. Among such goods was, for example, Balkan "honey" flint or *Spondylus* shells from the Aegean Sea Basin. Following this phase (dated to 6.300–6.000 BC), in the next phase the Neolithic groups spread over the entire Iron Gate region (6.000–5.900 BC).

Anthropological investigations into the populations of the Lepenski Vir culture, carried out by M. Roksandić (2000), show that, besides temporal trends within whole, fairly homogeneous groups, there is a greater homogeneity of female groups. We can, thus, assume that the allogenic element in Mesolithic groups was related, primarily, to the migration of male adult individuals. This is manifested in the differing funeral rites. There seems to have been little hostility between the local and the allogenic populations as the traces of violence on bones from grave are infrequent.

In the Adriatic zone the Mesolithic/Neolithic interactions had, certainly, different nature. They were, at least partially, related to the gradually growing importance of Neolithic components in the Castelnovian, at the end of the seventh and in the first half of the sixth millennium BC. In this process the system of information exchange must have played a vital role; this included contacts with the south-east part of the Apenine Peninsula. Neolithic components were very flexibly adapted to diverse ecological conditions; hence, relatively large differences in the frequency of Neolithic traits at particular sites.

The phenomena registered in the Late Mesolithic context in Greece indicate contacts with the Early Neolithic farming groups that inhabited Argolide and Thessaly in the first half of the seventh millennium BC. In view of the presence of some Neolithic attributes at several sites (Franchthi, Theopetra, Sidari) and the absence of opposite situation (i.e. Mesolithic attributes in Neolithic contexts) we are inclined to put forward a hypothesis that cultural transmission occurred in one direction. It seems, that – unlike in the Adriatic zone – at none of the sites in Argolide and Thessaly was the initial neolithization successful; for there are no traces of continuation of the evolution of local communities in the direction of the full Neolithic package. The question about the fate of hunter-gatherer groups inhabiting e.g. the caves of Franchthi and Theopetra, who had some contacts with their Neolithic neighbours, remains unanswered.

The discussion of interactions between Neolithic and Mesolithic populations in the Middle Danube and the Tisza Basins is much more difficult, especially in the territory of adaptation of Anatolian-Balkan culture patterns to central European conditions and in the Linear Complexes formation zone. The state of knowledge of the Late Mesolithic settlement is insufficient, while the manifestations of the influence of Mesolithic traditions on the formation of the Linear Complex (e.g. in the sphere of lithic industry) are few. On the other hand, it is hardly conceivable that the areas under consideration should have been totally abandoned by Late Mesolithic populations. Rare sites (e.g. Ciumeşti) confirm the presence of the Mesolithic which, nevertheless, must have been very poorly represented.

Again, the question can be posed: what happened to Late Mesolithic groups? The absence of Mesolithic elements in the Linear chipped stone industries justifies the assumption that they underwent neolithization only during the subsequent evolution of Linear cultures (see: Kozłowski & Nowak in this volume). In the same way, it might be possible that neolithization reached more southern Mesolithic groups also relatively late, in the period of formation of the Vinča Cultural Complex.

The cultural situation in the Balkans in the second half of the sixth millennium BC appears as a mosaic. This mosaic was made up of: typical Mesolithic foragers and Neolithic food producing populations, as well as the whole gamut of intermediate phases between the "pure" Mesolithic and the "pure" Neolithic. These intermediate units derived from foraging groups as a result of a variety of contacts and interactions. This process cannot be restricted to the material sphere only; it took place, as well, on the mental and ideological level. On the other hand, signs of an opposite process (that is: a kind of mesolithization) are not easily detectable in typical farming communities of the First Neolithic. The infrequent changes of this kind in the material culture, settlement or minor changes in economy – as compared to the Near Eastern-Anatolian model – are treated as a expressions of unavoidable contacts and adaptation to changing environmental conditions.

References

AKSU, A. E., HISCOTT, R.N., KAMIŃSKI, M.A., MUDIE, P.J., GILLESPIE, H., ABRAJANO, T. & YAŞAR, D. (2002a) Last glacial-Holocene paleoceanography of the Black Sea and Marmara Sea: stable isotopic, foraminiferal and coccolith evidence. *Marine Geology* 190: pp. 19-49.

AKSU, A.E., HISCOTT, R.N., YAŞAR, D., IŞLER, F.I. & MARSH, S. (2002b) Seismic stratigraphy of Late Quaternary deposits from the southwestern Black Sea shelf: evidence for non-catastrophic variations in sea-level during the last ~10.000 yr. *Marine Geology* 190: pp. 61-94.

ALLEN, H. D. (2003) Response of past and present Mediterranean ecosystems to environmental change. *Progress in Physical Geography* 27: pp. 359–377.

ALLEY, R. B. & ÁGÚSTSDÓTTIR, A. M. (2005) The 8k event: cause and consequences of a major Holocene abrupt climate change. *Quaternary Science Reviews* 24: pp. 1123–1149.

ANDRIČ, M. (2001) The Holocene vegetation dynamics and the formation of Neolithic and present-day Slovenian landscape, *Documenta Praehistorica* 28: pp. 133-75.

BAILEY, D. W. (2000) *Balkan Prehistory. Exclusion, Incorporation and Identity*. London: Routledge.

BALLARD, R. D., COLEMAN, D. F. & ROSENBERG, G. D. (2000) Further evidence of abrupt Holocene drowning of the Black Sea shelf. *Marine Geology* 170: pp. 253–261.

BÁNFFY, E. (2000) The Late Starčevo and the Earliest Linear Pottery groups in western Transdanubia. *Documenta Praehistorica*, 27: pp. 173-187.

BÁNFFY, E. (2004) *The 6th Millennium BC Boundary in Western Transdanubia and its Role in the Central European Neolithic Transition (the Szentgyörgyvölgy-Pityerdomb Settlement)*. Budapest: Archaeological Institute of the Hungarian Academy of Sciences.

BARKER, G. W. (1985) *Prehistoric Farming in Europe*. Cambridge: Cambridge University Press.

BARTOSIEWICZ, L. (2005) Plain talk: animals, environment and culture in the Neolithic of the Carpathian Basin and adjacent areas. In BAILEY, D., WHITTLE, A. & CUMMINGS, V., eds. *(Un)settling the Neolithic*. Oxford: Oxbow, pp. 51-63.

BARTOSIEWICZ, L. & BONSALL, C. (2005) Prehistoric fishing along the Danube. *Antaeus* 27: pp. 253-272.

BARTOSIEWICZ, L., V. BORONEANŢ, C. BONSALL & S. STALLIBRAS. (2001) New data on the prehistoric fauna of the Iron Gates: a case study from Schela Cladovei, Romania. In KERTÉSZ, R. & MAKKAY, J. eds. *From the Mesolithic to the Neolithic. Proceedings of the International Archaeological Conference held in the Damjanich Museum of Szolnok, September 22-27, 1996*. Budapest: Archaeolingua. pp. 15-23.

BENECKE, N. (2006) Animal husbandry and hunting in the Early Neolithic of South-East Europe – A review. In GATSOV, I. & SCHWARZBERG, H. eds. *Aegean – Marmara – Black Sea: the Present State of Reasearch on the Early Neolithic*. Langenweisbach: Beier & Beran. pp. 175-186."

BIAGI, P. (2001) Some aspects of the Late Mesolithic and Early Neolithic periods in Northern Italy. In KERTÉSZ, R. & MAKKAY, J. eds. *From the Mesolithic to the Neolithic. Proceedings of the International Archaeological Conference held in the Damjanich Museum of Szolnok, September 22-27, 1996*. Budapest: Archaeolingua. pp. 71-89.

BIAGI, P. & SPATARO, M. (2005) New observations on the radiocarbon chronology of the Starčevo-Criş and Körös cultures. In NIKOLOVA, L. & HIGGINS, J., eds. *Prehistoric Archaeology & Anthropological Theory and Education*, pp. 35-52. (RPRP 6-7).

BIAGI, P., STARNINI, E. & VOYTEK, B. (1993) The Late Mesolithic and Early Neolithic settlement of Northern Italy: recent considerations. *Poročilo o raziskovanju paleolitika, neolitika in eneolitika v Sloveniji* 21: pp. 63-73.

BOGAARD, A. (2004) The nature of early farming in Central and South-East Europe. *Documenta Praehistorica* 31: pp. 49-58.

BOYADJIEV, Y. nd. - Neolithic and Eneolithic cultures on the territory of Bulgaria. http://archweb-bg.cilea.it/neol.htm.

BÖKÖNYI, S. (1970) Animal remains from Lepenski Vir. *Science* 167: pp. 1702-1704.

BÖKÖNYI, S. (1974) *History of Domestic Mammals of Central and Eastern Europe*. Budapest: Akadémiai Kiadó.

BONSALL, C., COOK, G. T., HEDGES, R. E. M., HIGHAM, T. F. G., PICKARD, C. & RADOVANOVIĆ, I. (2004) Radiocarbon and stable isotope evidence of dietary change from the Mesolithic to the Middle Ages in the Iron Gates: New results from Lepenski Vir. *Radiocarbon* 46: pp. 293-300."

BONSALL, C., G. COOK, R. LENNON, D. HARKNESS, M. SCOTT, L. BARTOSIEWICZ & K. Mc SWEENEY. (2000) Stable isotopes, radiocarbon and the Mesolithic-Neolithic transition in the Iron Gates. *Documenta Praehistorica* 27: pp. 119-32.

BONSALL, C., LENNON, R., MCSWEENEY, K., STEWART. C., HARKNESS, D., BORONEANŢ, V., PAYTON, R., BARTOSIEWICZ, L. & CHAPMAN, J. (1997) Mesolithic and Early Neolithic in the Iron Gates: a palaeodietary perspective. *Journal of European Archaeology* 5: pp. 50–92.

BONSALL, C., MACKLIN, M. G., PAYTON, R. W. & BORONEANŢ, A. (2002) Climate, floods and river gods: environmental change and the Meso–Neolithic transition in southeast Europe. *Before Farming: The Archaeology of Old World Hunter-Gatherers* 3–4: pp. 1–15.

BORIĆ, D. (2001) Mesolithic and Early Neolithic hunters and fishers in the Danube Gorges: An analysis of archaeozoological data. In KERTÉSZ, R. & MAKKAY, J. eds. *From the Mesolithic to the Neolithic. Proceedings of the International Archaeological Conference held in the Damjanich Museum of Szolnok, September 22-27, 1996.* Budapest: Archaeolingua. pp. 101-125.

BORIĆ, D. (2002) The Lepenski Vir conundrum: reinterpretation of the Mesolithic and Neolithic sequences in the Danube Gorges. *Antiquity* 76: pp. 1026-1039.

BORIĆ, D., & MIRACLE, P. (2004) Mesolithic and Neolithic (dis)continuities in the Danube Gorges: new AMS dates from Padina and Hajdučka Vodenica (Serbia). *Oxford Journal of Archaeology* 23: 341-371.

BOTTEMA, S. (2003) The vegetation history of the Greek Mesolithic. In GALANIDOU, N. & PERLÈS, C. eds., *The Greek Mesolithic: Problems and Perspectives*. London: The British School at Athens. pp. 33-49.

BOŽILOVA, E., FILIPOVA, M., FILIPOVICH, L. & TONKOV, S. (1996) Bulgaria. In BERGLUND, B. E., BIRKS, H. J. B., RALSKA-JASIEWICZOWA, M. & WRIGHT, H. E. eds. *Palaeoecological Events During Last 15.000 Years: Regional Syntheses of Palaeoecological Studies of Lakes and Mires in Europe*. Chichester...: John Wiley & Sons. pp. 701–728.

BREUNING, P. (1987) *[14]C-Chronologie des Vorderasiatischen, Südost- und Mittel-europäischen Neolithikums*. Köln-Wien: Böhlau.

CHAPMAN, J. (1989) Demographic trends in neothermal south-east Europe. In BONSALL, C., ed. The Mesolithic in Europe. Papers Presented in the Third International Symposium, Edinburgh 1985. Edinburgh: Edinburgh University Press. pp. 500-515

CHAPMAN, J. (1992) Social Power in the Iron Gates Mesolithic. In CHAPMAN, J. & DOLUKHANOV, P., eds. *Cultural Transformations and Interactions in Eastern Europe*. Aldershot: Avebury. pp. 71-121.

CHAPMAN, J. (1994) Social power in the early farming communities of Eastern Hungary - Perspectives from the Upper Tisza region. *Jósa András Múzeum Évkönyve*, 36: pp. 79-101

CHAPMAN, J. & SHIEL, R. (1993) Social change and land use in Prehistoric Dalmatia. *Proceedings of the Prehistoric Society* 59: 61-104.

CULIBERG, M. & ŠERCELJ, A. (1996) Slovenia. In BERGLUND, B. E., BIRKS, H. J. B., RALSKA-JASIEWICZOWA, M. & WRIGHT, H. E. eds. *Palaeoecological Events During Last 15.000 Years: Regional Syntheses of Palaeoecological Studies of Lakes and Mires in Europe*. Chichester...: John Wiley & Sons. pp. 687-700.

CRAIG, O. E., CHAPMAN, J., HERON, C., WILLIS, L. H., BARTOSIEWICZ, L., TAYLOR, G., WHITTLE, A. & COLLINS, M. (2005) Did the first farmers of central and eastern Europe produce dairy foods? *Antiquity* 79: pp. 882-894.

DEMOULE, J-P. & PERLÈS, C. (1993) The Greek Neolithic: A New Rewiev. *Journal of World Prehistory* 7: pp. 355-416.

DENNEL, R. (1978) *Early Farming in South Bulgaria from the VIth to the IIrd Millennia BC*. Oxford: British Archaeological Reports.

DERGACHEV, V. A. & DOLUKHANOV, P. M. (2007) The neolithization of the north Pontic area and the Balkans in the context of the Black Sea floods. In YANKO-HOMBACH, V., GILBERT, A. S., PANIN, N. & DOLUKHANOV, P. M. eds. *The Black Sea Flood Question: Changes in Coastline, Climate and Human Settlement*. Springer. pp. 489-514.

DERGACHEV, V., SHERATT, A. & LARINA, O. (1991) Recent results of Neolithic research in Moldavia. *Oxford Journal of Archaeology*, 10: pp. 1-17.

EDWARDS, K. J., HALSTEAD, P. & ZVELEBIL, M. (1996) The Neolithic transition in the Balkans – archaeological perspectives and palaeoecological evidence: a comment on Willis and Bennett. *The Holocene* 6: pp. 120-122.

ERDOGU, B. (1999) Pattern and mobility in the prehistoric settlements of the Edirne region, Eastern Thrace *Documenta Praehistorica* 26: pp. 143-153.

FEURDEAN, A. (2005) Holocene forest dynamics in northwestern Romania. *The Holocene* 15: pp. 435-446.

FORENBACHER, S. & MIRACLE, P. (2005) The spread of farming in the Eastern Adriatic. *Antiquity* 79: 514-528.

GARDNER, A. (1999) The ecology of Neolithic environmental impacts - ree-evaluation of existing theory using case studies from Hungary & Slovenia. *Documenta Praehistorica*, 26: pp. 163-183.

GATSOV, I. (1982) The archaeological cultures of the late Pleistocene and early Holocene in the western Black Sea region and their significance for the formation of the Neolithic flint industries. In KOZŁOWSKI, J. K., ed. *Origin of the Chipped Stone Industries of the Early Farming Cultures in the Balkans*. Warszawa: Państwowe Wydawnictwo Naukowe. pp. 111-130.

GATSOV, I. & ÖZDÖGAN, M. (1994) Some Epi-Palaeolithic sites from NW Turkey. *Anatolica* 20: pp. 97-120.

GÖRSDORF, J. & BOJADZIEV, J. (1996) Zur absoluten Chronologie der bulgarischen Urgeschichte. *Eurasia Antiqua*, 2: 105-173.

GÖRÜR, N., ÇAĞATAY, M. N., EMRE, Ö., ALPAR, B., SAKINÇ, M., İSLAMOĞLU, Y., ALGAN, O., ERKAL, T., KEÇER, M., AKKÖK, R. & KARLIK, G. (2001) Is the abrupt drowning of the Black Sea shelf at 7.150 yr BP a myth? *Marine Geology* 176: pp. 65-73.

HAAK, W., FORSTER, P., BRAMANTI, B., MATSUMURA, S., BRANDT, G., TÄNZER, M., VILLEMS, R., RENFREW, C., GRONENBORN, D., ALT, K. W. & BURGER, J. (2005) Ancient DNA from the First European Farmers in 7.500-Year-Old Neolithic Sites. *Science* 310: pp. 1016-1018.

HOWARD, A. J., MACKLIN, M. G., BAILEY, D. W., MILLS, S. & ANDREESCU, R. (2004) Late-glacial and Holocene river development in the Teleorman Valley on the southern Romanian Plain. *Journal Of Quaternary Science* 19: pp. 271–280

JAHNS, S. (2002) An improved time scale for the Holocene history of vegetation and environment on the South Dalmatian Island of Mljet. *Vegetation History and Archaeobotany* 11: pp. 315-316.

JERAJ, M. (2002) Archaeobotanical evidence for early agriculture at Ljubljansko barje (Ljubljana Moor), central Slovenia. *Vegetation History and Archaeobotany* 11: pp. 277-287.

JUHÁSZ, I. (2004) Palynological evidence of preneolithization in South-West Tarnsdanubia. *Antaeus*, 27: pp. 213-225.

KALICKI, T., KOZŁOWSKI, J. K., NOWAK, M. & VIZDAL, M. (2005) A settlement of the Early Eastern Linear Pottery Culture at Moravany (East-ern Slovakia): palaeogeographical and archaeology-cal perspective. In GÁL, E., JUHÁSZ, I. & SÜMEGI, P., eds. *Environmental Archaeology in North-Eastern Hungary*. Budapest: Archaeolo-gical Institute of the Hungarian Academy of Sciences, pp. 187-207.

KALICKI, T., NOWAK, M. & VIZDAL, M. (2004) Geomorphology and palaeogeography of Early Neolithic site at Moravany (Eastern Slovakia). *Geomorphologica Slovaca*, 4: pp. 62-69.

KALICZ, N., VIRÁG, Z. M. & BIRÓ K. T. (1998) The northern periphery of the Early Neolithic Starčevo culture in south-western Hungary: a case study of an excavation at Lake Balaton. *Documenta Prehistorica*, 25: pp. 151-189.

KERTÉSZ, R. & SÜMEGI, P. (2001) Theories, critiques and a model: Why did the expansion of the Körös-Starčevo culture stop in the centre of the Carpathian Basin? In KERTÈSZ, R. & MAKKAY, J., eds. *From the Mesolithic to the Neolithic. Proceedings of the International Archaeological Conference held in the Damjanich Museum of Szolnok, September 22-27, 1996*. Budapest: Archaeolingua, pp. 225-246.

KERTÉSZ, R., SÜMEGI, P., KOZÁK, M., BRAUN, M., FÉLEGYHÁZI, E. & HERTELENDI, E. (1994) Mesolithikum im nördlichen Teil der Großen Ungarischen Tiefebene., *Jósa András Múzeum Évkönyve* 36: 15-63.

KOSSE, K. (1979) *Settlement Ecology of the Körös and Linear Pottery Cultures in Hungary*. Oxford: BAR Publishing. (BAR Int. Series; 64).

KOZŁOWSKI, J. K. (2005) The importance of the Aegean Basin for the Neolithization of Sout-Eastern Europe. *Journal of the Israel Prehistoric Society* 35: pp. 409-424.

KOZŁOWSKI, J. K. & KOZŁOWSKI, S. K. (1982) Lithic industries from the multi-layer Mesolithic site Vlasac in Yugoslavia. In KOZŁOWSKI, J. K., ed. *Origin of the Chipped Stone Industries of the Early Farming Cultures in the Balkans*. Warszawa: Państwowe Wydawnictwo Naukowe. pp. 11-110.

KOZŁOWSKI, J. K. & KOZŁOWSKI, S. K. (1983) Chipped stone industries from Lepenski Vir, Yugoslavia. *Prehistoria Alpina* 19: pp. 259-294.

KOZŁOWSKI, J. K., KOZŁOWSKI, S. K. & RADOVANOVIĆ, I. (1994) *Meso- and Neolithic Sequence from the Odmut Cave (Montenegro)*. Warszawa: Wydawnictwa Uniwersytetu Warszaw-skiego.

KOZŁOWSKI, J. K, KACZANOWSKA, M. & PAWLIKOWSKI, M. (1996) Chipped stone industries from Neolithic levels at Lerna. *Hesperia* 65: pp. 295-372.

KOZŁOWSKI, J. K. & KACZANOWSKA, M. (2006) Palaeolithic traditions, Mesolithic adaptations and Neolithic innovations as seen through lithic industries. In SAMPSON, A., ed. *The Prehistory of the Aegean Basin*. Athens: Athrapos. pp. 67-87.

KOZŁOWSKI, S. K. (1989) *Mesolithic in Poland. A New Approach*. Warszawa; Wydawnictwo UW.

KOZŁOWSKI, S. K. (2001) Eco-Cultural/stylistic zonation of the Mesolithic/Epipalaeolithic in Central Europe. In KERTESZ R. & MAKKAY, J., eds. *From the Mesolithic to the Neolithic. Proceedings of the International Archaeological Conference held in the Damjanich Museum of Szolnok, September 22-27, 1996*. Budapest: Archaeolingua, pp. 247-260.

LAZAROVA, M. & BOZILOVA, E. (2001) Studies on the Holocene history of vegetation in the region of lake Srebarna (northeast Bulgaria). *Vegetation History and Archaeobotany* 10: 87-95.

MAGRI, D. 1996. The Neolithic transition and Palaeoecology in the Balcans: a comment on Willis and Bennett. *The Holocene* 6: 119-123.

MAJOR, C. O., GOLDSTEIN, S. L., RYAN, W. B.F., LERICOLAIS, G., PIOTROWSKI, A. M. & HAJDAS, I. (2006) The co-evolution of Black Sea level and composition through the last deglaciation and its paleoclimatic significance. *Quaternary Science Reviews* 25: pp. 2031–2047.

MANTU, C-M. (1998) Absolute chronology of Neolithic cultures in Romania and relations with the Aegeo-Anatolian world. In OTTE, M., ed. *Préhistoire d'Anatolie. Genèse de deux mondes*. Liège. pp. 159-173. (Études et Recherches Archéologiques de l'Université de Liège; 85).

MARINOVA, E. (2006) *Vergleichende paläoethnobotanische Untersuchung zur Vegetations-geschichte und zur Entwicklung der prähistorischen Landnutzung in Bulgarien*. Berlin-Stuttgart: Borntraeger.

MENK R. & NEMESKÉRI, J. (1989) The transition from Mesolithic to Early Neolithic in southeastern and eastern Europe – an anthropological outline. In HERSKOVITZ, I. ed. *People and Culture in Change*. Oxford. pp. 531-540 (BAR International Series; 508).

MIHAJLOVIĆ, D. (1999) The Upper Palaeolithic and Mesolithic stone industries in Montenegro. In BAILEY, G. N., ADAM, E., PANAGOPOULOU, E., PERLÈS, C. & ZACHOS, K., eds. *The Palaeolithic Archaeology of Greece and Adjacent Areas*. London: The British School at Athens. pp. 343-356.

MIHAJLOVIĆ, D. (2001) Technological decline of the Early Holocene chipped stone industries in South-East Europe. In R. KERTÉSZ & MAKKAY, J.,

eds. *From the Mesolithic to the Neolithic. Proceedings of the International Archaeological Conference held in the Damjanich Museum of Szolnok, September 22-27, 1996*. Budapest: Archaeolingua. pp. 339-347.

MIHAJLOVIĆ, D. (2004) Chipped Stone Industry from horizons A and B at he site Padina in the Iron Gates. *Acts of the XIV Congress of UISPP, Liege, vol.7, The Mesolithic*. Oxford. pp. 61-68 (BAR International Series; 1302).

MIRACLE, P. (1997) Early Neolithic foragers in the karst of northern Istria. *Poročilo o raziskavanju paleolitika, neolitika in eneolitika v Sloveniji* 24: pp. 43-62.

MLEKUŽ, D. (1999) Landscape dynamics on the Ljubljana Moor. *Documenta Praehistorica* 26: pp. 185-192.

MLEKUŽ, D. (2003) Early herders of the Eastern Adriatic., *Documenta Praehistorica* 30: pp. 139-151.

MLEKUŽ, D. (2005) The ethnography of the Cyclops: Neolithic pastoralists in eastern Adriatic. *Documenta Praehistorica* 32: pp. 15-52.

MLEKUŽ, D., BUDJA, M. & OGRINC, N. (2006) Complex settlement and the landscape dynamic of the Iščica floodplain (Ljubljana Marshes, Slovenia). *Documenta Praehistorica* 33: pp. 253-271.

MYERS, P. G., WIELKI, CH., GOLDSTEIN, S. B. & ROHLING, E. J. (2003) Hydraulic calculations of postglacial connections between the Mediterranean and the Black Sea. *Marine Geology* 201: 253-267.

NEMESKÉRI, J. & SZATHMÁRY, L. (1978) Taxonomical structure of the Vlasac Mesolithic subpopulation. In SREJOVIĆ, D. & LETICA, Z. eds. *Vlasac. A Mesolithic settlement in the Iron Gates*. Beograd. pp. 177-229.

NIKOLOVA, L. (1998) Neolithic sequence: the upper Stryama valley in western Thrace (with an appendix: radiocarbon dating of the Balkan Neolithic). *Documenta Praehistorica*, 25: 99-131.

ÖZDÖGAN, M. (1997) The beginning of Neolithic economies in Southeastern Europe. An Anatolian perspective. *Journal of European Archaeology* 5: pp. 1-33.

PĂUNESCU, A. (1972) *Evolutia uneltor si armelor de la pietra cioplita descoperite pe teritoriul Romanei*. Bucuresti: Editura Academiei.

PERLÈS, C. (2001) *The Early Neolithic in Greece*. Cambridge: Cambridge University Press.

PERLÈS, C. (2003) An alternate (and old-fashioned) view of Neolithisation in Greece. *Documenta Praehistorica* 30: pp. 99-113.

PRENDI, F. (1990) La Néolithique ancien en Albanie. *Germania* 68: pp. 399–426.

PRENTICE, I. C., HARRISON, S. P., JOLLY, D. & GUIOT, J. (1998) The climate and biomass of Europe at 6.000 yr BP: comparison of model simulations and pollen-based reconstructions. *Quarternary Science Reviews* 17: pp. 659-668.

RACZKY, P., SÜMEGI, P., BARTOSIEWICZ, L., GÁL, E., KACZANOWSKA, M., KOZŁOWSKI, J. K. & ANDERS, A. (*in press*) Ecological barier versus mental marginal zone? Problems of the northernmost Körös culture settlements in the Great Hungarian Plain.

RADOVANOVIĆ, I. (1996) *The Iron Gates Mesolithic*. Ann Arbor: International Monographs in Prehistory. (Archaeological Series; 11).

ROKSANDIĆ, M. (2000) Bertween foragers and farmers in the Iron Gates Gorge: physical anthropology perspective. Djerdap population in transition from Mesolithic to Neolithic. *Documenta Praehistorica* 27: pp. 1-100.

ROQUE, C., GUIBERT, P., VARTANIAN, E., BECHTEL, F., TREUIL, R., DARCQUE, P., KOUKOULI-CHRYSSANTHAKI, H. & MALA-MIDOU, D. (2002) The chronology of the Neolithic sequence at Dikili Tash, Macedonia, Greece: TL dating of domestic ovens. *Archaeometry* 44: pp. 613-633.

RUNNELS, C., PANAGOPOLOU, E., MURRAY, P., TSARTSIDOU, G., ALLEN, S., MULLEN, K. & TOURLOUKIS E. (2005) A Mesolithic landscape in Greece: existing site-location model in the Argolid at Kandia. *Journal of Mediterranean Archaeology* 18: pp. 259-285.

RYAN, W. B. F., MAJOR, C. O., LERICOLAIS, G. & GOLDSTEIN, S. L. (2003) Catastrophic flooding of the Black Sea. *Annual Review of Earth & Planetary Sciences* 31: pp. 525-555.

RYAN, W. B. F., PITMAN, W. C., MAJOR, C. O., SHIMKUS, K., MOSLALENKO, V., JINES, G. A., DIMITROV, P., GORÜR, N., SAKINÇ, M. & YÜCE, H. (1997) An abrupt drowning of the Black Sea shelf. *Marine Geology* 138: pp. 119-126.

SAMPSON, A. (ed) (2006) *The Mesolithic site in Cyclope Cave, Island of Youra, vol. 1*. Athens.

SHERRATT, A. (1982) The development of Neolithic and Copper Age settlement in the Great Hungarian Plain, part I: regional setting.. *Oxford Journal of Archaeology* 1: pp. 287-316.

SHERRATT, A. (1983) The development of Neolithic and Copper Age settlement in the Great Hungarian Plain, Part II: Site survey and settlement dynamics. *Oxford Journal of Archaeology* 2: pp. 13-42.

SREJOVIĆ, D. (1969) *Lepenski Vir. Nova praistorijska kultura u Podunavlju*. Beograd.

SREJOVIĆ, D. (1972) *Europe's First Monumental Sculpture: New Discoveries at Lepenski Vir*. London: Thames & Hudson.

STARNINI, E. (2001) The Mesolithic/Neolithic transition in Hungary: the lithic perspective. In KERTÈSZ, R. & MAKKAY, J., eds. *From the Mesolithic to the Neolithic. Proceedings of the International Archaeological Conference held in the Damjanich Museum of Szolnok, September 22-27, 1996*. Budapest: Archaeolingua. pp. 395-404.

STEFANOVA, T. (1996) A comparative analysis of pottery from the "Monochrome Early Neolithic Horizon" and "Karanovo I Horizon" and the problems of the Neolithization of Bulgaria. *Poročilo o raziskovanju paleolitika, neolitika in eneolitika v Sloveniji*, 23: pp. 15-38.

SÜMEGI, P. (2003) Early Neolithic man and riparian environment in the Carpathian Basin. In JEREM, E. & RACZKY, P., eds. *Morgenrot der Kulturen. Frühe Etappen der Menschheitsgeschichte in Mittel- und Südosteuropa. Festschrift für Nándor Kalicz zum 75. Geburtstag*. Budapest: Archaeolingua. pp. 53-60.

SÜMEGI, P. (2004) Environmental changes under the Neolithisation process in Central Europe: before and after. *Antaeus* 27: pp. 117-127.

TANTAU, I., REILLE, M., DE BEAULIEU, J-L., FARCAS, S., GOSLAR, T. & PATERNE, M. (2003) Vegetation history in the Eastern Romanian Carpathians: pollen analysis of two sequences from the Mohoş crater. *Vegetation History and Archaeobotany* 12: pp. 113-125.

THISSEN, L. (2000) Thessaly, Franchti and western Turkey: clues to the Neolithisation of Greece? *Documenta Praehistorica* 27: pp. 141-154.

THOMAS, E. R., WOLFF, E. W., MULVANEY, R.,. STEFFENSEN, J. P., JOHNSEN, S. J., ARROW-SMITH, C., WHITE, J. W. C., VAUGHN, B. & POPP, T. (2007) The 8.2 ka event from Greenland ice cores. *Quaternary Science Reviews* 26: 70–81.

TODOROVA, H. (1999) Rec. "E. Alarm-Stern, Die Ägäische Frühzeit. Band 1. Das Neolithikum in Griechenland". *Archaeologia Austriaca* 82/83: pp. 545-546.

TRINGHAM, R. E., McPHERRON, A., GUNN, J. & ODELL, G. (1988) The flaked stone industry from Divostin and Banja. In McPHERRON, A. & SREJOVIĆ, D., eds. *Divostin and the Neolithic of Central Serbia*. Pittsburgh: University of Pittsburgh. pp. 203-254.

URSULESCU, N. 2001. Local variants of the Starčevo-Criş culture in the Carpato-Nistrean area. In DRAŠOVEAN, F., ed. *Festschrift für Georghe Lazarovici zum 60. Geburtstag*. Timişoara: Muzeul Banatului Timişoara. pp. 59-69

VIRÁG, Z. M. & KALICZ, N. (2001) Neuere Sidelungsfunde der Frühneolitischen Starcevo-Kultur aus Südwestungarn. In GINTER, B. *et al.*, eds. *Problems of the Stone Age in the Old World. Jubilee Book Dedicated to Professor Janusz K. Kozłowski*. Kraków: Jagiellonian University. pp. 265-281.

WHITTLE, A. (1996) *Neolithic Europe. The Creation of New Worlds*. Cambridge: Cambridge University Press.

WHITTLE, A. (2001) From mobility to sedentism: change by degrees. In KERTÈSZ, R. & MAKKAY, J., eds. *From the Mesolithic to the Neolithic. Proceedings of the International Archaeological Conference held in the Damjanich Museum of Szolnok, September 22-27, 1996*. Budapest: Archaeolingua. pp. 447-461.

WHITTLE, A., BARTOSIEWICZ, L., BORIĆ, D., PETTITT, P. & RICHARDS, M. (2002) In the beginning: new radiocarbon dates for the Early Neolithic in northern Serbia and south-east Hungary. *Antaeus* 25: pp. 63-117.

WILLIS, K. (1994) The vegetational history of the Balkans. *Quaternary Science Reviews* 13: pp. 769-788.

WILLIS, K. J. & BENNET, K. D. (1994) The Neolithic transition – fact or fiction? Palaeoecological evidence from the Balkans. *The Holocene* 4: 326-330.

WILLIS, K. J., SÜMEGI, P., BRAUN, M. & TÓTH, A. (1995) The late Quaternary environmental history of Bátorlieget, N.E. Hungary. *Palaeogeography, Palaeoclimatology, Palaeoecology* 118: pp. 25-47.

WILLIS, K. J., SÜMEGI, P., BRAUN, M., BENNETT, K. D. & TÓTH, A. (1998) Prehistoric land degradation in Hungary: who, how and why? *Antiquity* 72: pp. 101-113.

ZVELEBIL, M. (1998) Agricultural frontiers, Neolithic origins, and the transition to farming in the Baltic basin. In ZVELEBIL, M., DOMAŃSKA, L. & DENNEL, R., eds. *Harvesting the Sea, Farming the Forest. The Emergence of Neolithic Societies in the Baltic Region*. Sheffield: Sheffield Academic Press. pp. 9-29.

ZVELEBIL, M. (2001) The agricultural transition and the origins of Neolithic society in Europe. *Documenta Praehistorica* 28: pp. 1-26.

www.ingramcontent.com/pod-product-compliance
Lightning Source LLC
Chambersburg PA
CBHW061004030426
42334CB00033B/3362